F. S Clifford

A Romance of Perfume Lands

F. S Clifford

A Romance of Perfume Lands

ISBN/EAN: 9783744675048

Printed in Europe, USA, Canada, Australia, Japan

Cover: Foto ©Thomas Meinert / pixelio.de

More available books at **www.hansebooks.com**

CAPTAIN BRADFORD COLE.

A ROMANCE

OF

PERFUME LANDS,

OR, THE

Search for Capt. Jacob Cole.

WITH INTERESTING FACTS ABOUT

PERFUMES AND ARTICLES USED IN THE TOILET.

(ILLUSTRATED.)

BY

F. S. CLIFFORD.

"Every country and clime offers up its ripened odors from the earth to the Most High."
— *Forster Kerr.*

BOSTON:
PUBLISHED BY CLIFFORD & CO.,
23 SCHOOL STREET.
OCTOBER, 1881.

Entered, according to Act of Congress, in the year 1875, by
FRANK S. CLIFFORD,
In the Office of the Librarian of Congress, at Washington.

25 CENT

Trial Bottles

OF

PERFUMES,

50 Different Kinds.

CLIFFORD, Perfumer,

23 School Street, Boston, Mass.

A few doors from Washington Street.
Near City Hall.

CONTENTS.

READING NURSERY,

ESTABLISHED 1854.

JACOB W. MANNING.

The proprietor, after an experience of thirty-four years in the nursery business, is fully engaged in growing trees and is able to give advice in selecting and planting them, being often called to lay out grounds. During this time nearly all the varieties of grapes and many other large and small fruits that are now popular have been introduced into cultivation; also many ornamental trees and shrubs.

RESIDENCE of the PROPRIETOR, who laid out his own grounds.

The nursery covers fifteen acres, and in it visitors can *see growing* every variety of ornamental and fruit trees and shrubs usually seen growing in nurseries, and many more rare plants not usually found, and some which we are introducing to the trade, and which cannot be found in other grounds. Visitors can learn useful lessons by calling on us and seeing our methods in the care of trees.

Among ornamental trees we call attention to our trimmed hedges, and single trees in conical and round forms for the lawn. These can be removed with perfect safety, owing to frequent transplanting.

We have a very large stock of evergreens. Seventy species and varieties, many of which are very rare. Thuja Woodwardii, of our introduction, a dwarf Arbor Vitæ, will make a perfect hedge without pruning, which will not have the stiff, formal outline of a close clipped hedge.

We have a splendid stock of Maples and Elms, also a full list of deciduous ornamental trees of desirable kind, including blood-leaved, fern-leaved, and variegated-leaved forms.

The following is a partial list :—

1000 Chestnut Oaks, 12 to 18 inches. 2 years from seed.

7000 White Oaks, 6 to 18 inches up to 6 feet.

3000 Red Oaks, 8 to 18 inches up to 8 feet.

1000 Scarlet Oaks, 6 to 12 inches up to 5 feet.

CONTENTS.

LIST OF ILLUSTRATIONS.

THE JOURNAL OF THE SOCIAL CIRCLE.

Home Life in America

AND THE

AMERICAN GASTRONOMIST.

A SEMI-MONTHLY REVIEW,

DEVOTED TO

*THE ART OF LIVING WITH ELEGANCE, COMFORT AND ECONOMY;
THE SCIENCE OF FOOD IN ITS RELATIONS TO HEALTH;
ETIQUETTE, FASHIONS, PERFUMES, Etc., and all the
Domestic and Useful Arts.*

EDITED BY LEO DE COLANGE,

Editor of "Zell's Encyclopædia," "The National Encyclopædia," "Zell's Monthly
Magazine," "The Picturesque World," "Colange's Dictionary of Commerce and Manufacturers," etc., etc.

*Price of Subscription, $3 per year (postage prepaid), invariably
in advance.*

Office of Publication (where all communications are to be addressed),

5 AND 7 MURRAY STREET, NEW YORK.

FINIS PERFUMES.

MR. WILLIAM HALFORD is the Sole Proprietor of the Celebrated Sauce bearing his name. Its undoubted precedence over all the English and American Sauces is now thoroughly established. In consequence of this it has been and is, like all other successful productions, subjected to spurious imitations.

Observe Trade Mark below on each bottle.

ADULTERATION is one of the evils of these high-pressure times. Nothing that is useful or edible escapes its contaminating touch. Respecting the genuine article in Halford Sauce, read the following:—

WM. HALFORD, Esq.:

Sir,—I have analyzed and used the "Halford Leicestershire 'Table Sauce,'" and consider it an excellent relish. It is free from anything unwholesome or injurious, and is composed of such spices and other ingredients as we all know to be the best for a sauce of this kind.

Respectfully,
    S. DANA HAYES,
State's Assayer and Chemist, Mass.

HALFORD
LEICESTERSHIRE
For *Soups,* *Fish,* *Steaks*   *For* *Gravies, Chops,* *Game,* *Cold Meats, etc.*

TABLE SAUCE.

SOLD BY ALL GROCERS.

A ROMANCE OF PERFUME LANDS.

CHAPTER I.

AN OLD FRIEND.

"ALBERT," said my wife, entering my study one afternoon in the spring of 1873, "a gentleman, calling himself Captain Bradford Cole, is in the reception room, and would like to see you."

"What!" I exclaimed in surprise, "Bradford Cole!" and descending the stairs, two steps at a time, mentally abusing the architect and builder for making them so long, I soon had Brad by the hand. He was an English lad, but had lived in Boston, and while here, we were chums. His father was wrecked at sea, and supposed to be on an uninhabited island. It was the object of Brad's life to become a thoroughly educated navigator, so as to be able to go in search of, and find his father; for this purpose he shipped under his uncle, who was captain and part owner of a trading vessel. I remember the day he sailed how I played truant to see him off, but was prevailed upon by a philanthropist to go to a church vestry, to help scrape lint and tear bandages for the soldiers, for this was during the first year of the late civil War; and how grieved I felt afterwards at not seeing him depart.

1

After all my devotion to my country's cause, when I went t. school next day, my excuses availed me nothing, for I was wel! punished for playing truant, which so aroused my indignation that I determined at the first opportunity to leave school, and at last the chance arriving, I enlisted as a Chaplain's boy in the —th. Mass. Vols., but after a year's service was glad to return home and resume my studies, which I followed till I entered business circles.

From that time to this, a period of nearly a dozen years, I had neither seen Brad or heard any tidings of him, and here he stood before me, grown from the slim, pale youth, to a broad shouldered, and well-formed man, imbrowned by exposure to the sun, but with the same merry twinkle in his black eyes, and the same pleasant smile on his full bearded face. I had also changed; the little fellow whom he used to hold on his knee was now almost as large a man as himself, and with constant exercise and temperate living had become nearly as strong, and perhaps a little quicker in my movements; his strength was the result of toil, and mine was gained by a course of training in the gymnasium. Our conditions physically and pecuniarily were well matched. He had followed the sea continuously since he first sailed with his uncle, and had received a thorough nautical education, and by constant attention and assiduous study, he had become a first-class navigator, and with some money which was left him, in addition to that which he earned trading in foreign merchandise, he was quite well off. Still adhering to the resolution of his boyhood, to search for, and find his father, he had had built a beautiful ship according to his own ideas, and was sole owner and commander of her. Unfortunately, he as yet, in all his travels, had found only a slight trace of his father; this he was now fol-

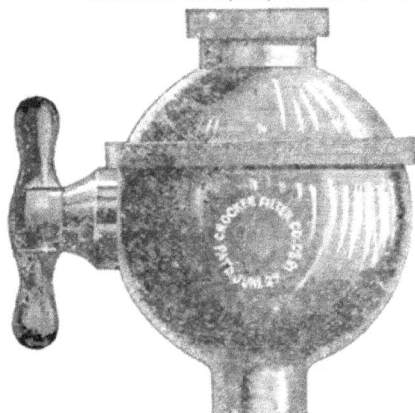

lowing, and he had stopped here to see his old friends, as his search was in this direction.

We were delighted to see each other and talked long into the night, and I finally persuaded him to make my house his home during his stay in this port, although it was an hour's ride into the city. A few years after the war, I had gone into business, and having married a good and economical wife, I was enabled to rise in the world much faster than I should have done alone, and as my business was very profitable and had become extensive, I had a surplus. In fact I had succeeded so well that I had frequently spoken to my wife about going abroad, and here was the opportunity, for Brad intended to induce me to accompany him in his search for his father, provided he could find me, and I was not tied down by business or otherwise; this he told me after several days stay with us.

" All things considered — your entertaining wife, palatial residence and lucrative business, of course you cannot go now," said Brad, " and I was depending so much on your company."

" Well, old fellow, don't be too sure about that; we have been thinking of travelling for some time, but not of making such a long trip as you will probably be obliged to make."

" Have you? I was afraid after finding you so pleasantly situated, it would be hard to get you away."

" There is only one difficulty," I answered, " and that is, I couldn't go and leave my wife alone, and I fear so long a sea voyage would be unpleasant to her."

" Oh! is that all!" said Brad. " That is easily arranged, for I have eight large cabins, and I will have one of them fitted up in the best of style, and with every convenience, so she will hardly know the difference between it and her own cozy parlor;

so it is understood you are to go, and be prepared as soon as possible, for I am impatient to be once more on the deep blue; the life of a land-lubber does not agree with me, and as a parting inducement, it will do your wife good, and deepen the roses in her cheeks; so good-bye for the rest of the day, as I go to make preparations, and when I come back I hope the decision of your wife will be in the affirmative."

This is the manner in which we were induced to set out on our travels; for after a long talk, my wife and I decided we would go, greatly to Brad's joy.

My trade and business being that of a practicing and manufacturing perfumer, also a dealer in everything pertaining to perfumery and the toilet, I always had a great desire to visit the countries where the flowers and plants grew and flourished in the greatest profusion, of which I used the products; and also to make a collection of each and every kind, with a view of forming a conservatory, in which could be seen growing all the Flora from which are derived those pleasant odors which so delight our senses; and also to secure specimens and samples of each of the animals and curiosities pertaining to, or from which any perfume or articles of the toilet owe their derivation, as well as to observe and study all the methods of extracting and manufacturing, and to obtain all new ideas which would advance the interest of the perfumery business and teach others the value and the benefits accruing from the use of perfumes.

"I am sorry, for your wife's sake, I am not married," Brad was saying the day after we had decided to go, "then my wife would be a companion for yours; there is room enough as I have five cabins unoccupied, and I can have two more built if we should need them."

JEAN.

Page 5.

" It would make it much pleasanter," I said. " Do you suppose Susie would like to go?" I asked of my wife.

" She would be delighted," was her reply, " and she could be of great assistance to you no doubt, for she is quite an expert botanist, and would like to examine the growing Flora of the different countries."

" Suppose you write to her and see what she says," I replied.

" Do," said Brad, " I should be happy to have her accompany us; and would it not be well to have your chemist with you? I should think he would be a great help, as he appears to be quite learned, and seems also entirely devoted to your interests. Where did you first meet him?"

" I will answer your question by telling you his story, which is a very sad one," I replied. " I presume you mean Jean Souplesse. Well, one dark, stormy evening in November, several years ago, as I was closing the store, having stopped a little later than usual to complete writing up the result of some experiments I had been making, a dirty, ragged, and as I supposed drunken man, with pale face, sunken eyes and hollow cheeks, reeled toward me; I stepped aside to let him pass, and was proceeding on my way, intending not to notice him, for I despise a drunkard, even the smell of liquor sickens me, and I keep as far from it as possible, and would never give employment to any one addicted to the use of liquor or tobacco in any shape. As he did not move along, I glanced at him again, and he gave me a piteous look. stretched out his hands seemingly imploring for help, staggered, and would have fallen had I not caught him; he had fainted, and as I could smell no stench of liquor about him, I opened the door of the store and carried him in; by the aid of ammonia and brisk rubbing he quickly revived and called for water, speaking in

French. He said he had begged and questiored so many who had not or would not understand him, that that was the reason he had not spoken to me; that he was almost starved, having eaten nothing for three days. Taking him to a restaurant near by I ordered a hot supper for him, after which I took him to a lodging house and hired a room for him to sleep in, and told him to come to the store in the morning, which he did, and then told me that he was from the south of France, and had been in Paris for several years employed as a chemist in a large toilet soap manufactory; but some of the other employées, having become jealous of him on account of his rapid advancement in the factory, he left, and for awhile led an idler's life, strolling in the Parks and Boulevards, and visiting the theatres and other places of amusement. At one of these places a troupe from the United States were performing, and among them a very pretty girl, and as he became enamoured of her, he went nightly to see her acting. At last the engagement of the troupe being concluded, they were about to sail for New York, and he determined to follow her. He said, ' he could not lose her thus,' and spent near to his last sou to pay his passage. He hoped that during the voyage, an opportunity would be offered to form her acquaintance; obtaining an introduction, and pushing his suit with all the ardor of a Frenchman, he soon gained her heart and a promise of her hand on their arrival in America. But alas! during a terrific storm the steamer foundered, and nearly all on board were lost. In the confusion he tried, but could not find his lady-love, and finally concluded she was among the lost. After floating for two days, clinging to a spar, he was rescued by a Boston bound merchantman, and on his arrival at this port, the captain of the vessel supplied him with clothes, and all the money he felt he could spare,

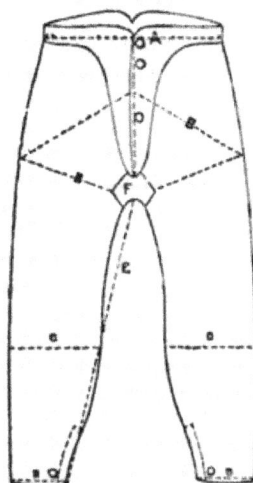

and he started out to find work. He had been here for weeks, but had only obtained an occasional job, just enough to keep body and soul together. For the last three days he had had almost nothing to eat, and the vessel that rescued him having sailed, he was left desolate and despairing. I had thought the matter over during the preceding evening and had concluded to offer him employment at my house as a gardener, but in the morning when he informed me that he was a practical chemist I changed my plans, and gave him employment in the store till I could ascertain how much he really knew. When I told him what I would do for him he was profuse in his thanks. Giving him a week's leisure to regain his health and strength, he commenced work at the store and I have never regretted his coming, as his devotion is unequalled, and by his help I have been able to make many improvements in my manufactures, and have always found him trustworthy, industrious and agreeable. He cannot however seem to overcome his sorrow for the loss of his first love, whom he considers was beyond comparison, for he says, ' one in her calling who resists the many temptations to which she is subject has by far a stronger principle of right and virtue than another who is not so tried.' That is why you will see him standing and apparently looking into the far distant, probably imagining himself again amid the scene of the shipwreck and its horrors."

" When you first saw him he was not under the influence of liquor as you supposed?' asked Brad.

" No," I replied, " he neither drinks nor uses tobacco in any form; he knows well the ill effects of drinking and of what poisons the majority of liquors are made, and would no more think of polluting his system with such fluids than he would think of eating arsenic for dessert; and as for tobacco, he considers that

COLUMBIA BICYCLE.

The Bicycle as a permanent, practical road-vehicle is an acknowledged fact, and the thousands in daily use are constantly increasing in numbers. It combines speed and endurance that no horse can equal, and for pleasure or health is far superior to any other out-door sport. The art of riding is easily acquired, and the exercise is recommended by the medical profession as a means of renewing health and strength, as it brings into action almost every muscle of the body.

Send 3-cent stamp for 24-page illustrated catalogue, containing price-lists and full information.

THE POPE M'F'G CO.

597 Washington Street . . BOSTON, MASS.

GREAT LUNG ᴀɴᴅ CHEST CORDIAL

— AND —

GREAT HEALING VITAL OIL.

Reader, why will you suffer and die with Consumption when a remedy is at hand? Both of these remedies taken and applied in connection with each other, are confidently recommended as a sure cure for all cases of Consumption, except in its last stages. All other affections of the Chest and Lungs are removed in a few days.

Prepared by

J. H. PORTER, M. D.,

SOLE PROPRIETOR OF THE

Rhode Island Medical and Electrical Health Institute, Providence, R. I.

Two Bottles, one for internal and the other for external use, will be sent to all parts of the country by Express, **C. O. D.**, or on receipt of price, **$4.00.**

[The Institute has all modern conveniences, wide southern front, large piazza, heating and ventilation complete, large lawn, shade and fruit trees; near steam and horse cars, church and school and Roger Williams Park. Elmwood horse cars pass Atlantic Street, near the Institute, every ten minutes.]

Address,

DR. J. H. PORTER'S AGENCY,

13 TREMONT ROW (Room 9)   ·   ·   ·   ·   BOSTON, MASS.

nicotine, which is the chief constituent in tobacco, has caused
more softening of the brain and put more people in the insane
asylums than any other one thing; but here he comes, so we will
adjourn to the sitting room and he will tell you more of his history."

Jean was but a few moments preparing for supper; he greeted
us as he entered the room and we then sat down.   Jean Souplesse
was of medium height, with dark, curly hair, deep black eyes,
a short, thick, black moustache and goatee, and red cheeks;
he was quick of movement, and most graceful in action and
polite in manners.

We had received a letter from my wife's sister in reply to ours,
saying, " she should like nothing better than to accompany us, and
would be with us in a few days."   We were now awaiting her
coming, as she had arrived and would soon be down.

Miss Susie Stearns, a really handsome girl, a blonde, not one
of the dumpy, lackadaisical kind, but of lively disposition, of
medium height, slender form, with regal bearing, a graceful carriage, a pleasant smile, and bright blue eyes, which would darken
almost to black when she was excited; an intelligent face, showing
both determination and womanly tenderness; and her hair was
like the finest spun gold, which when left to fall untramelled.
reached far below her waist, clothing her in its wealth and beauty.
like a cloud with a golden lining.   Thus she presented herself to
Capt. Cole, Jean and myself.   After introducing her to my companions, and a few commonplace remarks were exchanged, the conversation turned to our proposed tour.   Susie seemed delighted.
and expressed her satisfaction and gratification at our thinking of
her and opening to her such a field for the practise of her favorite
study.   I saw that both Brad and Jean were well satisfied that

she was to accompany us, and from the many admiring glances bestowed upon her, it looked as if they would lose their hearts or peace of mind if they did not keep themselves under restraint. Supper being announced, we adjourned to the dining-room, where further plans concerning our anticipated journey were discussed.

ASK YOUR DRUGGIST FOR

CLIFFORD'S LIQUID BANDOLINE.
    CLIFFORD'S BRILLIANTINE.
CLIFFORD'S FRENCH COLOGNE.
    CLIFFORD'S VERBENA COLOGNE.
CLIFFORD'S LAVENDER WATER.
    CLIFFORD'S FLORIDA WATER.
CLIFFORD'S HAIR OIL.
    CLIFFORD'S EMOLLIENT.
CLIFFORD'S BALSAMIC TOOTH WASH.
    CLIFFORD'S TOOTH POWDER.
CLIFFORD'S LIQUID BLANC DE PERLE.
    CLIFFORD'S HAIR DRESSING.
CLIFFORD'S TOILET VINAIGRE.
    CLIFFORD'S FLAVORING EXTRACTS.
CLIFFORD'S BAY RUM.
    CLIFFORD'S SEA FOAM SHAMPOO.
CLIFFORD'S ROSE WATER.
    CLIFFORD'S ORANGE FLOWER WATER.
CLIFFORD'S HANDKERCHIEF EXTRACTS (all odors).
    CLIFFORD'S SACHET PERFUME POWDERS (all odors).

All the above in 25c., 50c., 75c. and $1.00 bottles.

These articles below sent by mail to any address on receipt of price :—

CLIFFORD'S SERPENT EGGS, 15c. box.
    CLIFFORD'S CAMPHOR ICE, 25c. box.
CLIFFORD'S COSMETIQUE, 25c. stick.
    CLIFFORD'S MOUSTACHE WAX, 25c. cake.
CLIFFORD'S FACE POWDER, 20c. package.
    CLIFFORD'S SHAVING SOAP, 10c. cake.
CLIFFORD'S BATH SOAP, 20c. cake.
    CLIFFORD'S PERFUME POWDERS, 50c. ounce.
CLIFFORD'S 336-Page, Elegantly Illustrated "ROMANCE OF PER-
FUME LANDS," $1.50 per copy.

If your Druggist does not have them, send to

CLIFFORD & CO.,

Manufacturing Perfumers, Chemists,

AND DEALERS IN

DRUGGISTS' SUNDRIES AND TOILET ARTICLES,

23 SCHOOL STREET - - BOSTON, MASS.

Send for Free Price List.

THUS SHE PRESENTED HERSELF TO US.

CHAPTER II.

THE following day, Tuesday, we all proceeded to the city to view the steam yacht on which we expected to reside for many days. We reached the wharf, and there in the bay rode at anchor a magnificent clipper-built steam yacht, of about three hundred and twenty tons burthen. She had two masts, — a foremast with fore-sail, fore-top and fore-top-gallant sails, and a mainmast carrying a mainsail and fore-staff. Her rigging was therefore sufficient, and she could profit by wind like a simple clipper; but she relied principally upon her mechanical power. Her engine was of an effective force of two hundred and eighty horse power, and being constructed on the most improved plans, possessed apparatus for overheating, which gave its steam a powerful tension. It was a high pressure engine, and produced motion by a double screw; "CYNTHIA" in large gold letters was brightly conspicuous on the stern. Under a full head of steam the Cynthia could acquire great velocity, and Capt. Cole assured us she could attain a speed of twenty miles an hour. On the forecastle we could see the shine of a pivot gun, reflected by the sun.

"No knowing what may happen," said Capt. Cole. "It is

10

better to have some means of defense than be taken unawares; we have also a good armory between decks, with abundance of small arms and amunition. Here comes the small boat; we will go on board, then you can continue your inspection at closer quarters."

"Isn't she a beauty!" exclaimed Susie, referring to the steamer.

"I think she is," replied Capt. Cole, — but he was not looking at the ship at the time he spoke. "I am glad you admire her, for I am very proud of my vessel."

The boat touching the steps at this moment, we embarked, and were quickly rowed to the ship, and soon on deck. Everything was clean and in the most perfect order; the sailors neatly dressed and intelligent looking. We descended directly to the main cabin; this was large, and the luxuriant style in which it was fitted was pleasing to us. Two large inlaid tables occupied the centres of each half; above each was a chandelier of rich bronze, supplied with gas, made by a gas machine on board; around the room were elegant reclining and easy chairs and two lounges; let into the wood-work on one side was a library, filled to repletion with works by the best authors on Science, Poetry and Fiction. A superior piano, with a rack full of the latest music, occupied the rear of the saloon, under a skylight.

"How nice," said Susie, "no necessity of time dragging heavily on our hands."

"I expect to hear some excellent singing by you," said Capt. Cole. "I have been informed that you are a very good singer, and that Jean is quite a musician, so you two must make it your duty to amuse us during our leisure hours."

"We will entertain you to the best of our ability," they both replied.

PETERSILEA
ACADEMY OF MUSIC,
Elocution and Languages,

281 COLUMBUS AVE., BOSTON, MASS.

In alliance with the ROYAL ACADEMY OF MUSIC, LONDON;
and the ROYAL CONSERVATORY OF MUSIC, LEIPZIG.

Best Possible Instruction

AT LOWEST POSSIBLE RATES.

FINISHING FINE SOLOISTS AND TEACHERS A SPECIALTY.

BEGINNERS, ONLY $10 PER TERM,

English Literature, Concerts, History and Theory of Music, Readings, Piano Recitals
and Ensemble Lessons, Free to Pupils.

DIPLOMA AND HANDSOME GOLD MEDAL PRESENTED TO GRADUATES.

"Now let me show you your cabins," said Brad.

Into this large saloon eight smaller cabins opened; these were each of good size, and fitted in the same luxurious manner, corresponding with the large saloon, and each supplied with gas, water, and every convenience necessary for comfort. They were, however, arranged peculiarly. Two doors opened into each one; two berths, oblong shape, were in the centre, and hung at each end on a post firmly set, sufficient space being left for passage-way at either end. A woven, nickel-plated wire mattrass, bound with bands of elastic steel, was suspended within two brass hoops, like a ship's compass, and heavily weighted to keep them in position; these moving upon each other formed a universal joint and thus counteracted the motion of the vessel.

"No danger of your suffering from sea-sickness," said I to my wife.

"That *is* a blessing for which I am truly thankful," she replied.

"If you feel the least nausea," I said, "you can lie down and immediately recover from it; and by taking short strolls in the saloon to accustom yourself to the motion of the vessel, and returning to your berths, you will soon be good sailors; at night the ship may pitch and rock and you will not perceive it."

"There will be no need to enter your berths if the motion is disagreeable," said Capt. Cole, "as I have had four chairs constructed, on a plan similar to that of these berths, which I intend to have set up in the large cabin; they look like a large ship's lamp; in each of the gimbals is a section swinging on hinges and fastened with a spring catch; the front of the box or chair part is open, but the back and sides are closed, padded and covered with material similar to the other furniture; there are arms pro-

jecting from the sides and a rest for the feet, and I think you will find them the most comfortable of easy chairs. You must, however, keep your eyes as much as possible from surrounding objects, or you might feel slightly sick."

"Words are inadequate to express our thanks, Brad," said I, "for all the trouble and expense you have incurred to protect us from that terror of sea-travellers."

Scarcely noticing my remarks Brad continued, — "This, Albert, will be your cabin; I occupy the one opposite; adjoining yours is Miss Susie's; opposite Miss Susie's and next to mine is my first mate's. He is ashore at present, but I will introduce him to you when we meet. Adjacent to his is Jean's, and the one facing Jean's is used as a store and work room."

All were fitted in the same rich manner as the main cabin; no expense had been spared to make them comfortable. The cabins of Capt. Cole and the first mate were not supplied with the swinging berths, but otherwise they did not differ from those to be occupied by us.

"I think I have a surprise in store for you, Albert," said Brad, after we had inspected the state-rooms.

"Another?" said I.

"Still another," he replied.

"What is it?"

"Follow me;" and leading us to the after part of the large saloon, Capt. Cole lifted aside some drapery which concealed a door in a partition that divided the large cabin from the stern. I looked into the room and was indeed surprised; the entire stern was arranged with shelves, covered with an assortment of vials with glass stoppers, graduates and measures, a pair of scales, a set of percolaters and receivers, a small copper still, and a glass

one; the shelves were divided into compartments with covers, to hold roots, seeds, grasses and dried flowers, and stands, in which were cut slots and holes to grasp the bottles which were to contain samples of ottos, essences, oils and extracts, that we expected to collect on our tour; these stands were made to slide into some of the compartments. A complete laboratory with every facility one could possibly wish for.

"Brad," said I, "how *can* I thank you?"

"By saying nothing about it in the way of thanks," said he; "all these arrangements have been made by Jean; he is the one to whom the praise and thanks are due."

"But you furnished the room, let me express my gratitude to you for that," I said. "Where is Jean? I must tell him how pleased I am for his thoughtfulness. There he is with Susie; I will go to him."

"Never mind now," interrupted my wife; "they are busily engaged in the library looking over the books and music; some other time will answer your purpose as well. You are very kind," she said, turning to Brad.

"Never mind, for we have no time to discuss that subject now, for there rings the dinner-gong; allow me to conduct you to the dining saloon."

Proceeding to the dining saloon, we there saw a table well filled with substantial fare; the arrangements were very attractive, and everything neat and inviting. Here we met Mr. Roscoe, the first mate, of the *Cynthia*. After Brad had done the honors of the vessel by introductions, we seated ourselves and did justice to the viands.

Mr. Roscoe, as a companion of our voyage, is worthy of a description. Possessed of a genial face, a firm mouth. indented

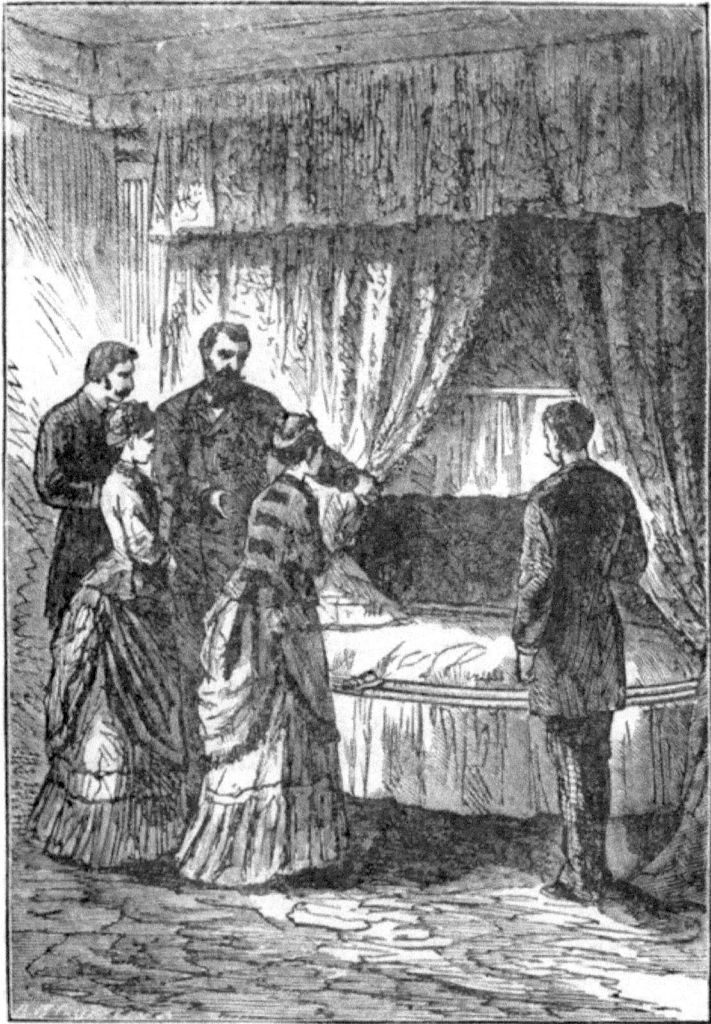

THEY WERE, HOWEVER, ARRANGED PECULIARLY.

Page 12

chin, showing cool understanding, sharp gray eyes, red side whiskers trimmed close, making the face look large and full; dark chestnut, wavy hair; six feet and two inches in height, with the chest and shoulders of a Hercules, of good form; a man to command and to be obeyed, yet not severe; agreeable in conversation, yet not talkative; a native of the eastern part of the coast of Maine, he had been a sailor from boyhood, and he became acquainted with Capt. Cole in London, England, and Bradford, finding in him a good and trustworthy friend, had given him the berth of second commander.

After dinner, Susie tried the piano, Jean and I inspected the laboratory and its contents to see if anything was required to make it complete, and my wife, Capt. Cole, and Mr. Roscoe sat on deck, conversing on general topics, and watching the vessels as they came up the harbor. At four o'clock we started home arriving there in about three hours.

"We have two weeks for preparation," I remarked to them on our way home, "and we must be fully prepared, for we ought not delay Capt. Cole any longer, as his anxiety to follow up the clew already obtained toward the finding of his father should not be prolonged. By the way; I don't know as I ever told you why he had directed his course this way. Well, during his last cruise with his uncle, they were dealing with traders in the East Indies, and while cruising among the Islands, fell in with a merchantman from London. Among the exchanges which they made were some London papers; looking over them, he saw an announcement of his mother's death, which had occurred six months previous according to the date of the paper; he was very anxious to get back to London, so obtaining permission from his uncle, he took passage on board a homeward-bound vessel.

" In due time he arrived at London, and immediately repaired to the house of his uncle, where his mother used to reside ; he visited her grave, but everything that was necessary had been done by his aunt, who was his mother's sister. A will, by which she left some money and other effects to him, was given to him. The will contained a clause, requesting him to use the money to ascertain the fate of his father, and to rescue him if he still lived ; his mother always refusing to believe that he was dead.

" Among other documents and papers left by his mother, he found an advertisement which she had clipped from the *London Daily Times*, and had pasted to a sheet of writing paper, on which were various memoranda, showing that she had tried to find the author of the advertisement, and had followed him to many places ; but having been unsuccessful in meeting him, she left the task to her son, Captain Bradford Cole, with a dying request that he should use all means to find his father. The search for the writer of the advertisement probably hastened the death of Brad's mother, as his aunt said she was out in all kinds of weather, and being in poor health, the exposure, in addition to the worry consequent from her repeated failures, was too much for her constitution.

" Brad hastened to the last address on the memorandum, without, however, much hope of gaining any information, as it was almost a year since it was made. The people with whom the writer of the advertisement had stopped, told Brad that the man had gone to Liverpool. Brad went there to the address given him, but could not find the writer of the advertisement ; in fact, all trace of him was lost for the time being, till one day, happening to be in the office of the Cunard Steamship Line, conversing with one of the clerks, an old school friend of his, an officer of one of

THE "HARVARD" ROADSTER.

THE HARVARD TRICYCLE.

the steamers just arrived in port, entered the office, and reported one of the sailors to be crossed from the roll.

" ' What name?' asked the clerk.

" ' John Gagler, com—'

" ' Who!' exclaimed Brad, interrupting him.

" The officer repeated the name, — ' John Gagler, common seaman.' Brad, seeing they noticed his agitation, explained to them that it was the man for whom he had been searching for months. 'Could he forget that name?' It was before him always; even the wording of the advertisement had not slipped his memory; it read thus :

" ' An old sailor would like to find some friends or connections of Capt. Jacob Cole, of the ship " Godolpha," foundered at sea about seventeen years ago.

" ' JOHN GAGLER, No. 24 Hackett's Lane.'

" Brad had a copy of the advertisement with him, and showed it to the officer and clerk.

" ' You have no necessity for haste to find him,' said the officer, ' as we left him sick in the hospital, and he will not recover probably for several months; and on our return we can bring him back with us.'

" So Brad make an agreement with the officer to do so.

" After the steamer arrived in New York, Brad received a telegram from the officer that John Gagler had recovered sooner than expected, and had left the hospital.

" Soon after his return to London from the East Indies, Brad had made a contract for the building of the *Cynthia*, the vessel we have visited to-day. It being nearly completed, he determined to wait until it was finished, and to sail to the United States in his own ship, telegraphing to the officer to have the attendants

THE
Sparrow Kneader and Mixer.

This kneader produces bread that is perfect in quality and entirely free from impurities liable from perspiration; the whole work being done with the Kneader, the hands do not come in contact with the dough at all. In addition to cleanliness, by its use, time, labor and material are saved; considerations of the utmost importance in every family.

THE SPARROW MIXER

FOR

MAKING CAKE,

Beating eggs and sugar for Ice Cream, and for mixing purposes of every kind, is the most perfect and rapid of any device for the purpose ever made. In sizes from six quarts to fifteen gallons.

FOR
Economy and Comfort.

All persons using Smoothing and Pressing Irons for any purpose should purchase the

NONPAREIL LAMP AND IRONS.

The Utility Roaster is splendid for roasting meats of all kinds, is Self-Basting, and requires no attention while cooking.

Our Improved Double Bail Hollow Ware for Stove and Kitchen use is just splendid; no burning the hands with hot bails or scalding with steam.

We manufacture and sell the above and many other useful articles, to which we invite your attention.

SPARROW & NOBLE,
234 HANOVER STREET, BOSTON.

at the hospital ascertain where John Gagler had emigrated. Brad is now here in Boston, to find, if possible, this man; from information received from the Superintendent of the Hospital he thinks he can, so we must do all in our power to further his purposes. We sail from here to New York, as Brad wishes to see if he can get any further information from the employés at the hospital, than was telegraphed to him. Thence to Jacksonville, Florida, and from there to a small town called Green Cove, situated twenty miles from Jacksonville, at which place he was informed that John Gagler had settled."

UNEQUALLED!

Essex's Improved Nickel Silver Atomizers.

For the Atomization of Liquids for Inhalation, Freezing for producing Local Anæsthesia, Odorizing or Face Baths, and for Perfuming and Disinfecting the Sick-Room. They also constitute a perfect Douche for Bathing the Head, Sensitive Eyes, Painful Surfaces, Burns or Inflamed Sores, Throat, Nasal and other Local Application.

By these Atomizers, a single drop of perfume is converted into numberless minute particles, which fill the surrounding air with fragrance. The toilet of no lady or gentleman is complete without one of these instruments.

Artists, Architects, Draughtsmen and Amateurs use and recommend Essex's No. 5 Atomizers as superior to all others for producing fixation directly and instantaneously upon the surface of all designs in Water Colors, Charcoal, Sepia, India Ink, Chalk, etc., etc. The application of the Fixatif is, by these instruments, rendered very simple, and the results are durable and otherwise entirely satisfactory.

No. 5, F, Atomizer.

No. 5, C, Atomizer.

Ocean Vapor Nickel Silver Atomizer.

No. 5, D, Atomizer.

MANUFACTURED ONLY BY

THE ESSEX MANUFACTURING COMPANY, NEWPORT, R. I.

Under Patent June 27, 1871, Reissued May 29, 1877.

Sole Manufacturers and Proprietors of the only Atomizer which has an Atomizing Tube, combined with an External Vent passing through the same opening in the Stopper as the Jet or Suction Tube; also, of the only Atomizer which has, in combination with the Suction or Jet Tube, an External Vent passing through the same aperture in the Stopper, and provided with a Drip Cup and Return Passage, leading into and forming part of the Vent Tube. For sale at the store of

CLIFFORD & CO., Perfumers, 23 School Street, Boston.

CHAPTER III.

ON the twenty-third of July, 1873, all being in readiness, my business left to the control of my father, we started for the ship, — Susie, Jean, my wife and self.

After bidding farewell to our relatives and friends, we entered a car and in about three hours were aboard the *Cynthia*. We weighed anchor in the cool of the evening, and steaming down the harbor, passed the forts and beacons, and at midnight we were on the broad Atlantic, nothing in sight save the bright, twinkling stars above, and the dark green, sparkling water beneath us. Captain Cole had had the new chairs arranged, and we of the land found them admirable.

The evening passed pleasantly to all and we did not retire till very late. We reached New York before eight o'clock next morning, and lay here for Brad to make his inquiries, and to procure and store the necessaries for a long voyage, allowing us time to make whatever short excursions we wished. We made good use of the opportunity thus offered.

The first day we visited many of the places of interest in this great business mart of the New World. Knowing we had time, I determined to take a trip to the town of White Pigeon, St.

19

Joseph county, Michigan, where the principal Peppermint Farms of America are situated.

Boarding a small steamer we had a delightful sail up the Hudson; stopping a few hours at West Point, thence to Albany, then by rail to Niagara Falls, reaching there late in the evening. We were obliged to wait until morning to view them. Although much fatigued with our ride, we were up early, and going to the foot of the inclined railway, a magnificent spectacle met our eyes.

Leaving here, before sunset we reached White Pigeon, where the sight of the numerous acres of peppermint plants was alone sufficient to show the public taste for this odor, though strictly speaking, peppermint is consumed more to gratify the sense of taste ather than that of smell. It is used too much as a confection flavor ever to become a favorite as a perfume; nevertheless a large percentage is used in scenting soaps and mouth washes; for these, however, it is used by the French perfumers more than by those of any other nation. The fact is, pure peppermint is a more uncommon article with them than with us, so by a law of human nature, — ever seeking that which is most difficult to obtain, — the European people esteem it more of an odor than we do.

Seeking the proprietor of the distillery of the Otto of Peppermint, introducing ourselves, and informing him of the object of our visit, we were invited in, and he generously devoted a portion of his time for our benefit.

He first described to us its growth and manner of cultivation.

"The roots," he said, "are planted thickly in rows, between which spaces are left for the cultivator to pass, great care being exercised to prevent weeds growing among the plants, thus insuring a pure article of otto. The fields are ploughed and changed once every five years; the first year's crop is generally

F. HUBBARD & CO.
Picture Frame Makers.

GILDED AND PLAIN OAK FRAMES A SPECIALTY.

GILDING AND CABINET WORK.

SHOW CASES.

All kinds of Easels.   Also, Repairing.

23 WINTER STREET - BOSTON.

ORDERS PROMPTLY ATTENDED TO.

Samples can be seen at Clifford & Co.'s, 28 School Street.

H. M. POTTER'S
PRACTICAL AND POSITIVE METHOD
— OF —

DRESS AND CLOAK CUTTING.

IT CAN PRODUCE ANY GARMENT WORN.

PRICE, $5.00.   ORAL INSTRUCTION, $7.50.

DRESS PLAITING AND PLAITING MACHINES FOR SALE.

M. E. REED, 129 TREMONT STREET, ROOM 9 - - - BOSTON.

AGENTS WANTED.   General Agent for Massachusetts.

MRS. S. C. FENNER,
Root and Herb Doctress,

71 Carpenter St., Providence, R. I.

TREATMENT OF THE HAIR AND SCALP,
···→A SPECIALTY.←···

Letters answered in regard to restoring the Hair for $1.00.   Hair Restorative furnished
if requested.

the most abundant and purest, and is raised exclusively for its otto, about seven pounds of which is the average yield for an acre of plants. We usually cut it during the latter part of August."

He then led the way to the distillery, and we were just in time to see it in operation, as they were now bringing in the plants to be put into the still.

"These plants have been cut about a week," he said, "and have been standing in cocks at night, and spread during the day to dry, the same as in hay-making. If you will step this way," he continued, as he opened a door, "I will show you into the manufactory."

We passed from the office into a large place, with two openings on each side, in which were two large hay-riggings being unloaded.

"The loads have been weighed outside on scales at the rear end of the building," said the proprietor, "and a record is kept by one of my clerks of the weight of each load."

The plants were being carried to two large wooden stills and packed in. As one still was almost fully charged, we waited half an hour, and the lid of the still was put on, and steam admitted at the bottom by a pipe from a boiler. When it was heated to about 212° Fahrenheit, its aromatic principle went with the steam into the worm which is placed in a cooler to condense the otto and steam; it then passed out into a connected receiver, where the otto, as it floated on the surface, was lifted out with shallow dippers, poured into conveying vessels, and carried to the re-distilling and purifying room, where it was distilled again, then was taken to the packing room, to which we followed it, where were several men and girls filling bottles; the same kind

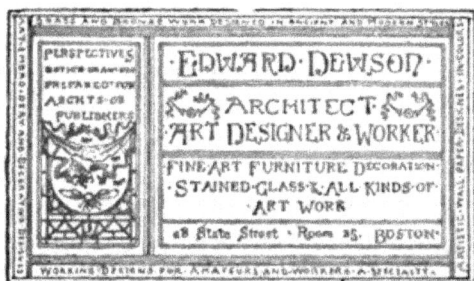

RAILROAD ADVERTISER

PUBLISHED BI-WEEKLY

At 79 Milk Street - - - Room 12.

SUBSCRIPTION

60 cents per year, 30 cents for six months, in advance, postage prepaid.

ADVERTISING RATES $1.00 per inch.   SPECIAL RATES on long Contracts.

Contains Time-Tables of Railroads running from Boston, also information regarding Horse-Car Lines, Coaches, Soldiers' Messenger Corps, Hack Fares, P. O. arrangements, Fire Alarm Telegraph, etc.

Is printed on fine tinted paper, having original and selected reading-matter; and being given free distribution at the depots, and throughout the city and country, makes it one of the best mediums for advertising.

MERCHANTS' NEWSPAPER LIST.

as are used for old English porter and stout, they being the safest for transportation, — and labelling them ready for delivery.

"Will you please tell us what use you make of the refuse mint?" Jean asked.

"We place it in stacks, and dry it," replied the proprietor; then it becomes tolerable fodder for sheep, and we sell it to the neighboring farmers. The meat of the sheep fed on this refuse is liked by a great many; for, as they say, 'it gives it an aromatic and agreeable flavor.'"

He also, in answer to our many inquiries, informed us that "about twenty thousand pounds per annum, of otto of peppermint are exported to England from this county, New York state, and Ohio, where there are also extensive Peppermint Farms. This farm is the largest in the country, having over one thousand acres under cultivation." He invited us outdoors to inspect some of the growing plants, a few acres of which had not as yet been gathered.

"The plants, you will observe," he remarked, "are of course much larger than those which we meet with in the fields."

"And how exhilarating the odor is," said Susie.

He gave us some fine samples, which were the first of our collection, to which we hoped to add many more. Susie classed it as *Mentha piperata*, an aromatic, pungent, deciduous, and herbaceous plant.

As we were returning on the cars, and were examining a small quantity of the otto which I had received, Jean remarked, "that dried peppermint herb affords by distillation over a naked fire a greater quantity of otto than by steam distillation."

"Why do they not distil it always by direct heat?" asked Susie.

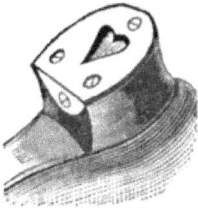

PAT. ARMOR
HEEL PLATES

—FOR—

Ladies' and Children's Boots and Shoes.

THEY DO NOT TEAR THE SKIRTS OR CARPETS;

THEY DO NOT RATTLE, OR CATCH AND PULL OFF,

AS THE OLD-FASHIONED KIND DO.

Ask your Shoe Dealer for Them.

THEY PROJECT OVER THE EDGE IN FRONT OF THE HEEL, THOROUGHLY PROTECTING IT.

How shabby a woman looks — if well dressed otherwise — with her boot heels all run down. For 15 cts. a shoe dealer will put a pair of **Pat. Armor Heel Plates** on your boots and add 100 per cent to their looks and wear.

EDWARD HENSHAW,

Manufacturer,

48 and 52 HIGH STREET · · · · · BOSTON, MASS.

"Because the otto obtained by steam distillation, is specifically lighter and of a brighter color than that obtained by a direct fire, also, there is no danger of burning the herb where such large quantities are operated upon, as the slightest scorching would spoil the otto, or give it an empyreumatic odor," replied Jean.

"Fresh peppermint herb gives by steam distillation and by distillation over a naked fire an equal quantity of otto," I remarked.

"Yes," said Jean, "and dried peppermint herb contains two different ottos, possessing different boiling points, and different specific gravities. The otto of higher specific gravity is formed from that of the lower specific gravity during the drying of the herb, as the fresh herb affords only one otto of specific gravity .910."

On reaching New York, we forwarded our samples and specimens by express to Boston, as we thought it safer than to keep them in the ship. We then went on board and saw Brad, who informed us that he was ready to start, and would sail in the evening; we then repaired to our cabins, laid aside our travelling clothes and donned those more suitable for the sea.

CHAPTER IV.

THE second day out from New York, near noon, we were sitting in the large saloon, differently engaged, when suddenly we heard on deck a stamping of many feet, cheers and exclamations like the following: "Hi yah!" "Whoop la!" "Hup there!" We could not have reached China yet, but it sounded as if we had been boarded by a crowd of Chinese. Brad, Mr. Roscoe and myself rushed up on deck to see what could cause such a commotion. Forward, we saw a group of the sailors, seemingly watching something very interesting, for they did not notice our approach. Coming up behind them cautiously as we looked over their heads, we saw near the bow a short, thick-set man or boy, — he was neither the one or the other, but a combination of the two, — with nothing on as wearing apparel, but a ragged shirt and short pants. He was coming from the bow towards us at full speed; we saw that in front of us, and extending some distance towards the bow, were spread some old sails; just as he reached the edge of them, he turned quickly on his hands, ejaculating at the same time those same phrases we had heard before, and with lightning-like rapidity turning over and over from his hands to his feet, he had almost reached within a few feet of the

24

sailors in front of us, when with one immense leap, he shot up
into the air as high as ten feet, and turned completely over and
around, and came down lightly and gracefully on his feet in
front of us. Then the stamping of the sailors' feet and their
cheering were renewed. At this juncture Capt. Cole pushed in
among the sailors and exclaimed, —

"What is the meaning of this? Where is the officer of the
watch?"

The sailors dispersed, standing in groups a short distance
away. The gymnast stood on the sails where he had landed from
his last somersault, grinning comically at us. The officer presented himself to Capt. Cole who asked him for an explanation.

"Aye! aye! sir; this boy sir, is a stowaway."

"Why was he not brought directly to me?" asked Capt.
Cole.

"Well, sir," the officer answered, "he was caught near the
steward's room, looking for something to eat, and he pleaded so
hard for food, that we gave him some, intending then to take him
to you. I asked him 'Where he wanted to go.' And he said, 'to
Ireland.' When we told him we were not going there he seemed
surprised. Going on deck, towards your cabin," the officer continued, "to take him to you, one of the men banteringly asked
him, 'What could he do on board ship.' The boy immediately
sprang on to one of the hauling lines, and went up, hand over
hand as quickly as a monkey, clean to the gasket, and then came
down like a flash. 'Shure an how's that?' he asked. 'Bring
on an ould sail,' he said, in his quick sprightly manner; and supposing that he wanted to show us that he was also a sail-maker,
one of the men brought him one; then he asked for another, and
we got it, forgetting in our curiosity to see what he could do, that

we were disobeying orders in not bringing him to you. He spread
the sails out and then performed something similar to that which
you just now saw; then the men gathering around cheered him,
and he repeated it; I hope I shall not forget again, sir, but we
were very much interested."

"Enough!" said Capt. Cole, who had waited patiently until
the explanation was concluded, "if anything unusual occurs
again, report to me immediately; now have the boy washed and
neatly dressed; give him a good dinner, then after we have dined,
send him to me."

"Aye, aye, sir," said the officer. We then descended to the
saloon, commenting upon this queer accession to the ship's crew,
and related to my wife and Susie what had occured. Soon after,
we dined. About half an hour later, the stranger was ushered
in. I judged that he was about twenty-five years old; he was
short in stature; the clothes he had on giving him a comical appearance, as they were probably the property of some one of the
sailors, who was a foot or two taller than he; he had a droll face,
snub nose, heavy black eyebrows, meeting over the nose, black
hair, cut too short to be called any length, round head, and small
twinkling gray eyes."

"What is your name?" asked Capt. Cole.

"Patsey Dunn, yer honor."

"How did you get on board, and where do you want to go?"

"Well, yer honor, yer must know that I was travelling with
a circus, way out West, an' they busted up intirely, heving bad
business all the sayson, an' be jabers I hed to wurruk me way
back to New York, an' whin I got there, yer honor, divil a cint
did I hev, so I kep loafing 'round trying to git sumthing to do,
for to git sumthing to ate wid, whin the evening before yees

William N. Frizzell,

Engraver and Plate Printer,

22 Winter Street, Boston.

EUGENE BERNINGHAUS'
(CINCINNATI, OHIO)

Revolving & Adjustable Barber and Dental Chair "Paragon."

The accompanying illustration represents our latest and entirely new invention, the REVOLVING BARBER and DENTAL CHAIR. The frame, of beautiful design, is made of iron (excepting arm-rests and back frame), handsomely japanned and embellished with gilding. The superior advantages in a Revolving Barber or Dental Chair are apparent to every one: it can be placed in any position to command the advantage of light; it is adjustable by a foot lever (so popular for its simplicity in my other chairs) in whatever position the same may be placed. The foot-stool is not connected to body of chair, but to a revolving plate just below, to this being also attached the hinges holding chair in position and by means of which the same is adjustable to the various angles. The seat can be taken out and replaced by a summer seat. The foot-stool is trimmed to match chair; platform covered with polished sheet brass, put on with fire-gilt nails. The casters facilitate moving about. *This chair can also be had with Improved Adjustable Head-rest, price, $4.00.*

(Patent applied for.)

PRICES OF CHAIR.

Covered in best Silk Plush (crimson or maroon) ..... }
Covered in pure Mohair (green, crimson or maroon). } **$60.00**
Covered in Moquette (very handsome and durable).. }
Extra Perforated Seat for Summer Use $3.50
Adjustable Barber Chairs of all Prices and Coverings.

CLIFFORD & CO. - - - 23 School Street, Boston, Mass.
SOLE NEW ENGLAND AND CANADIAN AGENTS.

sailed, I was near this illegant vissil, and a gintleman and lady were talking on deck, an' I heard thim say sumthing about raching Ireland."

"You must be mistaken," said Capt. Cole, "we do not intend to go to Ireland; anyway not for the present."

"Perhaps," I interrupted, "as Jean and Susie were talking together on deck, they might have said something about reaching Ireland; if we found your father, you would of course take him to London, then we should be near Ireland."

"Yis sir," said Patsey. "Well, yer honor, whin I heard the name of me ould sod spoken, the thought struck me that I would loike for to see me ould muther and fayther once moore, an' as I hed got disgusted with the show business, I thought I would ship wid yees. I axed one ov the sailors if ye wantid any moore men, an' he sid 'No.' I hed nary a cint to pay me fare, an' as the feeling was still strong widthin me for to see the ould folks, I was bound to go wid yees; so watching me chance, I hid in the hould. Shure, an' I thought I culd stan' the hunger longer, but it were hard, wid the smell of all the nice things near me, an' I hedn't hed a square male of vittels for a week or moore; so I stole out, an' wus jist agoing to git me hand on sumthing to stay me stomach, whin sumthing loike a strapping big fellow got his hand on me."

"What shall I do with you?" said Capt. Cole.

"An' ye wouldn't be after punishing a poor fellow that's got himself into a scrape from the love to his ould folks would yees?" pleaded Patsey.

"You tried to steal passage in my ship to Ireland, as you supposed, and also to steal my food," said Capt. Cole, looking sternly at him. "Do you not think you deserve it?"

WITH ONE IMMENSE LEAP HE SHOT UP INTO THE AIR.

Page 25.

"I niver giv it a thought, yer honor," replied Patsey. "I niver was on a ship before, excipting whin I came over from Ireland with me uncle, thin I was a small, wee bit of a gossoon; but, yer honor, I can wurruk an' do onything fur yees, only let me aff this time, and yees can put me on shore at onst, or whiniver ye loikes; but I shuld like iver so much to go to ould Ireland, if yees was iver expecting to git there."

"I must punish him some way," said Capt. Cole aside to me, "so as to make him obey in future. I rather like the boy, he is so spry, and as we have no especial servant here in the cabins, I will try him awhile and see how he behaves."

"You may go now," he said to Patsey, "and report to the officer of the watch."

Patsey went out, saying as he did so, "Thank yees, Captain," but looking rather dubious as to his fate.

Afterwards we talked the matter over, and I told Brad I would engage him as my attendant, as he would be very useful to me to climb and gather leaves, flowers, and curiosities.

After a few moments Captain Cole called the officer of the watch, and told him to compel Patsey to stand on the head of a barrel for one hour, as punishment. The officer went out, but in less than ten minutes one of the sailors entered, and said, "Captain, please sir, the hofficer of the watch sent me to say that Patsey was dancing jigs and 'ornpipes like mad, hon the top of the barrel; and the first thing we knew, the 'ead broke, and 'e fell into the brine water hin the barrel, — hit was an hold pork barrel he was hon, — and we pulled 'im hout wet through."

"Give him dry clothes, and mast-head him," said Capt. Cole; "make him stay there till further orders."

It was but a short time before the man came in abruptly,

and reported that Patsey was "'anging by 'is toes, standing on 'is 'ands, and swinging from the top-sail left to the back-stay, and doing various other capers; han' 'e'll break 'is neck," said the man.

"Order him aloft to the main truck," said Capt. Cole; "let him hang on there for half an hour," and turning to me he said, "I'll take the courage out of him."

The man had not been gone more than five minutes, when in he rushed, seemingly demoralized.

"What *is* the matter now?" asked the Captain.

"That boy, please sir. No sooner was 'e hordered to the truck than 'e went hup, han' 'ung there a minute or two, when my hattention was called to 'im by hexclamations of my shipmates near me. I looked hup, and there 'e was standing on his 'ead on the main truck, with 'is legs pointing hout like a weather-vane, and the mast bending like a reed hin the wind. The hofficer called to 'im, han' now 'e is sitting hon the truck looking as hunconcerned as you please."

"He is irrepressible," said I to Capt. Cole.

"You may order him down and send him to me," said the Captain to the man.

"Aye, aye, sir," was the response.

In a few minutes Patsey came in with a sly gleam in his eye; he was making a great effort to look sorry, but with poor success, for it made him look droller than ever.

"What shall I do with you, Patsey?" asked the Captain.

"Nuthing, plase yer honor," he answered.

"You say you were never on a ship before. Do you think you would like to be a sailor?" asked the Captain.

"Shure an' I wuld, sir," said he, "only yees give me some-

thing to do, an' ye won't find me lazy; but I can't kape still for the soul of me."

"Well, report to the officer again and tell him to find something for you to do. I think the steward would like some extra help, and be careful that you don't get into any more mischief."

From that day, Patsey was the pet of the crew, and many a leisure hour did he beguile for them, with songs and stories; he knew every step of all the dances he ever saw executed, and would go through with them; you could hear the rattle of his feet, making music for them during many a quiet evening. After awhile he became a good sailor, and with his nerve and dexterity in handling himself, he surpassed them all. He seemed to like the cabin best, and never appeared so contented as when he was doing something to help us, especially my wife and Susie.

CHAPTER V.

REACHING Hampton Roads, we anchored off Fortress Monroe. Brad and I wishing to visit this place, we went ashore and made a tour of the Fortress. Brad had a desire to see so memorable a fort, and I wanted to see the Virginia Cedar growing, and to obtain a piece of the wood, and a sample of the otto, as there was a distillery close by where the cedar-wood otto was manufactured.

"This wood has been famous since the days of Solomon, who employed it in the construction of the Temple," said Jean, "probably to have the structure last for all time, and protect it from ruin by insects, and according to Vitruvius, a celebrated architect in the time of Augustus, Cedria, an otto or gum extracted from the cedar, was smeared over the leaves of the papyrus to prevent the ravages of insects; and Pliny states that the Egytians applied it with other drugs in the preparation of their mummies."

"The wood now and then finds its way into the perfumer's warehouse," said I; "when ground it does well to form a body for sachet powders. Strips of the cedar-wood are sold as lighters, because while burning, an agreeable odor is evolved; some peo-

31

JOHN L. WHITING & SON,

Whitings' Celebrated Brushes.

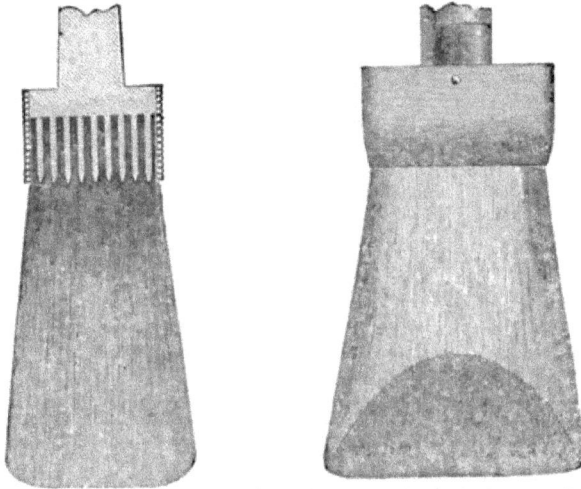

It is claimed for these Brushes, by the Manufacturers and all who have used them, that they are superior to all others in finish, compactness of design, working and wearing qualities.

Ask for Whiting's Patent Paint, Varnish, Sash, Wall, White-wash, Coach Painters' and Artists' Brushes and Pencils. Give them a trial, and you will buy no other make.

A LARGE ASSORTMENT OF

Bristle and Badger Shaving Brushes,

AT LOWEST PRICES.

MANUFACTORY OF GOODS,

Nos. 132 TO 146 OLIVER ST., BOSTON, MASS.

ple use it also in chips distributed among clothing to prevent moth, though any perfume will keep moths away, and also destroy them, and perfumes will also prevent and arrest mould and decay. So long as the odoriferous qualities are retained in any substance, so long will it last; as soon as its power is gone, the article so depending for its life quickly decays. This will be noticed particularly in flowers having perfume, they keeping so much longer after being picked than those possessing none; perfume seems to be their breath and life. It is well known that an apple which has been filled with the cloves, by pushing them into it and covering the entire outside, will last indefinitely."

"I like the taste of Extract of Cedar very much," said Susie; "it is very noticeable in the tooth-wash that I use."

"But Extract of Cedar cannot be used on the handkerchief," said I to Susie, "as its crimson color would make a stain; we, however, compound the Essence of Cedar from the otto, which is colorless. The 'Cedars of Lebanon' are so familiar, that we are obliged to give that title to the essence, though the true Lebanon Cedar — "

"Do you mean the *Cedrus Libani?*" asked Susie.

"Yes," I replied; "it yields a very indifferent otto. Perfumers could not afford to change the title of the scent, though they use the product of the Cedar of the West."

"Do not say 'Cedar of the West'; you should say *Juniperus Virginiana.*"

"Certainly," I replied, "but it is so hard to say such brain-entangling and jaw-breaking names; I will leave all that for you and Jean to do."

"Pathologically considered," said Jean, "the use of perfumes is in the highest degree prophylactic. The refreshing feeling im-

STANDING ON HIS HEAD; THE MAST BENDING LIKE A REED.

Page 29.

parted by the citrine odors to an invalid is well known. And the occasional sacrifice of incense in the fever chamber will prevent infection. The odors of plants are, in fact, all antiseptic."

Patsey stood looking at Jean with eyes staring and mouth wide open.

" Look at Patsey," I whispered to Jean; " as for myself, I shall have to carry my dictionary with me, if you are going to continue using such refined language."

" I will promise not to repeat the dose," said Jean, laughingly.

" Come," said I, " the river steamer starts very soon; we shall have but time to get to the landing."

After a short, rapid walk, we reached the landing and stepped aboard the steamboat just as she was ready to start, and we sailed up the "roads," by the Rip Raps and New Port News, and landing at a small settlement we proceeded to the place of manufacture of the Otto of Cedar; it is procured from the chips and shavings by distillation. The manufactory was surrounded by a cedar forest, so the material was plentiful. We procured a sample of the otto and several pieces of freshly cut wood, and waiting the return of the steamer, we embarked, reaching the *Cynthia* by sundown. Brad, giving the signal, we steamed past the fortress on our way to Jacksonville, Florida, and I noticed we were making headway very fast. Brad was anxious to reach Jacksonville without loss of time, so as to find John Gagler. Towards night the breeze began to freshen, and for the first time since starting on our voyage, we anticipated bad weather. At midnight the wind blew a gale, the rain came down in torrents, the vessel pitched and rocked fearfully, but she was well built, and rode the seas like a thing of life.

At noon the next day we sighted Cape Lookout; the weather

3

had cleared, we reached the St. John's river and steamed up to Jacksonville, where we arrived in a few hours. The boat was soon lowered, and we were glad to put our feet once more on land, after our first experience of a storm at sea. The wharf was crowded with negroes, and a motley collection of the general class of loafers, who seem never to have anything to do but minding other people's business. The negroes strove with each other to have us hire them.

"I see'd yer fuss, Cappen," said one.

"Go way dar! show yer to hotle, Kunnel," said another.

"Dis way, Ginnewal," said a big fellow, almost lifting me from my feet.

Amid the scuffling we selected the neatest looking one; he brought us a carriage, which we entered and reached the hotel. After resting awhile we took a short stroll, it being late in the afternoon, and made arrangements for conveyance early in the morning to Green Cove. Brad inquired at the hotel if anyone knew of such a person as John Gagler; but they did not. We noticed he was very nervous and anxious, and no wonder; for the information he expected to obtain would perhaps inform him of the fate of his father, or would give him some clew by which he could find him.

We started early in the morning, as we had arranged; the ride was charming, the air bracing and the sky beautifully blue and clear; but the roads were sandy, and there was no grass, which gives such a rich tone to our more northern landscapes. Patsey gathered specimens for Susie, and chased insects and birds, taking any chance that offered to make a dangerous leap, turning flipflaps and handsprings, throwing somersaults, climbing to the topmost bough of some lofty tree, or swinging from branch

t) branch, pursuing some impertinent paroquet or bright-hued insect, almost scaring our wits out of us.

Green Cove appearing in the distance, our attention was directed to it; it appeared to be a small, but pretty place, and is a resort for invalids, who come here to drink and to bathe in the waters of its sulphur springs. Just before entering the town, we passed through a large grove of Magnolia Trees, in full bloom; the perfume of the large white blossoms, soft, pleasant and most agreeable, had reached us sometime before we came to the trees; but when in the midst of the grove the perfume was overpowering.

"The Magnolia," said Jean, "was named for Pierre Magnol, Professor of Botany at Montpelier, in the seventeenth century."

"Yes, and there are several species of this genus of trees and shrubs, all of great beauty, and usually bearing large fragrant flowers. Patsey show your skill and agility by reaching for me that large blossom," said Susie, pointing as she spoke to a magnificent, creamy, waxen one, swinging temptingly on the topmost bough of a tree directly ahead of us.

Patsey gained it after some hard climbing, and its rare, aromatic perfume was delightful.

Going through the grove we soon reached the town, and put up at the Magnolia House. After dinner we whiled away the time in conversation till the heat of the day was over. Then Brad and myself went searching for John Gagler. Walking up the main street, we took a turn to the left, and passing several large estates, we took a road to the right, going according to directions obtained at the hotel. At last we arrived at the house, a small one, unpainted and well patched. Our summons was answered by an old man and woman, of whom we

inquired for John Gagler. Alas for poor Brad! The old man informed us that he had left only the week before, as he became discontented, having no relations or particular friends to associate with; and although quite an old man, he determined to return to the old life and its associations; the sea was his home; so he went away with a captain of a sailing vessel, who was visiting the Springs. This captain traded between the Sandwich Islands and San Francisco, and was on his way to the former place.

Brad was greatly disappointed, and could hardly conceal his chagrin, but being one of those to whom obstacles are but incentives for greater exertions, he determined to follow John Gagler, if it was to the ends of the earth. So, thanking the people for such information as they had given, we hurried back to the hotel, and informed the others of our ill success. Expressing their sorrow they tried to console Brad, and make him forget his disappointment.

Having decided to take a bath in the Sulphur Spring, separate bath-houses for the convenience of ladies and gentlemen being numerous, we soon found one that suited us. These baths are considered very healthful; and we were much refreshed. We had a delightful sail by steamer down the St. Johns, the moon shone bright, the evening air was cool, and we reached Jacksonville by ten o'clock, staying at the hotel during the rest of the night, then going on board the *Cynthia* in the morning. As the weather looked threatening we did not sail till late in the afternoon, the prospect then being much brighter.

The three days which elapsed before we sighted Key West, were spent in reading, experimenting, arranging the shelves, labelling the bottles for our expected prizes, and in the evenings by story telling, familiar conversation about ourselves, and singing by

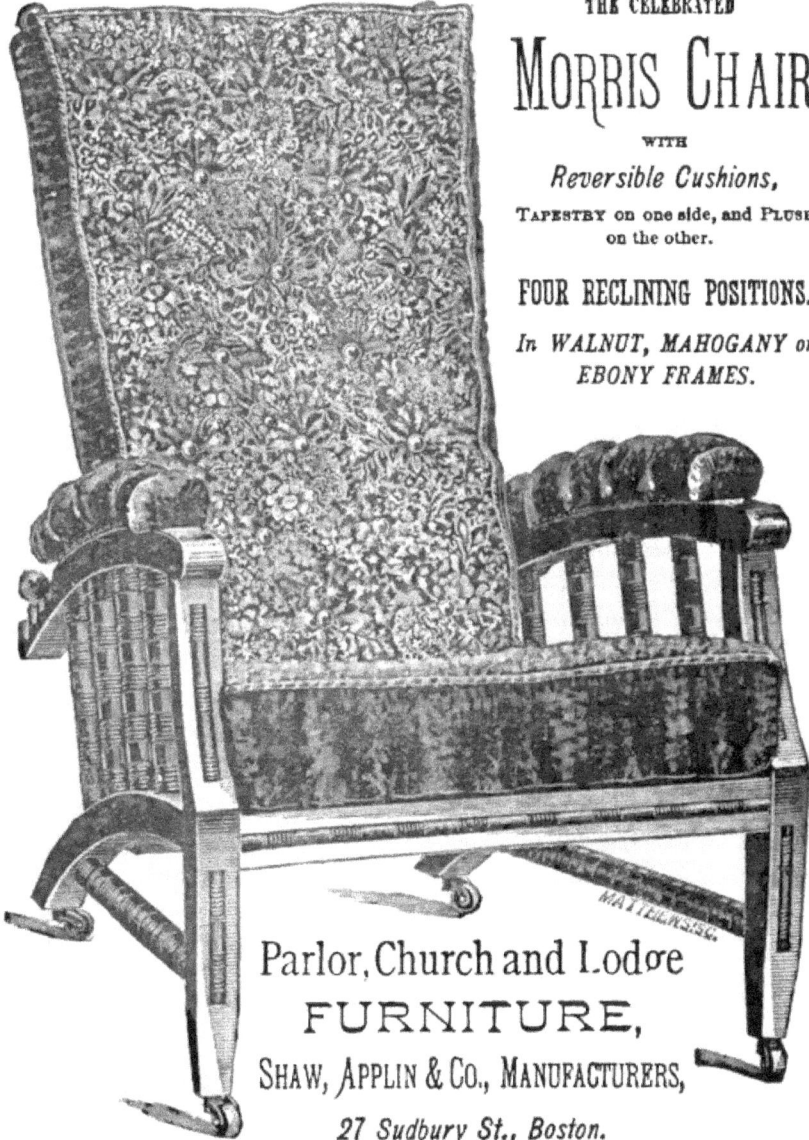

Susie and Jean, together and separately. This was the only thing that seemed to make Brad forget his disappointment. When Susie sang, he gazed upon her in rapture. He often watched Jean, seeming to study how much more advantage he had than himself; a good singer, a pleasant conversationalist, learned, good looking, and so much more used to the society of ladies, so graceful and easy; his chances looked dubious to himself, you could see by the changes in his face, that such was his opinion; after an evening passed in social conversation, he seemed rather to avoid Susie, and let Jean have it almost all his own way; but it was a sore trial. Susie had treated them both alike; but seeing Brad trying to avoid her, her pride was touched, and she tried the more to please him, and thought a great deal more of him than she probably did of Jean, who was almost constantly with her, in her walks and studies. Brad seeing the advantage he was gaining, was more fatherly to her every day, and she having all her life had her own way, thought it splendid to be commanded and made to obey and have some one to rely on, and so always went to him for any advice she wished. But Brad could not spare the time to be much with her, as he was constantly engaged in looking after the vessel and the welfare of his sailors, believing in making them comfortable and happy as the only true way to have his ship well taken care of, and his orders strictly obeyed.

INTRODUCED IN 1870.

HAVE STOOD THE TEST OF YEARS,

And are still ahead, as the easiest to operate, taking less air than any other make. Can
be easily cleaned from obstructions, as the Atomizer may be taken apart.

"FAVORITE."

Price, 50 cents.

"THE BOSTON PERFUMER."

UNDER PATENTS.

Aug. 23, 1870.
March 2, 1875.
July 18, 1876.

Price, $1.00.

"CENTENNIAL."

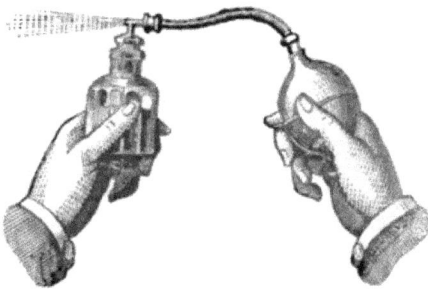

Price, $1.25.

Operated with one hand as well
as with both.

For sale by Druggists, Perfumers and Dealers in Fancy Goods.

T. J. HOLMES, Proprietor and Manufacturer,

BOSTON, MASS.

YOUNG, LADD & COFFIN, Sole Agents,
NEW YORK CITY.

CHAPTER VI.

BEAUTIFUL TONKA.

THE entrance beacon of Key West "dowsed its glim" just as the flush of the coming morn revealed its iron cage, suspended in the broad space of waters. We were up bright and early to catch the first glimpses of the Island. We steamed into the harbor, passing Fort Taylor, which commands the entrance, and made fast to the pier. It was a fine day, and like many in this latitude, fraught with cheering influences; and Nature on every side appeared in her best aspect. The island of Key West is nearly five miles in length, and one mile in greatest width, the town being situated at the western extremity, where the reef protects a large and safe harbor. We proceeded to the public house, around which Coco-Palms reared their crested heads to the height of fifty and eighty feet, and Banana Plants stood in splendid groups in the gardens. The Banana is not tree-like, the stem is annual in its growth, the root being perennial and permanent. In one year the banana grows about twelve feet high, bears its one bunch of fruit, and dies; other shoots meantime are coming up from the same root; they in turn bear fruit, each after a year's growth. The flower bud is purple, and contrasts finely with the rich glossy green of the leaves. Some of the handsomest trees

38

THE AUTOPHONE,

MANUFACTURED BY

THE AUTOPHONE COMPANY . . . . . . ITHACA, N. Y.

This engraving represents the instrument, and the mode of playing it. Requires no skill or musical knowledge, and even a child may play the most difficult pieces without instruction. We put this new musical instrument on the market solely upon its merits, and with confidence that it will give complete satisfaction. It is the invention of Mr. H. B. HORTON, whose genius and ability are well known, and who has been steadily engaged for many years in perfecting this instrument in various forms. While nearly every person, in greater or less degree, is attracted and pleased by music, comparatively but few can master the trained ear and facility of execution necessary to success. An instrument, therefore, which requires no previous practice, or costly education, but enables any one to play accurately even difficult and complicated tunes, is much to be desired. Most of the efforts in this direction have resulted in awkward and complicated inventions, lacking both simplicity and economy, and giving very imperfect results. The AUTOPHONE will be found to accomplish the desired purpose, and having been thoroughly tested, may be safely trusted to win its own way to public favor.

It is simple in its construction, not liable to get out of order and easily managed. Can be played by a child six years old. Will furnish amusement to all. It contains twenty-two notes and plays in three different keys. It is tuned so that it is a good accompaniment to the voice. The workmanship is of the best quality, the wood being black walnut, finished in good style. We invite comparison in regard to its musical as wel' as mechanical execution. It is truly wonderful what a scope and with what precision it executes. It is one of the kind that speaks for itself, and need only to be seen and heard to be appreciated. We quote from the *Scientific American*, Nov. 19, 1879 : —

"The most remarkable feature of this invention is the regularity and perfection with which the music is rendered. All of the parts are played, and the music is of no mean order."

It is securely packed and sent by express on receipt of price. Weight when boxed, five pounds. Both have attachments for holding cards with words of songs, which will be sent postpaid for $1.00 per 100.

Price, Style A, $5 00 with 5 tunes, amounting to 70 cents.
"   "   B, $7.00   "   "   "   "   "

Style B has the same number of notes as style A, but has rounded edges, handsomer finish and nickel mountings. Extra Music sent by mail, postpaid, on receipt of price as per catalogue. Price with music, $5.00.

DIRECTIONS FOR PLAYING.

Hold the instrument in the right hand, with the thumb resting in the hollowed centre piece; grasp the outside of the bellows with the ends of the fingers, and work the bellows with a *regular* motion, as the *instrument will beat its own time*. Give the bellows full expansion. Place the music in so that the end with the name printed on it will be first, and also will read corectly to the person holding the instrument. Be sure to place it in straight, so that the "feed" is even. Be careful to leave the back side of bellows free. If you wish to repeat the tune, draw it back.

Send for catalogue of music to

A. D. SMITH, SOLE AGENT,
197 TREMONT STREET, BOSTON, MASS.

of this garden, which attracted our attention, were the date-palm and oleanders, the latter being covered with a wealth of gay blossoms, and growing fifteen to twenty feet high. Vines and flowering plants climbed and hung gracefully over the walls. One of the most prolific in growth and perfume, is the Night Blooming Cereus, a native plant, growing luxuriantly upon trees and houses, fastening itself readily upon brick or wood by rootlets at each joint as they put forth their shoots. In our walks in the evening we saw houses and trees loaded with the great cups of this elegant plant, its waxen flowers of exquisite form, and the sepals of the calyx of a pale golden hue surrounding the intensely white petals like a halo. The air, made balmy by its perfume, the soft moonlight, the sweet whistling of the orioles, the gentle breeze stirring the great leaves of the coco-palms, that rasped together, giving forth a sound like a gentle fall of rain, filled our hearts with a feeling of repose and freedom from all care.

The next morning, we were all ready for an excursion along the shores of the islands, which we had planned the day before. The rich azure of the sky was heightened to wondrous beauty by the moving volumes of day clouds, and the now quiet sea mirrored the scene, adding deeper touches of olive and brown where the reef came nearest to the surface.

"Just the weather to view the many wonders of the deep," said Jean, looking with admiration at the beautiful sight.

Proceeding to the South Beach, we entered one of the ship's boats sent to meet us. The water was clear as crystal; it was so transparent that the boat seemed suspended in air. The tufts of pink and white coral that studded the bed of the ocean beneath, were as distinct as if they were growing at our feet. We seemed to be gazing down upon a beautiful garden, — the various colored

"PATSEY, SHOW YOUR SKILL AND AGILITY BY REACHING FOR
ME THAT LARGE BLOSSOM," SAID SUSIE.

Page 35.

corals intermingling with the most delicate and brilliant-hued algæ and mossy sea-weeds, exquisite in form, simulating the daisies and ferns of the forest, — deepened the impression.

Jean, having engaged a diver, with his boat and mate, they followed closely behind, ready at any moment to procure us specimens of these beautiful forms. Sea Fans and Sea Feathers, Brain, Star and Branch Coral, they brought to the surface. We watched the fishes, the Malthea, the Bellows Fish, and Porcupine Fishes, besides many others. It was a vast natural aquarium. As we were returning and passing near some rocks, my wife asked, —

"What is that man gathering?" pointing to a diver just distinguishable beneath the water between two large rocks.

We all turned and saw him pulling from the rocks what appeared to be bunches of moss.

"He is pulling sponge," said Jean.

Brad ordered the sailors to pull nearer, then we saw growing sponges of all shapes, pediculated, foliated, globular and digital.

"They certainly justify the names that the natives give them," said Jean, "such as baskets, cups, distaffs, elk's-horns, lion's-feet, peacock's-tails, Neptune's-gloves, and various others. You will notice a black membraneous tunic covers them, making them, unlike most other marine objects, less attractive in their living state; only when the soft parts are removed are they pleasing to the eye."

"What! Are sponges alive?" asked my wife.

"Yes, when attached to the rocks they form on," said Jean; "that tunic and the soft jelly-like portions that you see projecting into the pores and cavities, may be called its flesh or body;

the slight current you observe over the openings is the water which is drawn through them, from which nourishment is absorbed. The framework is made up of silica, in the form of spiculæ or splinters."

"Animal mucus and fat oil are found in their analysis," said I. "To remove the soft parts this diver will bury them in the sand until the matter which forms the flesh decomposes, then they are washed, collected upon strings of convenient length, and bleached in the sun. When we buy them at home they are full of sand, and in that state it is the best way to purchase them; then afterwards beat out the sand with a stick, and rinse them well in cold spring water. Nothing is better adapted for cleansing the skin than a good sponge thus prepared; hence, surgeons prefer it to any other material."

"In the regular way of using a sponge with soap for washing," said Jean, "they rapidly become greasy and are then frequently thrown aside before half worn out. The peculiar cellular, fibrous tissue of sponge enables it to decompose soap, retaining the grease and oil, which renders it slimy; when such is the case, a little ammonia in water will cleanse them; if this is not effective a lye of soda should be prepared, in the proportion of half a pound of soda to half a gallon of water, and the sponge allowed to soak in it for twenty-four hours; it should then be washed and well rinsed in spring water, and afterwards in water containing a small quantity of muriatic acid; about a wine-glassful of acid to half a gallon of water being strong enough; finally, rinse the sponge in plenty of spring water."

"That is a great deal of trouble," said my wife.

"The best sponges being very expensive renders it fully worth it," I replied.

COLTON
WATER-MOTOR CO.

CAPITAL - - $300,000.

100,000 Shares.   *Par Value, $3.00.*

Full-paid and Unassessable.

JAS. H. NASON, President.

A. H. DILLON, JR., Vice-President.

GEO. D. ELDRIDGE, Sec'y and Treas.

THE TREASURY STOCK IS NOW FOR SALE AT THE
OFFICE OF

RANSOM, ELDRIDGE & STRAINE,

Financial Agents,

31 MILK STREET, BOSTON, MASS.

(See next page.)

" If the trouble be taken to well rinse a sponge every time after using, as I do," said Susie, " the cleansing process will never be necessary."

We had by this time reached the beach; stepping out, we selected the best specimens the divers' boat contained, and had them taken on board the *Cynthia*, with a quantity of pure white coral, which Jean intended to pulverize in his mortar and use as tooth powder, it being highly recommended by some of the best authorities on the preservation of teeth.

We returned to the hotel, and the boat's crew pulled back to the ship. We passed the warmest part of the day in lounging on the piazzas and sauntering under the trees; late in the afternoon we strolled through the town, and saw many beautifully arranged gardens and estates. The next day we made a visit to a friend of the proprietor of the hotel. On this gentleman's estates were large numbers of Tonka Trees, which we wished to see. Arriving at the residence, we were hospitably received and shown over the grounds. The seeds of the Tonka Tree, or as Susie, in her scientific dialect called it, the *Dipterix odorata*, are the Tonka or Coumarouma Beans of commerce. When fresh they are exceedingly fragrant, having an intense odor of new made hay, and the *Anthoxanthum odoratum*, or the sweet smelling vernal grass, as Susie told us, to which new mown hay owes its odor, probably yields the same fragrant principle; and it is remarkable that both Tonka Beans and Vernal Grass while actually growing, are nearly scentless, but become rapidly aromatic when severed from the parent stock. Under the trees we picked up many of the seeds. They are about an inch long, shiny black on the outside, and light brown within, and exhaling a very strong perfume when broken.

We noticed something very curious in connection with these beans, on equally dividing one perpendicularly; at the lower part of the bean, that part where it was attached to the branch, is a tiny hand, showing the fingers perfectly, and a small part of the arm, seemingly encircled by a bracelet. The gentleman related to us a legend told to him by his old nurse, who said it had been handed down from generation to generation from the Indian natives, about this peculiar fact. On our return to the ship Jean put the legend into verse, and as it interested us at the time, we insert it here, hoping others will be as well pleased by its perusal as we were.

THE LEGEND OF BEAUTIFUL TONKA.

In a fair land, a sunny clime,
'Tis said that "once upon a time,"
(Thus all good legends, old and new begin,)
There lived a princess, lovely, young,
Beleaguered by a princely throng,
That fondly hoped her heart and hand to win.

More fair and beauteous she became,
Until she did all hearts inflame;
None could resist her beauty so bewitching.
Besides the princes of her nation,
Many there were of lower station,
Who for her hand were sighing, often fighting.

Yet still she chose not any one,
But tired at last,—all patience gone,
She sent her lovers all a proclamation;
That soon a trial would take place,
Needing much courage, skill and grace;
And warned them all to make full preparation.

A ROMANCE OF PERFUME LANDS.

Now they in manly vigor prime,
The islands of a southern clime
Inhabited, and sported in the waves,
Played in the surf, and boldly fought
With dread man-eater sharks, or aught
That ventured forth from out their ocean caves.

She promised him her heart and hand,
Who, in a race ten miles from land
Would swim, and win, and make a safe return,—
She would be his with all her beauty,
With all her love and all her duty;
For SUCH a BRAVE alone her heart could yearn.

Upon the day which was appointed,
With limbs all bare and well anointed,
Five hundred brave contestants lined the shore.
And throngs there came the race to view,
With trembling hearts, for well they knew,
Most of those brave ones would return no more.

For in their course there lay in wait,
To whelm them in a dreadful fate,
The huge man-eating sharks that swarm those seas.
So each must swim and fiercely fight,
With sharks to left and sharks to right,
And conquer all, his lady-love to please.

Upon a lofty cliff hard by,
While fiendish glee looked from her eye,
The princess on a downy couch was lying.
Already in her mind she views
The victims of her wicked ruse,
Exhausted, mangled, bleeding, sinking, dying.

Each lover then before her passed,
A wistful look upon her cast,
And bowed his head low, even to the ground.

Then on the beach they stood apart,
Waiting the signal for the start,
Each muscle strained and ready for the bound.

And now the signal conch was sounded,
And quick each manly swimmer bounded
Into the surf, and dashed aside the wave.
The crowd looked on with bated breath,
As, to the very jaws of death,
They swiftly swam to find a common grave.

Ah! Now the struggle did begin,
Each striving manfully to win,
Battled with waves and sharks that round did hover.
With mingled blood the sea was red;
Soon the last mangled swimmer dead;
And now the wily maiden had no lover.

The crowd that watched upon the shore,
Gave a deep groan like ocean's roar,
And vowed revenge upon the treacherous maid.
They all cried out as with one breath,
That, for their comrades' awful death,
Her life alone should be the forfeit paid.

Well now she knew what was her fate,
She rose in haste with eyes dilate,
And headlong cast herself into the sea.
Her voice was heard upon the strand,—
"I go to give to each my hand;
Those brave ones all, shall each my lover be."

Years having passed, the rolling tide
From off that dreadful spot had dried;
When from the soil a shoot sprang forth, and grew
Into a beauteous tree and bloomed,
Its fruit full richly was perfumed;
Tree, bloom and fruit were very fair to view.

And children played within its shade:
One day a tiny little maid,
In joyous sport broke ope the nut-brown shell;
When lo! before her enraptured eyes,
To her great wonder and surprise,
Into her hand a tinier hand there fell.

Go now, behold! this wondrous tree!
And pluck its perfumed fruit, and see
That in each seed a maiden's hand there lies.
'Tis for the swimmer bold, who died,
And perished in that bloody tide,
A maiden's hand to gain; that tempting prize.

'Tis thus we find the Tonka tree,
Sprang from a maid beneath the sea;
Tonka, her name, means "fairest in the land."
Redeemed, the maiden's pledge she gave,
The while she sank beneath the wave, —
"I go to give my lovers, each, my hand."

"Chemically considered," said Jean, "Tonka Beans are very interesting, containing when fresh, a fragrant otto, to which their odor is due; benzoic acid, a fat oil, and a neutral principle, coumarin."

"In perfumery they are valuable," said I, "as when ground they form, with other bodies, excellent and permanent sachets, and by infusion in absolute alcohol an extract is obtained which enters into many of the compound perfumes or bouquets; but on account of its strength it must be used with caution, otherwise the perfume will be called snuffy, owing to the predominance of that odor and its habitual use in the boxes of those who indulge in that brain destroying tobacco dust, called snuff."

Offering to purchase a quantity of the beans, the proprietor

SAW HIM PULLING FROM THE ROCKS WHAT APPEARED TO
BE BUNCHES OF MOSS.

Page 40.

would make no price, and generously forced upon us a large number of them.

Much pleased with our visit, we returned to the hotel, dined, and proceeded on board, though quite reluctant to leave so pleasant a place. About four o'clock we steamed away, all sitting on deck, gazing long at the luxuriant shores of Key West, fast fading from our sight. At dark we were heading in the direction of New Orleans. We should have sailed directly for the Sandwich Islands, but Brad said he had time to spare, as the ship in which John Gagler had gone would not reach there for some time, being only a sailing vessel, and that by putting on a good head of steam we would reach the Islands as soon as they; so the time might as well be utilized here, as to waste it there waiting for John Gagler to put in an appearance; and as there was no chance of meeting him on the high seas, it would be better to wait patiently, give him time to reach his destination, and then catch him on shore. So Brad took this course to particularly oblige us, and allow us all the time required to observe what we wished.

CHAPTER VII.

AFTER six days' sailing from Key West, here our good ship lays at the levee of New Orleans, and we are preparing to disembark to see all that is worth seeing. Passing up Canal street, going by the United States Custom House, the St. Charles Hotel, and several other places of note, we obtained information in regard to the whereabouts of a Sassafras distillery, and this we soon found. The Otto of Sassafras comes from the bark and wood of the *Laurus Sassafras*, which grows abundantly in the Southern States; the otto is procured by distillation with water and the bark, and yields a great quantity. Perfumers use it in the manufacture of hair washes and other articles, but it has rather a "physicky" than a flowery smell. It is used more by confectioners as a flavoring for lozenges and candies, than by perfumers as an odor. It is, however, extensively used in soap-making.

What we especially wished to see at this place, was the manufacture of Cotton Seed, Peanut, Benne, and Castor Oils. These being vegetable oils, they are much better for use on the hair than animal oils or fats, as they do not possess so much latent heat. It is the heating of the head which causes the falling

HUMANITY.

Popular Scientific and Radical Writings in German.

BY

FRITZ SCHUETZ.

PROSPERITY OF NATIONS.

1. PART I. *Judaism and Catholicism* — *Progress of Religion* — The Old Israelitic Religion — Christianity — The Evangelical Protestantism — Humanity — *Prosperity* — Welfare and Health — Mental and Moral Cultivation — Liberty — *Social Circumstances or Welfare* — *Riches of the Jews* — Reasons in Religion — Encouragement to get Rich — Commercial Spirit — Usury and Fraud — Religious Hatred — Jewish Pity and Charity — Reformed Judaism — Reciprocity between Religion, Fate, and National Character — *Impoverishment of Catholic Countries* — Weakening of Industrial Spirit — Social Enslavement — Christian Love and Charity — Prosperity in Free Cities — Reaction and Bloody Destruction — Result.

2. PART II. The Partial Flourishing Welfare in Protestantism — Spiritual Advantage of Protestantism — War of the Peasants and Luther — Confiscation and Robbery of Church Property — The English Robbing Nobility — Republicanism — Zwingli — Calvin — The Jesuits — The Quakers — Industry, Commerce and National Riches in Holland and England — Result.

3. PART III. Humanity (will appear next winter).

4. CRITICS AND DEBATES.

This book contains *Debates* with *the Clergy* and Laymen, with *Free-Thinkers* and *Socialists*, and with spiritual, *prominent women;* as also Treatise on *God, Law of Nature, Immortality, Moral Life, Christianity;* and Poems.

Each of these writings, containing 150–200 pages, costs 35 cents. Sent by mail, free of postage; and if your bookseller does not have them, send to

FRITZ SCHUETZ, Carver, Minn., Box 74.

More than 3,000 copies of No. 1 were sold a short time after publication. A second edition was printed, of which more than 2,000 copies were sold. The fourth edition has just been issued. Public criticism has pronounced upon them very favorably.

(Qualified American Translator Wanted.)

off of the hair, produced in many cases simply by using pomades made of lard. Bears Grease has somehow obtained a high reputation, but of all the unpleasant smelling substances ever known, it is the most nauseous. Pure bears grease is totally unfit for a hair dressing; a little added to beef body is beneficial for its healing qualities, but all it is fitted for, is a salve; for *that* it answers admirably, especially for frozen limbs. As oiling and greasing the hair is a custom almost universal among the inhabitants of civilized and uncivilized countries, it is well to know what oil is the best. Oiling the hair, besides promoting its growth, making it soft and glossy, and keeping it in place, has the infinite benefit of rendering it "uninhabitable," a consideration too often neglected in schools and similar institutions where children most do congregate. There are oil glands on the scalp, but their power of secretion is very slight, except in a few rare instances; in these cases the hair is said to be naturally moist and soft. The general rule is that the hair grows harsh and dry for lack of natural oily secretion, hence the instinctive application of an artificial oil, a practice hallowed by its ancient custom, and sanctioned as "necessary" from the Court beauty, to the Belle of equatorial Africa.

Baldness is very frequent at the present time, and may be attributed in many cases to the habit of using very close and tight fitting coverings on the head, wearing them indoors as well as in the open air. We have known many cases of baldness in quite young persons from this habit. Many are accustomed to wetting their hair with cold water, and never using oils of any kind; now the secondary condition of cold is heat, and the cold water being applied, and the head covered with a close fitting hat, the temperature of the head is greatly increased; hair resists decay in a

Menschenthum.

Populär-wissenschaftliche und radikale Schriften
von
Fritz Schütz.

Das Heil der Völker.

1, Theil I. Judenthum und Katholizismus. Fortschritt der Religion.

Die altismaelitische Religion. Das Christenthum. Der evangelische Protestantismus. Das Menschenthum.

Das Heil.

Wohlstand und Gesundheit, Bildung und Freiheit.

Soziale Verhältnisse oder Wohlstand. Reichthum der Juden.

Ursachen in der Religion. Antrieb zum Reichthum. Handelsgeist, Wucher und Trug. Glaubenshaß. Jüdisches Erbarmen und Mildthätigkeit. Reformjudenthum. Wechselwirkung zwischen Religion, Schicksalen und Volkscharakter.

Verarmung der katholischen Länder.

Abschwächung des Erwerbstriebes. Gesellschaftliche Knechtung. Christliche Liebe und Mildthätigkeit. Wohlstand in den freien Städten. Rückschlag und blutige Vernichtung. Ergebniß.

2, Theil II. Einseitige Blüthe des Wohlstandes im Protestantismus.

Geistige Vorzüge des Protestantismus. Bauernkrieg und Luther. Einziehung und Raub der Kirchengüter. Der neuzeitige, insbesondere englische Raubadel. Republikanische Strömung. Zwiegli. Kalvin. Jesuiten. Quäker. Industrie, Handel und Nationalreichthum in Holland und England. Ergebniß.

3, Theil III. Menschenthum.

(Erscheint nächsten Winter: 106 – 1881.)

4, Kritiken und Debatten.

Diese Schrift enthält Debatten mit kirchlichen Geistlichen und Laien, mit Freidenkern und Sozialisten und mit geistig hervorragenden Frauen, sowie Abhandlungen über Gott, Naturgesetz, Unsterblichkeit, sittliches Leben, Christenthum und Gedichte.

Jede dieser Schriften von 150 – 200 Seiten kostet **35** Cents und ist zu beziehen von

Fritz Schütz, Carver, Minn., B. 74.

Von No. 1 wurden in der kurzen Zeit ihres Erscheinens bereits über **3000** Ex. abgesetzt und eine zweite Auflage gedruckt, und von No. 2 über **2000** Ex. No. 4 wird im September versandt. Außerordentlich günstig hat sich die öffentliche Kritik ausgesprochen.

(Ein geschickter amerikanischer Uebersetzer wird gesucht.)

remarkable degree; it resists the action of acids and alkalies, except the strongest which dissolve it; it however will not resist boiling water, continued for a long time; the temperature, under the close fitting hat, will be found equal to that of boiling water, consequently the hair is soon destroyed and falls off. It seems almost necessary to use some kind of a dressing for the hair, and a little nice oil tends greatly to its growth.

If there are those who dislike to use oils, and wish to have their hair glossy and smooth, a better way than wetting it with water, is to frequently brush it with a stiff bristle, or a wire hair brush, and to continue so doing, until after awhile they will find their hair contains moisture enough of its own secreting to answer for dressing it.

I remember quite a laughable incident in regard to the habit of constantly wearing a hat, which, I before remarked, causes a great many cases of premature baldness. A salesman in one of the country stores of our most Eastern State, wore his hat from the minute he arose from his breakfast, till night, taking it off only at dinner and supper time. Slowly but surely the hair kept falling and wearing away, until at thirty-five there was hardly a hair to be seen on his head, except below the rim of his hat. One day, he went to a neighboring city on business, and to purchase himself a tall hat, for which he had long been denying himself many little luxuries, and thereby saving his money. Having determined he would possess the most stylish hat and the finest that was ever seen in his village, he hunted the city through, and came homeward well satisfied with his purchase. For style and gloss, there had probably never been seen such a beaver in town; and no doubt he was thinking to himself how envious would be the gaze of other fellows, when they saw how he had " come out."

A ROMANCE OF PERFUME LANDS;

— OR, —

THE SEARCH FOR CAPT. JACOB COLE.

With practical and interesting facts about Perfume and Toilet Articles. 336 Pages. Cloth Binding, Full Gold. Elegantly Illustrated with 33 full-page Engravings.

PRICE - - - - $1.50.

Sent by mail on receipt of price by any Bookseller, or by

CLIFFORD & CO.

23 School Street - - - BOSTON, MASS.

The Trade supplied by

MESSRS. A. WILLIAMS & CO. - - BOOKSELLERS,

Cor. of School and Washington Streets,

BOSTON.

Misfortune, however, overtook him before he reached his home. Crossing the river which separated the city from his native place, on one of the primitive ferries of those regions, the wind rose to a gale and made love to his hat and carried it from his head, and placed it on the bosom of the waters, which graciously received it, and bore it beyond his reach. It sailed majestically onward, mockingly rising on each wave which took off his hat to bow good-bye to him as it receded; he saw it floating down the river, and at last the distance was so great it was lost to view; but to him it was to memory dear and pocket too. His wrath knew no bounds; and then and there he took an oath that from that time henceforth he would never wear another hat, or in fact any covering for his head, and he kept his oath, for in rain or shine he was always to be seen bare-headed. His hair began to grow; unnoticed at first, but at last it covered his formerly bald head in profusion. He now never mentions that beaver hat, but to praise it.

We are, however, at the door of the factory, and must not waste time telling stories. We entered the office, as usual introducing ourselves. It was the counting-room of the manufactory, and several clerks stationed at desks in different parts of the room looked up as we entered. Addressing myself to an elderly gentleman, I stated our object, and with the natural hospitality of the Southern people he cordially received us.

"No trouble whatever, my dear sir," said he. "We are always glad to show our works to anyone who shows any interest in their operation. Mr. Atherton, show these ladies and gentlemen through the factory."

This was addressed to a middle-aged gentleman, very short and fat, with a pleasant face, who stood near him.

"Many thanks," said I, "but do not let us take him from other business."

"This is my Superintendent, Mr. Atherton, ladies and gentlemen," said the elderly gentleman, taking no notice of my remark. "He is at your service."

Thanking him again, we followed Mr. Atherton through a door in the left side of the office; crossing a hall he opened another door and we entered the receiving room.

"The three kinds of seeds, Cotton Seed, Benne Seed and Castor Seed or Beans, are received here by the cart load," said Mr. Atherton. "You see we have six bins in all; two for each kind of seed; one bin of each we try to keep filled all the time, and one we draw from. The bins used for the cotton seeds are sometimes also used for Peanuts or Castina nuts."

"What do you do with peanuts," asked Susie, "feed your workmen with them?"

"No, Miss," said Mr. Atherton, trying to conceal a smile. "Whenever the cotton crop is short, so that the seeds are scarce, we use peanuts or Castina nuts instead; they yield as good an oil as the cotton seeds, and I think a little better."

Mr. Atherton then ushered us into the main room or factory. Three of the most improved oil mills, driven by steam power were on the left side of the room, one for each kind of seed, and were grinding away at a tremendous rate. For quite a while we watched the working of these combinations of mill and press, then crossed to the other side of the room to see the clarifying process. Here were rows of very large Canton flannel filters, suspended from iron bars running horizontally and parallel. These filters were packed with freshly burned and coarsely powdered charcoal, from which all the dust had been taken by sifting

AND QUICK EACH MANLY SWIMMER BOUNDED INTO THE SURF.

Page 45.

and fanning. The oils are poured in and after filtering through
the pulverized carbon, drop into long troughs which are under
each line of filters, and thus conveyed into barrels, which when
filled are closed up, weighed, marked, and taken to the store-
room, ready for transportation. Cotton Seed yields by this
method of extraction about twenty-five per cent. of oil, which is
of a dark yellow color, almost inodorous, and is used very extensively as a cheap hair oil, is easily perfumed with ottos, but is not
delicate enough to perfume with flowers; it will not mix with
alcohol in any proportion. The benne seeds are imported from
the West Indies, but the cotton seeds and castor beans are
raised abundantly in the vicinity of New Orleans.

"The Oil of Benne, sometimes called Sesamum," said Mr.
Atherton, "is one of the finest oils the perfumers can use; it is
nearly free from color, taste, and odor, as you can see by this
sample. It remains for a lengthened time free from rancidity,
indeed, some claim it ' never becomes rancid.' We have a sample in the office which we keep exposed in a situation where all
other oils would spoil in a year, yet the sample of benne oil is
still sweet, although it is some of the first we made more than ten
years ago. It is an oil that deserves more attention than it has
hitherto received."

Jean remarked that, "For making cold cream and other unguents it has proved valuable, and also for enfleuring it answers
well; when perfectly pure olive oil is unattainable, the benne oil
is a serviceable substitute."

The castor oil, after being clarified, instead of being packed in
barrels, was put into square tin cans, holding five gallons each,
which when filled were hermetically sealed. Castor oil is very
heavy, of a light yellow color when good, and is the only oil sol-

uble in alcohol; when mixed with alcohol in equal proportions, it makes an excellent hair dressing; it is also used in pomades, and is mixed with other oils to make them thicker.

"It is, however, not so nice as oil of benne, or olive oil perfumed with flowers," said Jean, "and it is better mixed with these oils when any one wishes a heavier hair dressing than compounded with alcohol, as alcohol is very drying and heating."

"If castor oil could be wholly deprived of its odor, by some inexpensive method," said I, "it would be the best and most invaluable agent for extracting the perfume from flowers and other odoriferous substances, in place of the insoluble oils now used, for castor oil is soluble in alcohol; perfumers could then have ottos of violet, orange blossoms, tuberoses, and various others, using them in the same manner as other ottos. We hope this will be accomplished within a few years, as it would economize time and labor, besides giving a method of procuring standard strengths for perfumes. We hope this matter, full of interest, will be experimented upon by laborants."

"The study of perfumery opens a book as yet unread by the chemical philosopher," said Jean. "The odors of some flowers resemble others so nearly that we are almost induced to believe them to be the same, or at least, if not evolved from the plant as such, to become so by the action of the air oxidations. It is known that some are identical in composition, although produced from totally different plants, such as camphor, rosemary, and turpentine. Hence we may presume that chemistry will sooner or later produce one from the other, for with many it is merely an atom of water or an atom of oxygen that causes the difference."

"Yes," said I, "there is a wide field for investigation."

"It would show the power of Science over Nature," said Jean, becoming excited over the subject, "to produce Otto of Roses from Otto of Rosemary, or from Otto of Rose Geranium, and theory indicates its possibility. The Otto of Almonds, in a bottle containing a large quantity of air oxygen, and but little otto, spontaneously passes into another odoriferous body called Benzoic Acid, which is seen to form in crystals over the dry parts of the glass. That is a natural illustration of the idea."

"I should very much like to see all that accomplished," said Mr. Atherton, deeply interested, "and especially the deodorization of castor oil."

We merely glanced into the store-room while passing, and saw vast numbers of barrels and cans of oil, such as we had seen extracted, piled high. The superintendent informed us that this factory supplied a greater part of the South and West, also many Northern cities.

By this time we had made the entire circuit of the room, and returned to the office, and expressed our satisfaction at what we had seen. We invited the proprietor and Mr. Atherton to supper on board the ship, and they kindly accepted the invitation. As we returned to the ship, we saw many acres of the castor oil plants, *Ricinus communis*, or *Palma Christi*, as Susie called them; and of course there were cotton plantations to be seen on every side. In the evening we received Mr. Atherton and the proprietor of the oil works, with their wives, and the evening passed very agreeably to all. We consider them the most pleasant of our acquaintances in New Orleans.

Sailing from New Orleans, we directed our course towards Tampico, Mexico, which we reached in due time, and as Brad wished to stop here to visit the silver mines of San Luis Potosi, in which he had an interest, it gave us a fine opportunity to see the country, and examine the many interesting productions of this prolific soil. And one of these being the Vanilla plant, Susie, Jean, and I were very anxious to see it. We were also desirous of seeing how they manipulated the little cochineal bug which is raised here in such vast numbers, from which is made carmine, one of the most expensive of coloring matters.

CHAPTER VIII.

A VALUABLE INSECT.

ON our way to the silver mines, Susie called our attention to the *Vanilla planifolia*. Here, the Vanilla grows wild in the woods, and is also cultivated on the plantations. This beautiful creeper, which bears the vanilla bean or pod, grows parasitically on particular kinds of trees, extracting its nourishment from the bark to which it clings. The roots shoot out at short distances as the vine ascends, the long lanceolate leaves springing from the same points with the root fibres. The beans depend from the angles where the leaf unites with the stem, two or three together, and when full grown vary in length from three to nine inches. Three species of forest trees have a bark which affords nutriment to the roots of the vanilla vine. The vine can be propagated easily, by tying slips to the bark; they take root and grow freely. The vine can also be grown in pots, but it produces an inferior quality of bean. The vanilla beans yield a perfume of rare excellence, which, according to Johnson, "acts upon the system as an aromatic stimulant, exhiliarating the mental functions and increasing generally the energy of the animal system."

"Vanilla Beans, if kept for some time," said Jean, "become

covered with an efflorescence of needle-like crystals, possessing properties similar to benzoic acid, but differing from it in composition; these crystals may be sublimed by the heat of a sand bath. Few objects are more beautiful to look upon than these crystals when viewed by a microscope with the aid of polarized light. I will show you after we return to the ship, and the beans are old enough."

"Do," said my wife, and "I won't forget your promise," said Susie.

Stopping at one of the plantations, we had an opportunity of witnessing the preparation, and also a chance to purchase a small lot of vanilla beans. The process is very tedious; Indians being employed for the purpose at extremely low wages. The green pods are laid upon flannel in a broken light, that they may dry, but not too rapidly. The woman who watched them, turned them over, and moistened them occasionally with olive oil to prevent hardening. At nightfall they are covered to protect them from the dews; in the course of two or three weeks, according to the temperature of the air, they become brown, and wrinkled lengthwise, and the unrivalled perfume of vanilla is developed by the change. They are then rolled in soft cloths or tinfoil, and packed for exportation. Many millions of dollars worth are used annually, and more could be disposed of, but for the high price they attain when imported, owing to the importations or supply being very irregular. The West India Islands are well adapted to the growth of this bean. It would well pay any who would undertake its cultivation there. Both Europe and America would consume a hundred times as much vanilla, if the price was reduced, and that can be done only by increased production.

Reaching the silver mines, Brad, Jean and I descended into them, leaving my wife and Susie, with Patsey as guard, in a hut near the shaft. We thought the mines were very interesting; a full description of them is however, unnecessary; suffice it to say, we saw all that could be seen, and obtained some fine specimens of ore, then ascended to the surface, much pleased to see the light of day again. On our way back to the pier we witnessed the collection and preparation of the cochineal insect for the market. This Cochineal insect (*Coccus Cacti*), a small and very insignificant creature, would never have attracted any notice, but for the valuable coloring matter it contains.

"Shure, I've seen minny of thim little bougs on the plants in hot houses at home," said Patsey, "an' I niver thought they was any good at all."

"They look like them, Patsey, but they are far different," said I. "You will notice how they differ after you see them prepared. Formerly the culture of cochineal was confined to Mexico alone, the government taking great pains to keep secret the method of preparation. It is now abundantly raised in Brazil and the East Indies. Mexico still produces the greatest quantity, and the best quality. In the *Nopaleros*, — the Spanish name of the fields in the great mayorals, derived from the name *Opuntia Nopal*, — are acres of the Tuna Cactus, *Opuntia Tuna*, on which the insects feed and are raised."

"The *Opuntia Coccinellifera* or Cochineal Cactus," said Susie, "is used only in the West Indies and Brazil."

The provinces, in which the cochineal is so largely raised, are Oaxaca, Tlascola, and Guanaxuato. It is necessary to renew the plantations frequently, as the insects rapidly exhaust the juices, and so cause the plants to dry up and die. We accompanied a

man in among these Cacti; he had in one hand, a squirrel's tail, and with this he swept the fully developed insects into a receptacle filled with hot water, which he held in the other hand; by this means they were killed.

"Be gorra," said Patsey, seeing him do this, "an' its moity glad I am that its meself is not a corchinelly boug, for they don't ax ye how ye'll have yer bath, but give it till yere moity hot."

They are also killed by being laid in the sun, after they are swept from the plants. When the man had obtained the requisite amount, he strained off the water and spread the insects out to dry; after they were thoroughly dry, they were ready for market. Each pound of cochineal contains about seventy thousand insects. The preparing of carmine from cochineal, cannot be carried on profitably on a small scale; four or five manufacturers supplying the whole of the world, a Parisian manufacturer producing the finest article.

The preparation of the finest carmine is still a mystery, because, on the one hand, its consumption being limited, few are engaged in its manufacture, and upon the other, the raw material being costly, extensive experiments on it cannot be conveniently made. Carmine, owing to its costliness, is almost always adulterated, and in making rouges for commercial purposes, but a very small quantity is used, it being mixed with talc powder to reduce the expense as well as its intense color, and bring it to the right shade for the complexion. Many hundred pounds of rouge annually, are used in this country, not only for theatrical purposes, but by private individuals. We, however, discountenance the use of rouge or paint of any description on the skin. But so long as blooming cheeks and cherry lips are admired, and considered indispensable to beauty, it will be in demand; and

JACKSON & CO.

HATTERS & FURRIERS

Dunlap's New York Hats,

No. 59 TREMONT STREET - - BOSTON.

JOSEPH A. JACKSON.   WM. H. HOLLOWAY.

MISS ROSILLA BUTLER,

Artist in Hair,

AND DEALER IN

HAIR GOODS,

132 TREMONT STREET,

NEAR WINTER STREET.   BOSTON.

Ladies waited on at their residences.

if the ladies persist in tight lacing, and wearing corsets, and hanging their clothes on their hips instead of suspending them by straps from their shoulders and taking a generous amount of exercise, to have these adjuncts to beauty they will always be obliged, if they continue to dress so unhealthily, to resort to paints, powders, rouges and cosmetics of various kinds. To those who will, and do, use the articles, we would recommend them always to get the purest, consequently the best, as it is less liable to injure the skin than those which are cheap, and composed of deleterious substances.

Patsey appeared before us at this moment, his cheeks as red as the setting sun; he had evidently been into some mischief, having powdered some of the dry cochineal and rubbed it on his face.

"Its blooming I am, Miss Susie," said he. "Och, how the gurrils in ould Ireland wuld cast their eyes on me, ef they could only see me mees now."

"Go wash your face immediately," I said to him, "and consider yourself fortunate if you get it all off."

Pretty soon he came back to us looking like a Sioux warrior; he had rubbed his face hard to wash it, but had only distributed the coloring over his face and into his ears and hair. We had a hearty laugh at him, but he evidently enjoyed it as well as the rest of us. We turned ourselves about, and in a short time were on board our ship, and abed, while the head of the *Cynthia* was pointed toward the east.

CHAPTER IX.

MONS. SASPORTAS.

WE steamed into the pretty bay of St. Thomas about six A. M., and when we anchored, about half a mile off shore, heavy showers commenced, lasting nearly two hours. At length all signs of unpleasant weather having disappeared, we proceeded to the shore, landing at a little jetty on which stood a group of the dingy denizens of St. Thomas. Amid the chatterings and laughter of these light-hearted beings, we continued our walk beneath a row of pretty coconut trees, on which hung their fruit, and we presently found ourselves in the town. We were shown a comfortable hotel, and were glad to be once more on land, and live in a house. I became acquainted with Mons. Sasportas, the gentleman whom I intended visiting here, while he was on a visit to Boston. He had immense estates, and carried on the manufacture of perfumes and pomades on a small scale, but his especial business was the distilling of Bay Rum, and Otto of Bay. Mons. Sasportas, whilst in Boston, told me if I ever came to the Island, he should expect me to make him a visit. After dinner, I despatched a messenger to him, announcing our arrival. He came back with the messenger, and greeted us cordially, requesting us to come immediately to his house and make it our

62

TUTT'S PILLS

Are extracted from Vegetable products, combining in them the Mandrake, or May Apple, which is recognized by physicians as a substitute for calomel, possessing all the virtues of that mineral without its bad after effects.

AS AN ANTI-BILIOUS MEDICINE THEY ARE INCOMPARABLE.

They stimulate the Torpid Liver, invigorate the Nervous System, and give tone to the Digestive Organs, creating perfect digestion and thorough assimilation of food. They exert a powerful influence on the Kidneys and Liver, and through these organs remove all impurities, thus vitalizing the tissues of the body and causing a healthy condition of the system.

AS AN ANTI-MALARIAL REMEDY THEY HAVE NO EQUAL ;

and, as a result, act as a preventive and cure for Bilious, Remittent, Intermittent, Typhoid Fevers, and Fever and Ague. Upon the healthy action of the Stomach depends almost wholly the health of the human race.

DYSPEPSIA IS THE BANE OF THE PRESENT GENERATION.

It is for the cure of this disease and its attendants, Sick Headache, Nervousness, Despondency, Constipation, Piles, etc., that TUTT'S PILLS have gained such a widespread reputation. No remedy has ever been discovered that acts so speedily and gently on the digestive organs, giving them tone and vigor to assimilate food. This being accomplished, of course the Nervous System is braced, the Brain is nourished, and the Body robust.

Being composed of the juices of plants, extracted by powerful chemical agencies, and prepared in a concentrated form, they are guaranteed free from anything that can injure the most delicate person.

A noted chemist, who has analyzed them, says, "There is more virtue in one of TUTT'S PILLS than can be found in a pint of any other."

We therefore say to the afflicted, "Try this Remedy fairly; it will not harm you. You have nothing to lose, but will surely gain a Vigorous Body, Pure Blood, Strong Nerves, and a Cheerful Mind."

Principal Office, 35 Murray Street, New York.

Price 25 Cents per Box.

SENT BY MAIL ON RECEIPT OF PRICE.

SOLD BY ALL DRUGGISTS.

home during our stay on the Island. We waited, however, till morning. Riding through the town, we noticed that it was built upon the level and partly upon three hills, which abut down from the high range nearly to the shore, with savannas between, and we remarked how beautifully the place was located, and the large and substantially built stores and dwellings. The stores are owned principally by Americans and Danes. We met many Danish soldiers during our ramble.

We went through the main street, which runs parallel with the shore, and ascended one of the three eminences; after going some distance, we reached Mons. Sasportas' grounds. He conducted us through his estates, on which were growing Coffee, Coco, and Breadfruit Trees, and many beautiful flowers.

"See!" said Susie, "there is the *Moringa pterygosperma*, the *Hibiscus abelmoschus*, and the *Laurus nobilis*."

"Oh, Susie! don't distort your pretty mouth with such outlandish names," said I. "Tell us in plain English. So long as knowledge is bound up in such long-drawn, wearying words, it will never become universal; and as universal knowledge means universal peace, comfort, and happiness, let your information be expressed in the most simple terms."

"Well, to please you, I will," she replied. "The first one I spoke of is the Behen Tree, on which grow the benne seeds, such as we saw at New Orleans, from which the benne oil was taken; the next is the Musk Seed, or Ambrette Seed Tree, on which grow the grains d'Ambrette, so-called; and the last,— the large group to the right, — are the Bay Trees, from which Bay Rum and Otto of Bay are extracted."

"Thank you, that is better; but look at Patsey!"

There he stood, staring at Susie yet, with mouth wide open,

as was usual with him when he heard anything he could not understand.

"Perhaps he has thrown his jaw out trying to repeat the first names you mentioned. Patsey, what's the matter with you?"

"An' — an' — Miss Susie, sir, I hope she be well?"

"Yes."

"I didn't noo, sir, but what she were sunstruck, she talked so wild loike," he answered.

He had never before been in Susie's presence when she called plants by their botanical names, so he was naturally thunder-struck at first, but he soon became used to it, and when bringing her any of the plants she sent him for, he would try to give it the name he heard her call it; the blunders he made, and the way he pronounced the botanical names, kept us in a continuous roar of laughter.

After strolling through the gardens, we reached Mons. Sasportas' manufactory, in which we saw the distillation of Bay Rum. It was done in the ordinary way, the Bay leaves being put into a still with fine rum and distilled over, the product being the Bay Rum of commerce. The Otto of Bay is distilled from the Bay ber-ries; these berries, they are about twice the size of a clove, are put into the still with water; after passing over, the otto separates from the water, is taken off, put up in black junk bottles, and is ready for exportation. This otto when good is of a dark brown color, having a very penetrating odor. It is used very exten-sively by manufacturers of Bay Rum, by dissolving the otto in spirit, then distilling it; the otto possesses all the properties of Bay Rum in a concentrated form, and saves a great deal of ex-pense when imported thus. Otto of Bay is now distilled in New York, from the imported bay leaves and berries.

Patsey came to us with what seemed to be a handful of bird-shot; "An' phats thim, Miss Susie?" he asked.

"They are the produce of the plant *Hibiscus Abelmoschus*," answered Susie, "musk-seed or grains d'ambrette, as they are known in the perfumery trade."

"Kabb-el-Misk is the Arabic name," said Jean, "of which Abelmoschus is a vile corruption. Several other allied species are remarkable for a similar odor, one of which is called Sumbul."

"Musk Seed, when ground, certainly reminds our smelling sense of the odor of Musk," I remarked; "it is poor stuff at best; for making cheap sachet powder, it may be used for the sake of adulteration and variety, also to perfume hair and face powders."

Continuing on our walk, we came upon a workman at an apparatus, which, from its curious construction, arrested our attention. It consisted of a large glass tube in the form of a coil, and at the upper end divided into two tubes, in each of which was a tunnel.

"He is making Otto of Mirbane," said Mons. Sasportas, "a chemical imitation of Otto of Almonds, procured from Benzole, and Benzole is obtained from coal tar." The workman poured into one of the tunnels nitric acid, and into the other Benzole, the two substances uniting at the union of the tubes, a combination ensued, with the evolution of heat. As the newly-formed compound flowed down through the coil it became cool and ran into a receiver. The workman then washed it with water, and lastly with a diluted solution of carbonate of soda; it was then ready for use. Nitro-benzole, the chemical name, and Otto of Mirbane, the perfumery name of this artificial otto of almonds,

5

D. Lothrop & Co.'s Magazines for the Family.

I.

(For the Young People.)

WIDE AWAKE.

25 cts. a number. $2.50 a year.

This carefully edited magazine can be placed in the hands of young people with confidence and safety. A bright, clear, sunshine sparkle characterizes everything allowed to appear on its pages. Its stories, poems, narratives and adventures are chosen from the manuscripts of the best writers in the country, and then placed in the hands of popular artists for full illustration.

II.

(For the Very Little Ones.)

BABYLAND.

5 cts. a number. 50 cts. a year.

This beautiful eight-page quarto is the only periodical ever made especially for the babies. It is full of large gay pictures, sweet little stories and jingles, and very funny drawings for copying on slates and in drawing-books. Several new and amusing features are shortly to be added.

III.

(For Primary Schools, Home-Teaching and Kindergartens.)

LITTLE FOLKS' READER.

7 cts. a number. 75 cts. a year.

The LITTLE FOLKS' READER is a sixteen-page quarto, exquisitely gotten up in every detail of letter-press and illustration. Its success the last year in teaching children to "read at sight," in schools all over the country, has been something as marvellous as gratifying.

THE PANSY.

A PICTORIAL WEEKLY PAPER FOR YOUNG PEOPLE.

Edited by MRS. G. R. ALDEN, Author of the Pansy Books. 50 cts. a year.

The Weekly Numbers of each month are varied in subject. The First number of each month, complete in itself, contains Short Stories and Sketches, Illustrated. The Second contains Pansy's Serial for boys and girls. The Third, Young People Abroad. The Fourth, Young People at Home. And where there is a Fifth number in the month, its subject will be "Light in Many Lands," showing how the dark places of the earth are being enlightened. The First number of each month will be issued as a monthly. Single subscriptions, 15 cts. a year. 50 copies, one year, $5.00. The First and Second numbers of each month will be sent as a Semi-Monthly, 25 cts. a year. 50 copies, one year, $10.00.

D. LOTHROP & Co. also publish over 1000 choice books for Sunday-School and Home Libraries. Catalogues sent free.

D. LOTHROP & CO., 32 Franklin St., Boston.

has a different odor than the true otto of almonds, but is never-theless used in scenting soaps and common hair oils. After we had made the tour of the factory, we returned to the house, where we dined with the family of Mons. Sasportas.

Towards evening, we rode back to the hotel, accompanied by him and two of his sons. We invited them on board; they were much pleased with the ship, especially the boys, who were de-lighted with the chairs hung in gimbals, and kept continually rocking in them. They left late in the evening, pressing us to make our stay longer; but knowing that by so doing we should delay Brad, we thanked them, telling them we would come some other time and stay longer. They left, expressing their satisfac-tion for the pleasure we had afforded them.

Weighing anchor early in the morning, we stood out to sea, passing on our way out the large steamship, "The Seine," which plies between Northampton, England, and this Island. The first day out, we steamed by the islands east and south of St. Thomas, —Guadeloupe, Martinique and others. We remained on deck the greater part of the day, there being a cool, fresh breeze, mak-ing it the most comfortable place on board. In the evening we assembled in the large saloon, and with music and conversation the evening speedily came to a close. Brad told us many epi-sodes of his life, and Jean gave us some interesting information about perfumery and its origin.

"Pliny traced its origin to the East," he said, "and his opin-ion is fully borne out by the inspired writers, whose frequent allusions to perfumes and aromatics, prove the very early and extensive employment of the luxury by nations, in whose land flourish the aloe, cinnamon, camphor, sandal wood, nutmeg, and clove; the incense tree, which it was the sacred privilege of the

Sabæi to gather; the balsam trees; the sorrowful Nyctenthes, which pours forth its rich odors in the twilight; the Nilica, in whose blossoms the bees are said to hum themselves to sleep, and the sweet Elcaya, — these, and a forest of others, are indigenous to the East, and for ages, were disregarded by the rest of the world. Homer but twice alludes to anything of the sort being in use among the Greeks; and centuries after the Jews had been commanded to make incense, the Athenians were forbidden by Solon to use perfumery. Among the Lacedemonians, the luxury was always discountenanced, and perfumers were expelled from the city as wasters of oil, upon the same principle that they dismissed all who dyed wool, because they destroyed its whiteness. In Athens the case was different; in spite of Solon's prohibition, the taste for perfumery grew apace, and its indulgence was brought to a higher pitch of refinement than it ever enjoyed before or since. Though the East supplied the Athenians with the most valued gums and ointments, they added largely to the stock of fragrant plants already in use. Appollonius, of Herophila, wrote a treatise on perfumes. 'The Iris,' he says, 'is best at Phasalis and at Cyzicus; perfume from roses is most excellent at Phasalis, Naples and Capua; that made from crocuses, is in highest perfection at Soli, in Cilicia, and at Rhodes; the essence of spikenard is best at Tanius; the extract of vine-leaves at Cyprus and at Adramythium; the best perfume from marjoram, and from apples, comes from Cos; Egypt bears the palm for its essence of Cypirus, and the next best is the Cyprian and Phœnician, and after them comes the Sidonian; the perfume called Panathenaicum, is made at Athens; and those called Metopian and Mendesian are prepared with the greatest skill in Egypt.'"

"Still," said I, "the superior excellence of each perfume is

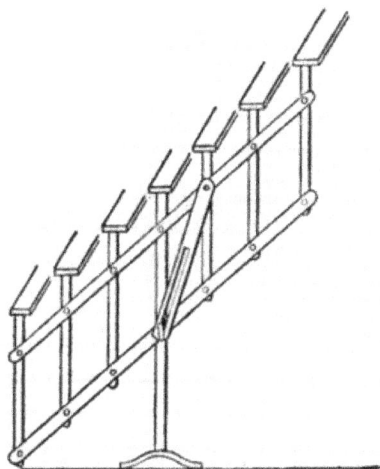

owing to the purveyors, the materials used, the artists and age, and not so much to the locality itself."

"True," replied Jean.

"The boxes of unguents, that were carried in ancient times," spoke up Susie, "must have formed expensive items in the jeweller's bill, for they were generally made of alabaster richly carved and ornamented with jewels."

"But," said Jean, "if we may believe a passage in the *Settler* of Alexis, even this extravagance has been exceeded :

> "'For he t'anoint himself
> Dipped not his finger into alabaster,
> The vulgar practice of a former age,
> But let fly four doves, with unguents drenched,
> Not of one sort, but every bird a perfume bore,
> Peculiar, and differing from the rest;
> And they, hovering around us, from their heavy wings
> Showered their sweets upon our robes and furniture.
> And I, — be not too envious, gentlemen, —
> I was myself bedewed with violet odours!'

"The room in which an entertainment was given was always perfumed, either by burning incense, or sprinkling the furniture with scented waters."

"An unnecessary proceeding, I should think," said my wife, "when we consider the lavish manner in which the guests were anointed."

"I should think so too," continued Jean, "for each portion of the body had its appropriate oil or essences. Mint was commended for the arms; palm oil for the jaws and breast; the eyebrows and hair were anointed with an unguent extracted from marjoram; the knees and neck with the essence of ground ivy. This last was beneficial at drinking parties, as also was the per-

fume obtained from roses; the quince yielded an essence suitable to the lethargic and dyspeptic; the perfume from vine-leaves kept the mind clear, and that from white violets was an aid to digestion. The habit of anointing the head at banquets, is said to have arisen from an idea that the heating effects of wine would be better borne when the head was wet, just as a patient who labors under a burning fever is relieved by the application of a lotion."

"Socrates disapproved of all perfumes," said I, "and he also believed it was wrong to bathe, and he never did; but his teachings made little impression upon his pupil Æschines, who turned perfumer. Alexander the Great was more attentive to the rebuke of his tutor, Leonidas, for his wasteful expenditure of incense in his sacrifices. His master told him it would be time for him so to worship when he had conquered the countries producing the frankincense. The king remembered the lesson, and when he had taken possession of Arabia, he despatched a cargo of frankincense and myrrh to his old instructor. From Greece, perfumes quickly made their way to Rome; and although their sale was strictly prohibited, their employment became more and more extravagant, until even the eagles and standards were thought unfit to face the barbarian hosts of Northern Europe, unless they had been duly anointed before battle; and should the engagement prove successful, the ceremony was repeated. Such was the demand for the luxury, that the chief street of Capua was occupied solely by perfumers' stores. The incense burnt by Nero upon the pyre of his wife, Poppœa, exceeded the annual production of spices in Arabia. At a rather earlier period Platuius Plancus, when proscribed by the triumvirs, was betrayed by his perfumes. His place of concealment got wind, and discovered him to his pursuers."

All of our preparations put up in 25, 50, 75 ct. and $1.00 Bottles.

$1.00 per bottle.

75 cts. per bottle.

50 cts. per bottle.

25 cts. per bottle.

CLIFFORD'S Pure **Bay Rum.** CLIFFORD, Perfumer, BOSTON.

CLIFFORD'S PURE **BAY RUM.** CLIFFORD, PERFUMER, BOSTON.

CLIFFORD'S PURE **BAY RUM.** CLIFFORD, PERFUMER, BOSTON.

Clifford's Pure **Bay Rum.** CLIFFORD, Perfumer, BOSTON.

18 ozs.

12 ozs.

8 ozs.

4 ozs.

SOLD BY ALL FIRST-CLASS DRUGGISTS.

"Describing the spectacles and Amphitheatre at Rome," I said, "Gibbon observes, 'the air of the Amphitheatre was continually refreshed by the playing of fountains, and profusely impregnated by the grateful scent of aromatics;' and also, 'In a magnificent temple, raised on the Palatine Hill, the sacrifices to the god Elagabalus (the sun), were celebrated, with every circumstance of cost and solemnity. The rarest aromatics were profusely consumed upon his altar.'"

"In the Romish Church," Jean went on to say, "incense is used in many ceremonies, and particularly at the solemn funerals of the hierarchy. Several passages in Exodus and also in other parts of the Scriptures, prove the use of perfumes at a very early period among the Hebrews. In the thirtieth chapter of Exodus the Lord said unto Moses, 'And thou shalt make an altar to burn incense upon; of shittim wood shalt thou make it. And Aaron shall burn thereon sweet incense every morning; when he dresseth the lamps he shall burn incense upon it. Take unto thee sweet spices, stacte, and onycha and galbanum; these spices with pure frankincense; of each shall there be a like weight. And thou shalt make it a perfume, a confection after the art of the perfumer, tempered together, pure and holy. And thou shalt beat some of it very small, and put it before the testimony in the tabernacle of the congregation, where I will meet with thee; it shall be unto you most holy. And as for the perfume which thou shalt make, ye shall not make to yourselves according to the composition thereof; it shall be unto thee holy, for the Lord. Whosoever shall make like unto that, to smell thereto, shall even be cut off from his people.' From this religious custom of employing incense, the royal prophet drew that beautiful simile of his, that his prayers might ascend before the Lord like incense."

All of our Preparations put up in 25, 50, 75 ct., and $1.00 Bottles.

$1.00 per bottle.

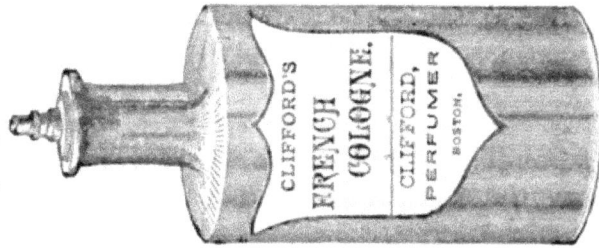

CLIFFORD'S
FRENCH
COLOGNE.

CLIFFORD,
PERFUMER
BOSTON.

12 ozs.

75 cts. per bottle.

CLIFFORD'S
FRENCH
COLOGNE.

CLIFFORD,
Perfumer,
BOSTON.

8 ozs.

50 cts. per bottle.

CLIFFORD'S
French
Cologne.

CLIFFORD,
PERFUMER
BOSTON.

4 ozs.

25 cts. per bottle.

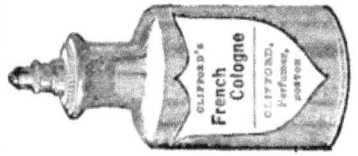

CLIFFORD'S
French
Cologne

CLIFFORD,
Perfumer,
BOSTON

1¼ ozs.

Sold by all First-Class Druggists.

" That the nations attached a meaning, not only of personal reverence, but also of religious homage, to an offering of incense," I remarked, " is demonstrable from the instance of the Magi, who having fallen down to adore the new-born Jesus, and recognizing his Divinity, presented Him with gold, myrrh and frankincense. The primitive Christians imitated the example of the Jews, and adopted the use of incense at the celebration of the Liturgy. The use of incense in all the Oriental Churches is continuous; nor do any of them ever celebrate their Liturgy without it, unless compelled by necessity, which seldom occurs. The Coptic, as well as other Eastern Christians, observe the same ceremonial as the Latin Church, in incensing their altar, the sacred vessels, and ecclesiastical personages."

" A reverend gentleman, describing the *precious ointment* of the Scriptures, says," Jean continued, after my interruption, " ' The sacred oil with which the tabernacle, the ark of the covenant, the golden candlestick, the table, the altar of incense, the altar of burnt offerings, the laver, and all the sacred utensils, and indeed the priests themselves, were anointed, was composed of a hin, — which is ten and one-tenth pints Hebrew measure, or twelve pints English measure — of the oil of olives, of the richest myrrh, of cassia, of cinnamon, and of sweet calamus. The proportions of the aromatics in the mixture were five hundred parts each of the myrrh and cassia, and two hundred and fifty each of the cinnamon and calamus. This ointment could not be applied to any other purpose.'

" Horace, in an ode celebrating the return of Augustus from Spain, bids his slaves go and seek for perfumes, and desires the tuneful Neaera to make haste and collect into a knot her scented hair. These passages sufficiently indicate the elegant direction

All of our preparations put up in 25, 50, 75 ct. and $1. Bottles.

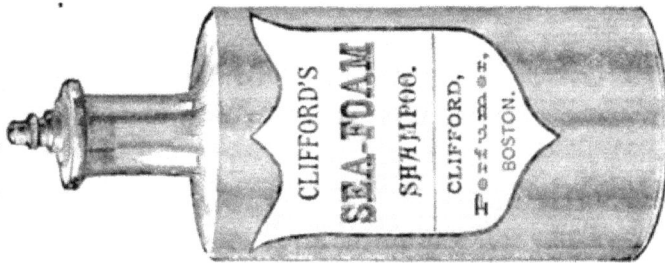

25 cts. per bottle.

CLIFFORD'S SEA-FOAM SHAMPOO. CLIFFORD, PERFUMER, BOSTON.

4 ozs.

50 cts. per bottle.

CLIFFORD'S SEA-FOAM SHAMPOO. CLIFFORD, Perfumer, BOSTON.

8 ozs.

75 cts. per bottle.

CLIFFORD'S SEA-FOAM SHAMPOO. CLIFFORD, PERFUMER, BOSTON.

12 ozs.

$1.00 per bottle.

CLIFFORD'S SEA-FOAM SHAMPOO. CLIFFORD, Perfumer, BOSTON.

16 ozs.

SOLD BY ALL FIRST-CLASS DRUGGISTS.

which the taste of the Romans took in the days of this poet, who himself was a voluptuary in flowers and fragrances. Perfumes were used in the Church service, not only under the form of incense, but also mixed in the oil and wax for the lamps and lights commanded to be burned in the house of the Lord. The brilliancy and fragrance which were often shed around a martyr's sepulchre, at the celebration of his festival, by multitudes of lamps and tapers, fed with aromatics, have been noticed by St. Paulinus, of Nola, a writer at the end of the fourth and beginning of the fifth century, who tells us : —

> "'With crowded lamps are these bright altars crowned,
> And waxen tapers, shedding perfume 'round
> From fragrant wicks, beam calm a scented ray,
> To gladden night, and joy e'en radiant day.'"

"Constantine the Great, provided fragrant oils, to be burned at the altars of the greater churches in Rome," I said, "and gold, frankincense, and myrrh, in silken bags, are still presented on Twelfth-day, at the Chapel Royal, in St. James Palace. Formerly the offering was made by the sovereign in person. At present it is by two persons connected with the Lord Chamberlain's office. It is related that after Edward, the Confessor, rebuilt Westminster Abbey, being so desirous of rendering the Abbey almost unique in its attractions, he endowed it with relics, — in those days beyond price ; among these were to be noted, 'part of the frankincense offered to Jesus by the Eastern Magi.'"

"In accordance with an ancient custom," Jean said, "the Pope of Rome every year blesses what is called the Golden Rose. This flower, which is made of the purest gold, and ornamented with precious stones, is rubbed with balm and incense. His

Holiness recites verses, explaining the mystic meaning of the benediction, after which he takes it in his left hand, then blesses the people. Mass is then celebrated in the Sistine Chapel. After the ceremony, this Gold Rose is ordinarily sent to female sovereigns, sometimes to princes, and sometimes, though rarely, to towns and corporations.

"Sophie Curvelli, the once celebrated opera singer, received the last Golden Rose, as she gave up her lyric career to become a wife and mother, and later a devotee, only singing for charitable purposes."

"It is time we left these classic scenes," I spoke up. "You can tell us more some other time, Jean, about the perfumed gloves and fatal caskets prepared by René, the chemist, astrologer, and perfumer, for the use of his mistress, Catherine de Medicis, and many other interesting facts. No doubt Brad and the others would be delighted to hear of them; but now it is late, so we had better retire."

THE "WHITE" IS KING.

Its Durability Demonstrated.

Its Success Unparalleled.

Its Sale 100,000 Machines Annually.

WE CLAIM — The " WHITE " is the simplest constructed shuttle sewing machine made.

WE CLAIM — The " WHITE " is the lightest running shuttle sewing machine made.

WE CLAIM — The " WHITE " makes less noise than any other shuttle machine.

WE CLAIM — The " WHITE " has the largest space under the arm of any family machine made.

WE CLAIM — The " WHITE " has a self-threading shuttle, which tension can be altered without removing it from the race.

WE CLAIM — The " WHITE " has a self-setting needle.

WE CLAIM — The " WHITE " has the strongest double-feed (on both sides of the needle) of any family machine.

WE CLAIM — The " WHITE " is adjustable in all its wearing parts.

WE CLAIM — The " WHITE " has the easiest working treadle of any machine made.

WE CLAIM — The " WHITE " will do the greatest range of work of any family sewing machine made.

WE CLAIM — The " WHITE " is unsurpassed for durability.

WE CLAIM — The " WHITE " has the most complete set of useful attachments of any machine.

WE CLAIM — The " WHITE " is not only the handsomest, but the best family sewing machine in the world.

WE CLAIM — That all our claims are incontrovertible.

THE BEST TEST OF DURABILITY.

COLUMBIA CORSET WORKS, NEW HAVEN, CT., Jan. 9, 1879.

DEAR SIR, — In reply to your favor would say we have been using the White Sewing Machine on corset work about one and a half years. We have in use nearly 500, running 1000 revolutions per minute, and find them the cheapest machine to keep in repair of any we ever had during an experience of eighteen years in the corset business. The machine is so simple in construction that we have no trouble in learning beginners to use it in comparatively very short time. The evenness of the tensions warrants us in using it on our finest class of goods as well as on the lower grades. It keeps the work free from oil spots, which is so very essential in white goods. We consider it the most perfect machine in the market for corset work, and recommend them equally as highly for family use.

Yours truly,   MAYER, STROUSE & CO.

CLARKE & FREEMAN, New England Agents.

N. I. ASHTON, Boston Agent.

SALESROOMS - - 163 Tremont Street.

CHAPTER X.

EMBRACED BY A NATIVE.

A LONG voyage was before us, for Brad had determined not to stop at any place between St. Thomas and the Hawaiian Islands, unless absolutely necessary. He had laid in a sufficient supply of fuel and provisions to last, covering all ordinary delays. We continued on our course, the uneventful days following each other in quick succession, Jean and I employing ourselves in the laboratory, and reading the scientific works contained in Capt. Cole's library. The ladies spent their time in reading, sewing and helping in any little matters where their deft fingers were needed and could be used to advantage. Brad and Jean were all attention to Susie, but she did not encourage either of them. Some days they were disconsolate, at others all excitement with hope at some favor shown them, which they construed as favorable to their cause. Patsey of course could not keep quiet. We had not been out more than a week, before he asked permission to get up an entertainment among the sailors, to pass away the time. Permission being granted, after a few days' rehearsing, he invited us to the opening performance. The acting on his part was very good; the gymnastics were admirable, and the others who helped him did quite well for novices; Patsey having that

MISS S. L. MORTON,

DRESS MAKER,

Cutting and Basting of Ladies' and Children's Suits by S. T. Taylor's
System a Specialty. Also, Pupils Received for Instruction
in the Taylor System.

No. 149 A, TREMONT STREET,

Room No. 81.   BOSTON, MASS.

JOSEPH WILLIAMS,

TAILOR AND CLOTHES CLEANER,

8 BOYLSTON STREET,

ROOM No. 1,

Near Washington Street - - - BOSTON.

DYEING AND REPAIRING DONE IN THE BEST MANNER.

managerial talent, of seeing what, and where, a performer would show to the best advantage. Three of the sailors being musically inclined, composed the orchestra; in some of the succeeding exhibitions Susie and Jean helped him out by singing and playing.

With the interest in preparing and the pleasure afforded by the performances, all the occupants of the ship were kept from feeling the time monotonously. Once every week the curtain was drawn aside to show us some novelty. Patsey's wonderful performances in the acrobatic line excited our highest encomiums, and as we watched the innumerable evolutions and gyrations that he accomplished with such grace and apparent ease, and saw his finely developed muscles, we thought, " Of what is the human form, when rightly trained, not capable?"

We experienced an occasional spell of bad weather, but none of any serious consequence, and we came across many curious sights and pleasant scenes; but as they have been so often and variously described by different writers, it would be superfluous to speak of them. We were now entering the temperate and colder latitudes, having crossed the tropic of Capricorn. One magnificent evening, about eight o'clock, we were abreast of Cape Blanc, thirty miles to the leeward of Patagonia, and the Straits of Magellan opened less than seven hundred miles to the south of us. Within the next eight days, the *Cynthia* would be ploughing the waters of the Pacific. We skirted the south-east coast of America with great rapidity; three days later we were at the opening of the Straits of Magellan. Capt. Cole concluded not to make the tortuous passage, but to double Cape Horn. Four days from this, about three o'clock in the afternoon, at fifteen miles to the south, we doubled the solitary island, — this lost rock at the extremity of the American continent, to which some Dutch sailors gave the

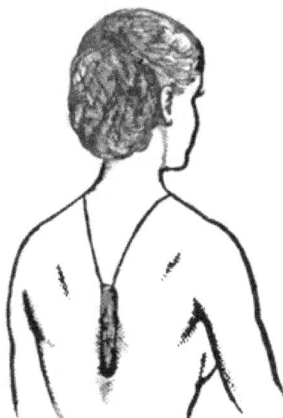

name of their native town, Cape Horn. We met many icebergs
in these waters, and were obliged to keep a sharp lookout to prevent being run into, or crushed. The temperature being too low
for comfort, we did not show ourselves much on deck. It was
not only cold, but the weather was remarkably clear. The course
was taken towards the north-west. The next day the screw
blades of our ship were at last beating the waters of the Pacific.
A week more and we were nearing the Island of Juan Fernandez,
where De Foe's hero, the famed "Robinson Crusoe" spent
a solitary life so many years. Brad could not but think that his
father was pursuing a like existence, and perhaps undergoing
greater hardships than even poor Robinson Crusoe did. We tried
to cheer Brad, assuring him that no doubt John Gagler could explain everything to him ; and it would be but a short time before
we should reach the Hawaiian Islands ; in fact we were ahead of
time, according to his own reckoning, as he had told me a few
days before. Brad, however, was rather quiet during that evening, but the next morning he was as bright and pleasant as
ever. I wanted to stop at Valparaiso, Chili, almost opposite the
Island of Juan Fernandez, but thinking Brad was anxious to push
on, I did not mention it then, but told him of it the next day,
when I thought it too late, and it was as much as I could do to
prevent him from turning the ship about.

"Always tell me, Albert," he said in his kindly way, "of any
place you desire to visit. I can spare what few hours you wish,
and make it up by putting on more steam. What did you desire
to see there?"

"I wished to see the Balsam of Tolu Trees," I replied, "and
to witness the method of procuring the Balsam of Tolu, a gum that
exudes from the—"

" *Toluifera Balsammum*," interrupted Susie.

" It closely resembles common resin, but with the least warmth it runs to a liquid like brown treacle," added Jean, " and the smell of it is particularly agreeable ; it is quite soluble in alcohol, so that we can make an extract of it; but it is never used as a perfume alone, but makes a good basis for a bouquet."

" A bouquet of brown treacle?" said Brad, inquiringly.

"A bouquet of odors," I explained, laughing, " that is, when dif· ferent perfumes are mixed together in certain proportions to form some odor not obtainable directly from the plant or flower, such as Extract of Jockey Club, New Mown Hay, and others, this gum helps to retain the perfume upon the linen longer than it would do without it. I, however, prefer Gum Benzoin."

" Balsam Tolu is sometimes adulterated with common resin," said Jean ; " in order to detect this adulteration, I pour sulphuric acid on the balsam, heat the mixture, and the balsam dissolves to a cherry-red fluid, without evolving sulphurous acid, but with the escape of benzoic and cinnamic acid, if no common resin is present. If the balsam is adulterated with common resin it foams, blackens, and much sulphurous acid is set free."

" I am sorry you would not let me bout ship for Valparaiso, so you could obtain and see the balsam procured," said Brad. " Remember, that I will put in at any port you wish to visit."

" It is of little consequence Brad," I replied, " but if you have time to spare, I should like to stop at La Union, State of San Salvador, Central America, to visit the forests in which grow the Balsam of Peru Trees, and I can there see how they procure the gum, the method differing but slightly from that of collecting the Balsam of Tolu."

" Certainly, Albert, and I can replenish our stock of provisions

NEW ENGLAND CONSERVATORY OF MUSIC,

Boston, Mass.

THE Conservatory of Music is now so established a fact in France, Germany, Belgium, England, and America, that scarcely any definition of its scope is requisite. It is to music what a college of liberal arts or the university is to education in general, and among certain European nations it is formally recognized by the government with the same liberality that is accorded to other institutions of learning. The great tone-masters, Mendelssohn, David, Joachim, and others that might be named, have earnestly labored to give to musical education the benefit of the advantages of a class system of instruction; for by this plan they secured to the scholar of average means the services of better teachers and more thorough training than they could otherwise afford, and the general student, instead of pursuing his study amid the solitude and disheartening atmosphere of his own room, was brought in contact with congenial minds, and kept abreast with all the musical influences, literature, and progress of his day. The very atmosphere of a college is favorable to learning. The crowd of students bent on one pursuit; the eminent teachers; the class-rooms; the costly and curious apparatus; the library, and daily drill, — all conspire to make study interesting. The Conservatory groups all these advantages around musical instruction. The system that is so beneficial to the study of mathematics, and the higher branches of learning, has been found equally serviceable in attaining a high musical education.

TWENTY-FIVE YEARS have now elapsed since Dr. E. Tourjée inaugurated the Conservatory system of musical instruction in New England. Beginning in a comparatively small way, as a School of Music, it soon developed into a Musical Institute, and in the year 1867 expanded into a full-grown and well-appointed Conservatory, on the same basis and offering the same advantages as those which have existed in Europe under the patronage of the governments, or have been founded by the great composers. The Director's critical personal examination of the most celebrated Music Schools in Europe, and his long experience in conducting the above institution, enable him to employ the most valuable methods; his aim being to broaden the area of musical culture in this country, by furnishing the instruction of the best masters, with the greatest number of collateral advantages, at the lowest possible cost to pupils.

The Director remembers with pardonable pride that more than 25,000 pupils have availed themselves of its advantages, many of whom are now prominent members of the musical profession; and the New England Conservatory is now known as the largest Musical School in the world.

there as well as at San Francisco, as I find I shall be obliged to do before sailing for the Islands."

We were pleased to hear that we were to set foot on land in a few days at La Union, as we had had a long voyage; fortunately no mishaps of any serious nature had happened, and everyone was in good health.

Two weeks and three days from the day of the above conversation between Brad and myself, we rounded Point Conseguinay, entered the Gulf of Fonseca, and rode at anchor in the harbor of La Union. After undergoing the preliminaries customary upon the arrival of a vessel in a foreign port, we went ashore, and strolled through the town. Finding a public house which was highly recommended to us, we halted, and induced the landlord to engage a guide and interpreter for us; he soon ushered into our presence a young man of very prepossessing appearance. Upon telling him our wishes, he promised to fulfil them to the best of his ability. In the morning, after an early breakfast, we went on the front piazza of the hotel, and saw our guide astride a mule and leading six others, too sprightly looking the ladies thought; but calming their fears we were soon mounted, and on our way to the "Balsam Coast," so called, as that part of the coast in the State of Salvador, reaching from Acajutla to Libertad is the only place where they collect the article known in commerce as the Balsam of Peru. This particular district is intermediate to the two ports, and does not reach either of them within three or four leagues. We considered it rough travelling, the whole track being almost impassable, and mule riding rather uncertain. Lying to the seaward of a low lateral ridge of mountains, this district is much broken up by spurs and branches, thrown off from the main eminence, and thickly covered by forests. From

STANDARD BLUE OF AMERICA.

H. SAWYER, being the only man in the United States who makes his own Bluing from the raw materials, is thus enabled to give a better quality for the same money than any other manufacturer.

ASK YOUR GROCER FOR SAWYER'S CRYSTAL BLUE.

Be sure and get the RED TOP and BLUE LABEL pepper box blue.

WARRANTED NOT TO SPOT.

Twenty-two years' constant use in families throughout the United States, always giving satisfaction, has demonstrated that this is the best and purest Blue for Laundry purposes.

SAWYER CRYSTAL BLUE CO., 135 STATE STREET.

A NEW BLUE.

SAWYER'S PATENT CONCENTRATED CRYSTAL FOR THE LAUNDRY.

This is the Purest and Strongest Blue ever Compounded,

THE BEST IS THE CHEAPEST.

One trial will convince every house-keeper. Once tested they will never use any other.

REASONS WHY:

1. The brilliant azurine tint has never been equalled in any other Blue.

2. It gives a clear, handsome appearance to Laces, Curtains, Linens, Shirts, Collars, and specially bright tints to old yellowed clothes.

3. It will not injure the most delicate fabric.

4. In this concentrated form a five-cent box will make a pint of Liquid Blue, or more than you can buy for 25 cents.

If you cannot find it at your grocer's, enclose two three-cent stamps, and we will mail you a box, post-paid.

The trade will apply direct for whole-sale prices.

Sawyer Crystal Blue Co., 135 State St., Boston.

this cause it is rarely visited by the residents of either Sonsonate or Salvador.

We travelled all day with the exception of a two hours nooning, and towards night, coming in sight of an Indian village, we entered it, intending to camp here over night. We informed the chief of the tribe that our object was to purchase of them a quantity of the balsam, otherwise we would probably not have been tolerated, as they hold no intercourse with the towns or travellers, only what is necessary for carrying on their peculiar traffic; their chief wealth being the balsam, of which they take to market from twenty thousand to twenty-five thousand pounds weight, annually. It is sold in small portions at a time in the before mentioned towns, to persons who purchase it for exportation. The trees yielding this commodity are very numerous on this privileged spot, and are apparently limited to it; for in other parts of the coast, seemingly identical in soil and climate, rarely an individual of the species, is met with. The Indians informed us, through our guide, that the trees that are well shaded yield a greater quantity than those which are exposed, but when they have been planted by hand and cultivated they yield most. During the months of December and January, the gum oozes away spontaneously, and when thus procured it is called "Calcauzate." It is orange-colored, weighs less than when drawn from the tree, emits a strong odor, and is pungent and volatile. Our guide informed us, that a very superior balsam is sometimes collected from the flowers, but is very scarce, and never found in commerce. We tried to obtain some of this superior balsam, but could not, though we secured a promise that some should be collected and sent to our guide, who agreed to forward it to Boston for us. We had arrived just in time to see them collect the common commercial balsam, as a

party of the Indians intended to set out the following morning, to some trees which had been prepared.

The tree having attained the proper age, five or six years, the " *coseche* " or collecting begins with the dry season, usually in the early part of November. When the season has been more rainy than usual, the product is less; but in order to supply the deficiency thus caused, the Indians heat the body of the tree by fire, by this means making the gum exude more freely; this operation invariably causes the decay of the tree, and should this mode of extracting the gum by heat be continued, the trees will soon disappear from the coast; otherwise, they will increase in numbers and attain to a great age. The method for the extraction of the gum is as follows: the bark, for some distance up, is well beaten on four sides with a beetle or wooden hammer, until it is separated from the woody part, but without injury or breaking; this requires great care. In performing this operation, four intermediate strips of bark are left untouched, so as not to destroy the vitality of the tree. Several notches or cuts are then made in the portions of the beaten bark with a sharp Kris or Malay dagger, and fire is applied to the openings by means of a blazing torch. The exuding balsam readily ignites, and is allowed to burn for a certain time, and is then extinguished. The tree, in this hammered and heated state, is left for fifteen days and carefully watched.

The above mentioned process had been performed previous to our arrival, the allotted fifteen days had expired, and a squad were going to help the watchers collect the balsam. We were awakened before daylight by the noise of preparation; not that we slept very soundly or comfortably in our quarters, for they were not the cleanest or most pleasant we had ever occupied. We had

but little time to eat our breakfast, for the company were almost ready to start. Bestriding our mules, we followed them. In less than an hour's time, we came in sight of the balsam trees. They are very handsome, rather widely branching below, tapering toward the top, and about fifty feet high. They were so odoriferous, that we scented the aroma of the flowers at a distance of more than a hundred yards. The flowers appear at the extremities of the branches, generally in pairs, numerous on each stem, white and unequal; the calyx of pale bluish green, and very glutinous from exuding balsam. The leaves were of a dark shining green, and the fruit almond shaped, winged, and containing a white kernel with much balsam.

Dismounting, we fastened our animals, and went to see the Indians manipulate the trees. The balsam was commencing to run copiously, and was being received on cotton rags stuffed into the cuts, and when saturated were pressed, and thrown into earthen-ware pots, containing boiling water, and the cut repacked with others. The heat detached the balsam from the cotton, and it being of less gravity than the water, floated on top, was skimmed off and poured into clean jars. When thus prepared, it was of a very dark brown color, dirty, and of the consistency of molasses. It was afterwards cleaned and clarified by settling and reboiling; the impure parts rising to the surface, were skimmed off, and sold for making an inferior tincture, used as a medicine among the Indians. The refined balsam is purchased on the coast at an average price of from three to four reals, that is, from thirty-eight to fifty cents per pound. It sometimes undergoes a second clearing, when it brings a higher price as "refinado." After the first cleaning, it is of an amber color, which darkens in cooling. The extraction from the tree is only

made during the four days of each week, that is, four *coseches*, courses or extractions, per month, for each tree, and the average produce is from three to five pounds per week. As soon as the supply begins to fail, fresh cuts are made in the beaten bark, fire again applied, and after fifteen days' rest the extraction is resumed. In this manner the collecting continues until the first ains appear, when all *trabajo* or work ceases. Jear told us that "For a long time this balsam was erroneously supposed to be a production of South America; for in the early period of the Spanish dominion, and by the commercial regulations then existing relative to the fruits of this coast, it was usually sent by the merchants here, to Callao, and being thence transmitted to Spain, it there received the name of Balsam of Peru, being deemed indigenous to that region. The real place of its origin was known only to a few mercantile men."

Returning to the camp we purchased enough to put the Indians in good humor, and show them we came for business, as well as curiosity, and stopping with them for the night, we set out early the next morning on our way back. During the return journey, our guide gave us some statistics regarding the value and quantity of the exports of this balsam.

He said that "as early as 1855 there were twenty-two thousand eight hundred pounds exported from Salvador, valued at about nineteen thousand eight hundred dollars, and probably now it is double that quantity and worth. In the district of Cuisnagua there are three thousand six hundred trees, which yield altogether only six hundred pounds of the gum annually; with proper care in the extraction, each tree would yield from two to three pounds, making the total quantity capable of being produced, in this district alone, about ten thousand pounds. On the coast of Chiqui-

mulilla, in Guatemala, there are many trees that would yield the balsam ; but hitherto it has not attracted the attention of the people of the country to collect it, and bring it to market."

" How long will a tree produce ? " I asked.

" A good tree." he replied, " with careful usage, will produce well for thirty years, after which if it is allowed to remain five or six years at rest, or, as the Indians say, ' to renew its strength,' it will again yield for several years."

He also informed us " that according to a manuscript copy of a Papal Bull, at present among the old records in Tzalco, ' Balsamo Negro' was in such high estimation, that in 1562 Pio IV., and in 1571 Pio V., issued edicts authorizing the clergy to use this precious balsam in the consecration of the ' Sagrada Crisma,' and pronounced it sacrilege to destroy or injure any tree producing it. Copies of these bulls are, — he told us, — still in existence among the archives of Guatemala."

The odor of this substance resembles very nearly that of vanilla, but is not so generally pleasing. On account of its dark color, it cannot be employed to any extent in liquid perfumery ; but added to soap, it imparts to it its fragrance, and at the same time causes the soap to wash with a soft, creamy lather. Balsam of Peru, having also the characteristic of a mild medicinal action upon the skin, soap containing it is said to be " healing " ; hence it is useful in winter for chapped skin.

Reaching the base of a mountain, we commenced the ascent ; the mules being accustomed to the ups and downs of this country, easily clambered up ; arriving at the notch or gap where we could pass to the other side, we dismounted for a nooning ; the view from our present elevated position was magnificent, and after we dined we sat for a long time enjoying the prospect. Our guide,

Special Notice, Based upon Truth.

Julye Myers.

To gratify the many requests of patients who have been benefited and their lives saved by the use of Mrs. JULYE MYERS' **Drawing and Healing Salve**, the following testimonial is respectfully submitted:—

BOSTON, Dec. 13, 1880.

MRS. JULYE MYERS—Madame: About the 3d of December, 1879, I was taken with a swelling in my foot, which settled into dry Gangrene. I was told that I had not twenty-four hours to live. My wife, catching at the last straw, applied your Salve; it kept the Gangrene from spreading any further, and saved my life. I am 78 years of age, and I owe the few remaining years of my life entirely to you. Yours, etc.,

WILLIAM WOOD, 45 Buckingham St.

And many more lie open for inspection in my office, **287 Shawmut Avenue.** Heretofore the lancet was used as the *only* remedy for Carbuncles, Felons and Tumors; *now my Drawing and Healing Salve* takes its place and *cures* the *most obstinate* cases like a *charm.* My Salve also cures Sores of long standing, Boils, Erysipelas, Ulcers, Soft and Ulcerated Corns, Piles, Salt Rheum and Inflamed Joints. My Rheumatic Cure is also widely known for its good properties and its benefits in using the same. Both can be obtained of all druggists. Consultation free at my office, **287 Shawmut Avenue.**

MRS. JULYE MYERS.

leading the mules, had gone far ahead, we preferring to walk awhile for a change. We were descending the mountain, following the rough road; my wife was strolling a few rods ahead; I was next behind, and the others some distance in the rear. My wife turned on a curve in the path, and was hid from our sight by a large mass of rock that had fallen across the way, and which the road had changed its course to avoid. A minute after losing sight of her, we heard her scream and call for help. I rushed forward as fast as possible, picking up, whilst running, a large stone; when I turned the curve, there before me stood my wife, confronted by a huge cinnamon bear. He was standing upright, and preparing to advance. I came upon them with such impetuosity that it carried me forward directly within reach of the beast, who, grasping me by the shoulder, pulled me into his embrace. I struck him a heavy blow on the head with the stone, but it did not seem to discommode him in the least, and the stone was thrown from my hand with the force of the rebound. I had just time to push my left arm up under his throat, and thus keep his head back, so that his great red mouth, with its rows of long, sharp, white teeth, were but an inch from my face. We stood thus for a second, when I felt his embrace growing tighter and tighter; felt his hot breath nearer, his great eyes staring into mine; felt my strength quickly oozing away, and my breath harder to draw, from the powerful pressure he was exerting; slowly, but surely, he was crushing me to death.

Why did not the others come to my assistance! Oh, for some help! What thoughts filled my brain! Was I to die thus! No! One more effort, even if it takes the last breath. Pushing my left arm up as hard as possible, — perhaps remembering some of my old wrestling tricks of my boyhood days, never dreaming

I should have to use them in a case of life and death, — we struggled around and around, till at last getting my right leg back of his right one, I made a lift; over we went, luckily he underneath, but he still kept that murderous embrace.

We crashed down, down, over and over, — for the declivity was steep, — each time that I came underneath it seemed as if every bone in my body was broken; still we kept on. Would we never stop! And horror of horrors! What is that I get a glimpse of! During one of our revolutions when I was uppermost, I perceived only a short distance below us, a frightful chasm, with steep, precipitous sides; we were fast approaching it, — death, inevitable death, for both of us. If I could loosen his grip; break those huge arms of sinews and muscles; but a sudden and powerful shock arrests us, almost throwing me from his grasp, and taking about the last atom of breath from my body. A huge boulder blocked the descent, and the bear struck it. If it had been me, I shudder to think of the consequences. For a moment it stunned both of us; the bear recovered first, and rising to his feet, he pulled me to an upright position. Again we were face to face, — man and beast, — in a terrible struggle for life, and again he commenced that mighty embrace. In lifting me up the beast raised me higher than before, so that my head was far above his, and my toes not touching the ground. I could look down into his face, with that red, cavernous looking mouth and throat, and those devilish eyes; my arm was still under his throat so he could not as yet reach me with his jaws, but having no rest for my feet, I could not again overthrow him; neither did I wish to, for over his head I could see that frightful precipice, only a few yards away. What could I do! My breath and strength were almost exhausted. If I only had some weapon, my right

arm, almost free, below his fore paws, I could use to advantage.
I felt in my breast pocket. Nothing, nothing, only a wicker covered flask. Of what use is a flask! A thought strikes me; the
bottle is of no use, but it contents may be; for it is, or was when
I started from the ship, filled with the strongest liquid ammonia, of
which I usually carried a small supply, to experiment with upon
odors, to find their composition, and for various other purposes.
If the stopple has not got out, or the flask broken in our mad
career down the mountain side, perhaps I can accomplish something with it.

I drew the bottle out slowly, it being almost impossible from
the immense pressure on it; but at last it came, and the space
left gave me one good breath. Now to raise my arm above his
head; I cannot get it by those crushing arms, neither can I reach
over them; my heart fails me, when I hear the shouts of Jean
and Brad. The bear on hearing the calls, released his hold for
a second, but only to resume it more powerfully, seemingly determined not be deprived of his prey. In that second's release I
had gained the freedom of my right arm, pulling the stopple of
the bottle with my teeth, the fumes of the ammonia escaping, almost overpowered me, so that I came near dropping it. Recovering myself, I dashed the ammonia into the bear's face; it entered
his eyes, his nostrils and his mouth, and such a howl as he emitted
probably never before awoke the echoes of those mountains.
He dropped me like a red-hot poker, and with somersaults which
would have put to shame the gymnastics of Patsey, he rushed
towards the precipice as if ten thousand demons were pursuing
him; when he reached the brink, his paws digging at his eyes,
he gave one tremendous bound, and making nearly one hundred
revolutions a minute, he disappeared from view into the frightful

chasm, carrying with him an avalanche of earth and stones. I heard my companions fast approaching, and Patsey calling to the departing bear : —

"Shure an' I hope ye'll find phat your'e lookin' after, and whin ye rach the bottom that ye'll bring up suddintly. Faith an' he bates me on somersets intirely."

My head began to swim, a faintness overcame me, and I knew no more until I awoke with my head in my wife's lap, and Brad, Susie and Jean were bending over me. Patsey had gone to see if the bear was still continuing his explorations to the lower regions.

These events happened in a much shorter space of time than it has taken to describe them. It seems that Brad and Jean, as soon as they saw me go to the assistance of my wife, followed me, but did not reach my wife, whom they found had fainted, until the bear and I had commenced our roll. They stopped a moment to try and revive her, but seeing my critical situation, they left her, and came to my assistance as fast as possible; then being certain of my safety, went back and restored her, assuring her of my escape; then they returned to me, Patsey following the bear as before mentioned. It was unfortunate that I did not carry any firearms, but as Capt. Cole and the others were armed, and I having no experience in their use, I had always refrained from carrying them. I was considerably scratched and bruised, and it was with difficulty that I could stand.

The guide having come back to see what delayed us, was told of the adventure, and had gone on again and brought back one of the mules; he held me on while we slowly descended the mountain, so slowly we did not reach the hotel till late into the night. After dressing my wounds we retired. I was confined to

my bed for two days; at the end of that time, though feeling
somewhat weak and sore, I concluded to wait no longer. I was
sorry to have delayed Brad, for perhaps by my wishing to afford
myself a short pleasure, I might be the cause of his again missing
John Gagler. We set sail immediately; full steam was put on
to make up for lost time, and we soon sighted the Sandwich
Islands

CHAPTER XI.

THE GHOST OF JACOB COLE.

ONE morning when I went on deck, having now almost fully recovered my strength, I saw about two miles ahead, Hawaii, the largest of the seven islands that form the group. We could see clearly the cultivated ranges, and the several mountain drains, that run parallel with the side, and the volcanoes that overtop Mauna Kea, which rises five thousand yards above the level of the sea. Brad was greatly excited at the appearance of land. He kept walking back and forth on the deck, his nervousness showing itself in every step he took.

"What if we should miss the ship now," he said to me as he passed me. "It seems as if fate only drew me on, and when just on the point of realizing my hopes, they are frustrated by some untoward accident. If I don't find John Gagler here, I will follow him, if I have to go around the world."

"Have a little patience, Brad," said I; "you have made all your calculations, and even the unavoidable delays which we have experienced, will hardly put us back and make us too late to meet the ship. Take it coolly; we are almost there now."

We soon approached the shore and no sooner was the anchor cast and the ship swung to, than Brad ordered a boat manned, and we both jumped in. He urged his men to pull with a will; reaching the landing, we went quickly to the Consul's office to see the report of arrivals. On the list we found the "Pegasus," which had arrived only the day before. Brad's spirits rose at this, and with slackened pace we proceeded again to the boat, and the sailors pulled toward the offing where we were told the ship lay. We soon came alongside her, and signaling, we were met at the gangway by the first mate. Brad introduced himself and me, and inquired if they had on board a man by the name of John Gagler.

"We have, sir," said the mate.

"Can I see him?" asked Brad.

"Aye, aye, sir; there he sits forward, near the capstan."

We both looked in the direction indicated. On a block sat an old man, his elbows on his knees, his chin resting in his hands, and his head turned partially to one side. Peering out into the distance, he seemed to be day dreaming. For a moment Brad hesitated to approach him; but advancing slowly he came close to him; still the man did not notice him. Brad touched him on the shoulder and said, —

"John Gagler, —"

Before Brad could continue, the old man turned and held up his hands as if to keep Brad from approaching him. His wrinkled, weather-beaten face, assumed a frightened aspect; he shook as with ague, and his eyes stared at Brad with a look of fear. What could be the matter! Brad was about to speak to him again, when the old man raised one arm, covering his face as if trying to shut Brad from his view, and with his hand motioned him away. In a low, mumbling voice he at last said, —

"Avast, Jacob. Why do you come to me? Why do you thus

happear, looking hexactly the same has I knew ye more than thirty years hago? Was I not always faithful? Did I hever do hanything to 'arm ye or yours? Last night I dreamt hof the spirits of old hacquaintances long gone to Davy Jones's. Now, hin broad daylight ye happear to me. Go, go, I beseech ye."

His voice had fallen to a piteous imploring tone, and sinking back on his seat, he buried his head in his hands. Brad hardly knew what to make of it, and stood staring at him not unlike a spectre, until he saw him sink back; then comprehending the situation, he said to him reassuringly,—

"My name is not Jacob. I am real flesh and blood. See!— take my hand! No ghost ever possessed the like. Perhaps my resemblance to my father has deceived you. My name is Bradford Cole."

John Gagler, for he it was, as it became clearer to him, slowly raised his head, looking yet a little incredulous, and cautiously stretching forth his hand, took that of Brad's, looking into his face long and earnestly.

"You see, now," said Brad, pleasantly and smiling, "you were mistaken."

"The same voice, form, heyes, 'air, heverything," muttered John Gagler, "'ow many ha time 'as your father stood afore me looking hexactly as you do. Shiver my timbers, me boy, don't wonder it made me blue habout the gills hat first." Then rising, he took both of Brad's hands in his, and pressing them lovingly, inquired, what brought him there, how he knew him, how he found him, and poured in questions upon him like grapeshot from a battery.

Brad answered them all, told him how his mother had read the advertisement, how she had followed him from place to place, and how she had left the task of finding John Gagler to him; how he had faithfully kept on the trail, till now he had fulfilled his mother's request and found him. Could he tell him about his father, as upon him he relied to solve the mystery.

"Your father, your father," said John Gagler, thoughtfully, "'ow strange hit seems. I am hafraid I can throw but little glim on his fate."

"But were you not with him on his last voyage?" Brad asked.

"Aye, aye, sir! I were, but not to the hend. Where that hend were I know not, but I'll tell you hall I do know, and ye can then see hif ye can make hanything hout of hit. Sit ye down; who's your mate, Bradford?"

Brad introduced me, and we sat down waiting impatiently for the old sailor to begin.

"Well, lad! Lord love ye! 'ow ye 'ave grown! You remember the day we started," he began, "your mother han' you came down to the ship to see us hoff; ye were but ha little mite then. We slipped hour cable, and went bowling hout of the 'arbor; the weather could'nt 'ave been finer; everybody prophesied ha pleasant han' successful viage. The weather continued fine huntil we 'ad halmost reached hour destination. Yer father traded then with the East Ingees, and 'ad hon ha cargo of Hinglish staple goods to hexchange for the productions of them hislands. The night hafore we hexpected to sight the hisland we traded with, h'it were clear and beautayus. Well, me 'arties, henough to say a squall struck us, one of the fierce hand sudden ones hof those latitudes. I won't tire ye spinning ha yarn about it, but 'ope hi may die hif I hever hexperienced the likes hafore, hor since. Hit were a regilar typhooner. Yer father were hat 'is post, and never left the deck for three days han' nights.

"We drove hon hall this time hafore the wind, we knew not whither, for hall control hof the vessel 'ad been lost. We 'adn't seen ha sign hof the sun during the 'ole time ; one mast was gone, and t'other swaying to, han' we, thinking hevery moment to be swamped. The gale blowed great guns, han' t'ords the hend hof the third day the wind seemed to hincrease, han' blowed from hall quarters and the seas which 'ad been kept down by the steady wind, rose 'igher han' 'igher, han' rolled hover the deck, one time carrying hoff two hof our men. I was one hof them. I never saw my messmate hagin. The last I saw hof your father, 'e were standing near the gunnell, looking to see hif we could be rescued, but 'e saw hit was hof no use. He cast over ha 'encoop han' ha box."

"Then you do not know where my father is, or what became of him?" asked Brad despondingly.

'Old 'ard, me lad," answered he. "The ship seemed to fly from me. Hafter ha long time I ran halongside the 'encoop han' boarded it, han' rested my haching limbs. 'Ow near land I was I couldn't tell. The day afore we 'ad 'eard breakers hindistinctly han' supposed we were passing some hisland ; but since daybreak we 'ad noticed but one such hindication. Night coming hon, I couldn't see me 'and before me heyes, hit were so pitchy dark.

"Hanother day han' night, still the storm continued ; 'unger gnawed hat me witals. I was not very thirsty, the rain supplying me with drink. The morning hof the second day hit broke haway, han' the sun came down upon me with ha scorching 'eat ; but the prospect seemed brighter. No signs has yet hof land. I now felt kinder shaky hin my timbers, for my 'unger was hin-

CORNS! CORNS!

Why use strong Mineral Acids and Alkalies to remove them, when the

PEERLESS CORN CURATIVE

Can be relied upon? It will remove

Hard and Soft Corns, Callouses, Etc.

IN FROM

FOUR TO SIX DAYS,

WITHOUT CAUSING ANY PAIN OR INCONVENIENCE.

FOR SOFT CORNS

The first application usually relieves all pain and soreness. It never fails when used a
directed. It is perfectly safe. Has no effect upon the healthy skin.

TRY IT ONCE AND BECOME CONVINCED.

Every Bottle Guaranteed or Money Refunded.

PREPARED ONLY BY

A. Littlefield & Company,

APOTHECARIES,

BOSTON, MASS.

PRICE ONLY 25 CENTS. For Sale Everywhere. Ask for PEERLESS CORN
CURATIVE. Take no other.

WE CRASHED DOWN, DOWN, OVER AND OVER.

Page 85.

tense. Thinking hof what were my resting place, I felt hunder-
neath, han' to me joy I found floating near the hupper deck hof
the coop ha 'en; breaking hoff ha slat, I pulled hit hout. The
salt water 'ad penetrated hit, but I tore hit hasunder han' de-
voured hit. It revived me for hawhile, but the 'eat, and salt in
the meat haggravated me thirst; many times was I tempted to
drink hof the water haround me, but I restrained meself, 'oping to
see ha ship or land.

"Hafter dark, 'oldin' to my now halmost waterlogged support,
I thought I 'eerd the break hof the surf. 'Ow anxiously I waited
for mornin', you can himagine. When day broke, land lay hafore
me, — a low coast, with ha long stretch of beach. The current
swept me halong the shore, but did not seem to be takin' me
to'rds land. Being hafraid I should be carried haway from the
shore, I left the coop, and swam to'rds it. I was so weak hit
took hall the remaining strength I 'ad to reach the beach, hon
which I lay for hours, hexausted. Hafter recovering me strength,
I wandered habout han' hobtained food han' water in habun-
dance.

"But where is my father?" asked Brad, again getting impatient.

"Your father," replied John Gagler, "I 'aven't seen from that
time to this."

"Then you cannot tell me anymore about him?"

"Only this," he continued. "For five long years I lived
halone hon this island, during that time never seeing ha 'uman
bein'. The sixth year I was captured by some natives hof the
neighboring islands, who surprised me hat night when returning to me 'ut. They 'ad landed hon the hother side hof the island, han' I 'adn't seen them; if I 'ad, I should 'ave kept haway

from 'em. I were kept a slave by these savages for two years, han' picked up a smatterin' hof their language. I questioned them hin regard to the 'urricane hof the time when I was washed hoverboard, han' foun' many who remembered hit well, saying hit were the worst hever known; they told hof many a wrecked vessel. One hin particular seemed as if hit might be our ship, which they said they 'ad 'eard hof, on han island many miles to the south; that there 'ad been 'uman bein's hon the shore, who 'ad come from the wreck han' 'ad stayed ha considerable time, has there were 'uts han' other hindications; but whoever they were they 'ad left hin ha boat built by themselves, han' 'ad never returned.

"I obtained all the information I could concerning the position hof the island. From hall I could gather it was near Australia, west, habout five 'undred miles from the coast. I made me hescape from these savages by floating down the river,— they lived some distance from the shore, — to the sea, where I 'ad seen ha vessel 'ove to; my 'ead covered with a gourd which I had dug out for the purpose, and hat night swam to the ship han' was taken haboard. Reaching London hafter many minor hadventures, I hadvertised for friends hof yere father, thinking per'aps 'e 'ad reached 'ome hafore me; han' 'avin' no relations, myself han' me friends hall hadrift, I wanted to find 'im hor some hof 'is connections."

For sometime after John Gagler had finished, Brad sat without moving. All his hopes were dashed to the ground.

"What can I do?" he at last said. "I do not see the least chance of finding my father. It would be an endless task to search among the many thousand islands which dot those seas, unless by chance I should land upon the right one."

"I don't think so," said John Gagler. "I can go to the island hon which I was ha captive; from there I could find the island on which I lived five years; then ye could judge by the currents han' the way hof the wind hat the time hof the wreck, very near what portion hof the sea the ship had drifted. Then 'twould be han heasy matter to hexamine the islands hin that 'icinity."

"Will you go with us?" asked Brad eagerly, grasping his 'and.

"Bless my heyes, won't I though. Nothing would give this 'old 'ulk more pleasure than to grasp me hold friend, Jacob Cole, by the 'and once more," replied John Gagler earnestly. "Wish I may die though hif I didn't think 'is spirit was hafore me when ye first spoke to me."

"Get your discharge," said Brad. "Tell the captain your reasons for the change, and we will take you on board immediately; and tell the captain we should like to see him."

"Aye, aye sir;" and he went to find the captain.

Meanwhile Brad and I talked together concerning which course we should take, but came to the conclusion to leave it all to John Gagler. The captain told us he was sorry to have John Gagler go, but if there was any chance in the world of rescuing a shipmate, he would not hinder in the least. So John Gagler packed his chest, and after adieus all round, his packages were lowered into the boat, we pushed off and were soon on board the *Cynthia*.

John Gagler was introduced, and every one felt glad that our captain had been so successful. Brad concluded to stop at these islands only till the next morning, then to head for the Chinese Seas, to commence the search immediately and in earnest.

CHAPTER XII.

CELESTIALS.

THE Celestial Empire is spread before us. We sail up the Canton river, our attention all absorbed by the novel and interesting scence. A prodigious number of boats covered the surface of the river, peopled with the odd appearing inhabitants, a large number of the boats being fixed residences, and the handsomest were the *hwa ting*, or flower boats. The form of the boats used as flower boats is very graceful, and their raised cabins and awnings are fancifully carved and painted. Brad wished to stop at Canton to lay in a supply of trinkets for presents for the savages whom we expected to encounter. We had been delayed by bad weather, but had reached our destination at last.

"To you, who have been here so often, it will probably seem tiresome," remarked Susie to Brad; "nevertheless, I shall oblige you to chaperon us, and we will try to make it pleasant for you, as we know you will for us."

"Thank you," he replied, "you know it is a pleasure to me to be your escort. To-morrow, we will go forth among celestial beings. Is it agreeable?"

"Aye, aye, sir," we answered in chorus.

With this sailor response we suppose Brad was satisfied, for

7

he started for his cabin, saying he "wanted to get his china together."

"Going to commence housekeeping, Captain?" Susie called after him.

"I am ready whenever you are," he replied.

"I'll think about it," said Susie, laughing.

Yes we were really to wander in Celestial land, — the place where perfumes have been known and used since the earliest times. An old Chinese proverb, attributed to Confucius or Kong-Foo-Tse, says, "Incense perfumes bad smells, and candles illumine men's hearts." Acting upon that principle, the Chinese use lavishly of both, in public and private, which would lead the hypercritical to conclude that their hearts needed a great deal of lighting up, and that the natural odors of their temples and dwellings were none of the sweetest.

Joss-sticks and tinsel paper, are the forms in which incense is usually burned. The consumption is so enormous that there are no less than ten thousand makers in the province of Canton alone. The joss-sticks are made principally of benzoin and ground sandal wood.

"But these pastils," Jean said, "for they are only pastils in a different form, are much finer if charcoal of willow wood, benzoic acid, and ottos, are used instead of ground woods. As every chemist knows, when such substances undergo slow combustion, the ligenous fibre contained in them produces far from a pleasant odor; in fact, the smell of burning wood predominates over the volatilized aromatic ingredients; it is for this reason that charcoal is used in lieu of other substances; it producing the requisite heat to quickly volatilize the perfuming materials, and does not interfere in any way with the fragrance of the pastil. It is true that there are certain kinds of fumigation adopted occasionally, where these products are the materials sought; such fumigation, as when brown paper is allowed to smoulder in a room for the purpose of deodorizing bad smells. Pastils are much neater and more agreeable, however, for such purposes."

Each morning and evening three sticks of incense are offered to their deity, being usually placed in stationary censers of elegant forms. Sometimes they are laid at the feet of the idols. In the Ti-vang-mia-o, or Hall of Ceremonies, at Pekin, incense is burned in twelve large urns, in memory of the deceased emperors.

When mandarins come and pay their respects to the present monarch, they also burn incense before him; if he is away, they offer the same homage to his empty chair, and a similar ceremony takes place every year at the festival held in honor of Confucius. Perfumes also play a conspicuous part at Chinese funerals, as the body is washed, perfumed, and dressed in the best apparel of the deceased, whose portrait is placed in the middle of the room above the incense burner, which forms an indispensable article in their household furniture, and in it are kept scented oils burning continuously while the corpse remains in the house.

The catalogue of Chinese and Japanese perfumery is somewhat limited. Besides incense sticks, they only use a few scented oils and essences, which are more pungent than agreeable. Musk is one of their favorite perfumes. They not only like its odor, but they believe it cures every disease which flesh is heir to, even headache; and in this opinion they are backed by their principal medical authorities. Sandal wood, camphor and *assafœtida*, are included in the list of Chinese perfumery ingredients.

In Japan, the list consists chiefly of a pomatum called *Nioiabra*, made of oil and wax; *Jinko*, an aromatic wood used for burning in temples and private houses; a sort of sachet called Nioi-bu-kooroo; and Hanigaki, a tooth powder, made of fine shells found on the coast and mixed with scented herbs. American and European perfumers are slowly introducing their wares into the country, but not much consumption can be expected until *paper handkerchiefs* are abolished.

Aromatics are used in funeral rites, somewhat in the same manner as they were by the ancient Greeks and Romans. The body is placed on a pile of fragrant woods, the youngest child of the deceased sets fire to it with a torch, and all persons present throw on it oil, aloes, and odoriferous gums. Cosmetics are universally used by ladies in Japan, as the duties of the toilet are an important matter with them. They pay great attention to their hair, which they arrange in all manner of fantastic styles, inserting into it natural flowers, and also an illimitable number of pins, made of tortoise shell or lacquered wood.

When a Japanese lady marries, she blackens her teeth, and extirpates her eyebrows. The men shave the fore part and the crown of their heads, and work up the back and side hair into a tuft over the bald scalp. Both men and women indulge in a great variety of styles and ornaments. Thus the Japanese men take great pains to get rid of what we are so anxious to preserve, and glory in a smooth and polished pate, while we endeavor to conceal it with wigs and false hair. So much for diversity of tastes in nations. Some shave their heads, and others their faces, and each calls the other uncleanly for not following the same fashion as themselves. The flowers of Japan are large and beautiful, but their perfumes are rank.

We were ready early in the afternoon of the day after our

HE SHOOK AS WITH AGUE, AND HIS EYES STARED AT BRAD
WITH A LOOK OF FEAR.

arrival, to accompany Brad, and arraying ourselves in Chinese apparel, which Brad had procured for us, the better to avoid attracting too much notice, we set out on our tour of inspection. We cut, to ourselves, the most comical figures, and many hearty laughs we had at the awkwardness of each other's movements. In the streets, many sights appeared strange to us. A great many kinds of business are carried on in the open air. The barbers are called here Te tow teih jin, or literally "shavers of the head," that being their chief occupation; we frequently came across them; they also combine with shaving, bleeding and other operations, like the barber-surgeons of old.

There is need of a great many barbers, as the Chinese men keep their heads shaved, allowing only a long tuft of hair to grow on the summit, of which they are very proud, although it was originally a mark of their subjection to the Tartars. When their hair is thin, they mix silk or horsehair with it to give their tails, as we call them, a respectable appearance. We saw no Chinese *ladies* walking in the street; in fact they cannot walk, their feet are so deformed by being compressed into a shape to wear a shoe smaller than we would put on the smallest infant. When they wish to leave their house they are obliged to be carried in palanquins. We saw but few of them. They have three styles of dressing the hair, which are generally adopted, and the particular style worn indicates whether she is a maid, wife or a widow. From her infancy to her marriage, a young girl wears the back part of her hair braided into a tail, and the remainder combed over her forehead, and cut in the shape of a cresent. On her wedding day, her head is decorated with a crown, covered with tinsel paper, and on the next day her hair is dressed for the first time in the well known *teapot style*. On holidays, she ornaments her

hair with flowers, either natural or artificial, according to the season.   When she becomes a widow, she shaves part of her head,
and binds around it a fillet fastened with numerous bodkins,
which are sometimes very costly.

The trinkets in the bazaars were in wonderful profusion, and
we purchased a few for curiosities, whilst Brad bought a great
many of them, to be used as peace offerings to the savages he expected to meet.   We found a Perfumer, but the variety of his
stock was small, as far as perfumes were concerned.   He had a
large quantity of cosmetics, which the Chinese ladies apply liber-
ally to the skin.   One, which was shown us, was a mixture of tea-
oil and rice-flour, which the ladies apply at night and scrape off
in the morning ; it is supposed to improve the complexion.   They
then apply a white powder called Meen Fun, touch up their
cheeks, lips, nostrils and the *tip of their tongue*, with carmine,
and sprinkle rice powder over their face, which finishes the elabo-
rate picture and softens its tone.   The perfumer showed us a sort
of cold cream, made from the pulp of a fruit called Lung-ju-en,
also a perfume for the clothes, called " e heang," which was very
powerful, but not the least flowery, as it contained assafœtida
among its other ingredients.   A pomade for the hair, called " heang
tsaou" was excellent, being perfumed with Ylang Ylang, the Chinese Lily or Flower of flowers.   The perfumer had some of the Otto
of Ylang Ylang, which was exceedingly fine.   It has an intense
jasmine odor, and is more costly than otto of roses.

" It smells precisely like the flower of the *Unona odoratissama*,"
said Susie.

" It should," said Jean, " for it is distilled from them."

Musk was shown to us in immense quantities, considering the
value of the article.   He had also a fruit of a cedar that grows

in the mountains of Tchong-te-foo, which is held in high esteem as a perfume, and is hung up in rooms to fill the air with its fragrance ; also Rondeletia or Chyn-len, one of the most gratifying perfumes to the olfactory nerve that has ever been produced.

Sandalwood and Otto of Saudalwood we also purchased. The sandalwood is a most valuable article to the cabinet maker of the East. The white ant which is so common here, eating into every organic matter that it comes across, appears to have no relish for it ; this quality, together with its fragrance, causes it to be used extensively in the manufacture of handkerchief and glove boxes, fans, deed cases and caskets. We saw and examined many of these ; they were elaborately and wonderfully carved, and their fragrance could be perceived at some distance, and left the odor clinging to our skin after we handled them. The Sandalwood Tree or *Santalum album*, as Susie designated it, grew plentifully in China, but the continued offerings to the numerous images of Buddha, have almost exterminated it from the Celestial Empire. It is burned by way of incense, to an extent almost beyond belief, in these religious offerings. The Otto of Sandalwood is readily obtained by distillation from the wood ; one hundred weight of sound wood will yield about thirty ounces of otto. Its peculiar odor is an old favorite with the lovers of perfume. The otto of sandal is remarkably dense and is more oleaginous in its appearance than otto extracted from any other substance, and when good is of a dark straw color.

The dealer in perfumes said the body of the still, used for its distillation, consists of a large globular clay pot with a circular mouth, and is about two and one-half feet deep, by about six and one-half feet in circumference at the bilge. No capital is used, but as soon as the still is charged, the mouth is closed with a clay lid, having a small hole in its centre, through which a bent copper tube, about five and one-half feet long, is passed for the escape of the vapor. The lower end of the tube is conveyed inside a copper receiver, placed in a large porous vessel containing cold water.

The distillation is carried on slowly for ten days and nights without cessation, by which time the whole of the otto is extracted. As the water from time to time gets low in the still, fresh supplies are added from the heated contents of the refrigeratory. The odor of sandal assimulates well with rose, and hence, prior to the cultivation of rose-leaf geranium, it was used as an adulteration for the Otto of Roses, but now is seldom employed for that purpose. The otto of sandal is often adulterated with castor oil, which, being soluble in alcohol, makes it difficult to detect the fraud.

But what is the matter with Patsey? While we were busily talking, he has been looking around, and is now trying to attract our attention, and grinning from ear to ear. Coming to where we were, he said : —

"Shure sir, here comes a whole rigiment of lame an' blind; shure lookit, they'er thryin' to loight the way wid candles, an' the sun out as bright as Miss Susie's eyes."

It was truly a strange procession. At the head were a number of men on crutches, hobbling along in the most painfully appearing manner; behind these a palanquin; those carrying it were burning perfumed matches, which they renewed as fast as they were burned up; behind this palanquin were others, from which proceeded loud lamentations.

After this procession had passed, which Brad informed us was a funeral, and that the men at the head were not lame, but were only showing how broken down they were with grief, we returned to our inspection of the perfumery and curiosities. and shortly went back to the ship, well pleased with our ramble.

Brad promised us another stroll, but not the next day, as there were matters about the ship requiring his personal attention. So the next day after, having nothing else to do, Jean experimented with the ottos we had purchased. The Ottos of Ylang Ylang and Sandalwood he found perfectly pure. He then added to a small portion of the otto of sandal a little castor oil, some which we had obtained at New Orleans, and proceeded to test the otto to discover the presence of the oil. Taking twenty drops of the adulterated otto he placed it in a capsule, and heated it over a sandbath, — which we had arranged on a small scale in the laboratory, — until the odor of the otto was no longer perceptible. To the residue he added five drops of nitric acid, and as soon as the action subsided, diluted it with a solution of carbonate of soda. The odor thrown out, once smelled, is not likely to be mistaken for any other, it being œnanthylic acid. This body is the product of the oxidation of castor oil, and is formed when the warm otto is treated with an excess of nitric acid. During the action much nitrous acid is disengaged, and there is found floating in the acid liquid, when the residue is mixed with water, a soft, unctuous mass. The acid liquid is neutralized with the carbonate of soda, so as to entirely removed the odor of nitrous acid; the smell of the œnanthylic acid can then of course be most clearly recognized.

Jean said " that as slight an adulteration as five per cent. of castor oil in an otto, could by this process be detected." He formed an Essence of Ylang Ylang and Sandal from the respective ottos, which were very agreeable odors. The bottles and shelves in our laboratory were fast filling up, and Jean was taking great satisfaction in watching the accumulation of the various rare articles and preparations.

Spending most of the day in the laboratory, towards evening we went on deck, and watched the strange sights going on around us. When the many colored lanterns were lighted, one who has not seen it cannot imagine what a brilliant scene was presented to our view.

The next day we again arrayed ourselves in our Chinese garbs for another trip; this time we were to ride in palanquins out into the suburbs some miles above Canton, to see the beautiful Hoqua Gardens. The ride was pleasant after we became used to the strange, easy, swinging motion. Reaching the Gardens, we found them indeed handsome, and we wandered for a long time amid their beauties. We saw here the Sandalwood Tree, and Susie pointed out to us the *Dryobalanops Camphora*, or Camphor Tree, and some *Laurus Camphora*, or Camphor Laurel of the Island of Formosa, which is almost opposite the mouth of the Canton river, a little to the north. From these plants Camphor, that beautiful and fragrant substance is produced. The kind mostly found in commerce is derived from the Camphor Laurel. The camphor exists naturally within the tree, ready formed; on splitting the wood it is found between the bark and the stem and in the pith, in masses twelve to eighteen inches long, sometimes weighing ten to twelve pounds. Every part of the tree, among its fibres, contains camphor, which is extracted by chopping the branches, and boiling them in water. The camphor rises to the surface and becomes solid as the water cools; in some instances, the boiler in which the operation is conducted is covered with an earthen dome lined with rice straw; as the water boils the camphor rises with the steam, and attaches itself to the straw, from which it is afterwards picked, and then packed for exportation. Canton supplies the markets of the world with this substance.

There is a race of men called Nyr-Cappoors, or camphor seers, who pretend to have the power of distinguishing the most profitable trees to fell. Many trees are, however, cut down at their instigation, without having any cryptæ of camphor in them. The camphor as found in the stores is refined, and is not in the original condition in which it is exported from here.

The purification or refining of camphor was held as a monopoly at Venice, but it is now done in all large cities of the United States and Europe. The process is simple, and consists of mixing the imported camphor with a little lime, and subjecting it to a heat sufficient to convert it into vapor, which readily condenses into the form of the receiver. The odor of the camphor is very characteristic, and to the majority of persons, very agreeable. It has the reputation of being highly prophylactic, and to this end is worn about the person in times of sickness, though any perfume would accomplish the same object. From its reputed antiseptic qualities, it is extensively used in the manufacture of dentifrices, soaps, aromatic vinegars, and other concomitants of the toilet. Many trees grow here whose woods are odoriferous, but the Chinese have not as yet availed themselves of these natural treasures.

The parterres were filled with many kinds of beautiful and fragrant flowers, such as the Kwei-Hwá or *Olea fragrans*, Lien-Hwa or *Nymphœa nelumbo*, Cha-Hwa or *Camellia sesanyna*, and a sort of jasmine called Mo-lu-Hwa, one blossom of which is sufficient to scent a large room. There were various other flowers very large, and some exceedingly curious and beautiful, but without perfume. We saw immense numbers of camellias and jasmines of every conceivable color; they bloom here the year round. Their wealth of golden, crimson, purple, and white blossoms are much used as floral adornments. The yellow, which are very rare, are allowed only in temple service; the crimson flaunt gaily over the boat or sedan chair, sent by the groom to convey his bride to their future home on their wedding day; the fair virgin white are laid on the pyre, as the last loving gift to the dead; and the purple are used as the insignia of royalty. The camellia has been so named after the Jesuit Camelli, by whom it was first discovered. We spent a long time wandering over these grounds. We saw the *Unona odoratissama* or Ylang Ylang growing luxuriantly, its uncommonly long, pendulous flowers, outside a bright orange color, and inside yellow, and their rich, grateful perfume attracting our attention from a distance; at last becoming weary we were glad to enter our palanquins, and return to the ship. We lodged on board during our stay here, as we could find no accommodations suitable ashore, and were a little afraid to trust ourselves in the outlandish city, feeling much safer in our floating hotel.

CHAPTER XIII.

ALL being in readiness, we weighed anchor, and the ship was headed for the Banda or Spice Islands. From there Brad's father sailed last on that unfortunate voyage when the good ship "Godolpha" fell a prey to Father Neptune. John Gagler wished to stop there first, to see if there had ever been any tidings from the ship, and to get his reckonings and bearings, as it was as good a way as any to get into a course that would bring us near that part of the sea in which the island was, upon which Captain Jacob Cole was supposed to have been cast.

"On these Islands that we shall soon reach," Jean said to us — in the afternoon of the day before we reached the Banda Island, — "are the principal nutmeg gardens of the world. They were colonized by the Dutch about two hundred and seventy-five years ago. Few fragrant substances are of more commercial importance than the nutmeg. Its history affords an instance of the extravagance to which the spirit of monopoly will urge us, and which has carried not only private individuals but even states. Soon after the subjugation of the original inhabitants, the Dutch endeavored to secure to themselves the entire trade in this aromatic spice. For this purpose they encouraged the cultivation

109

of the nutmeg tree in only a few of the islands, and being over-anxious for the sake of the monopoly, to have them exclusively under their own command, they destroyed the trees in the neighboring isles."

"Yes, I remember," said Susie, "and they pursued the same policy with respect to the clove plant. More than once, however, they have paid dearly for their insatiable avarice; for the dreadful hurricanes and earthquakes, which swept harmlessly over the other islands, nearly annihilated the nutmeg trees of Banda."

"While the Dutch held the Spice Islands," Jean told us, "the quantity of nutmegs and mace exported from the nutmeg grounds, circumscribed as they were, was truly enormous, amounting to a total of some four hundred thousand pounds. When the islands were taken by the British in 1796, the importation by the East India Company into England alone, in two years following the capture, were of nutmegs, about one hundred and thirty thousand pounds, and of mace, about three hundred thousand pounds. It is thus evident that the odor and flavor of nutmeg and mace is not disliked."

When the crops of spice have been superabundant, and the price in consequence, likely to be reduced, the same ignorant spirit as before mentioned, actuated the Dutch to destroy immense quantities of the fruit rather than suffer the market price to be lowered.

When Sir William Temple was in Amsterdam, a merchant who had returned from Banda assured him that at "one time I saw three piles of nutmegs burnt, each of which contained more than a church of ordinary dimensions could hold;" and a Mr. Wilcox relates that he beheld "such a conflagration of cloves, nutmegs and cinnamon, upon the Island of Newland, near Middleburgh,

New Zealand, as perfumed the air with their peculiar fragrance for a circuit of many miles." Balfour says, "that in 1814, when the Moluccas were in the possession of the English, the number of nutmeg trees planted, was estimated at five hundred and seventy thousand, five hundred, of which four hundred and eighty-six thousand were in bearing." The produce of nutmegs in the Moluccas has been reckoned at from six hundred thousand to seven hundred thousand pounds per annum.

Sighting land about midnight, we lay to till morning, then ran into the harbor, and in the afternoon we went on shore. The Island is lofty and volcanic, the harbor beautiful, well sheltered and easy of access. We landed amid a crowd of Coolies and China-men, each doing his best to induce us to engage him as guide ; but John Gagler knew the place too well to need any assistance. He had been ashore in the forenoon to inquire of the merchants with whom Brad's father used to trade, if they had ever heard any tidings of the "Godolpha." But they had never seen or heard of any of those who belonged to her, except himself. Some of the older ones who had seen Brad's father, remarked the striking resemblance of Brad to him.

John Gagler was at our service to conduct us to any place we wished to visit. Expressing a desire to examine one of the largest of the Spice Gardens of the Island, he engaged convey-ances and we were soon on the road. After riding about a mile we came to one that was said to yield next to the largest amount of nutmegs, mace and cloves, of any in the Island, the exception being a garden quite a long distance from the city, too far to allow us to go during the short stay we were to make here. En-tering the gates we proceeded for some distance through a beauti-ful grove of nutmeg trees, which extended to the right and left of us like a forest, the trees rising to a height of twenty and twenty-five feet. Beyond these were some handsome evergreen trees, rising from fifteen to thirty feet, with large elliptic leaves and purplish flowers, arranged in corymbs on short stalks.

" See the *Caryophylli aromaticus*," exclaimed Susie.

" Faith, an' where is it? Let me kill it!" said Patsey.

" Clove Trees, I mean," explained Susie.

Among one of the groups of these trees were two magnificent specimens in full bloom, or bud we should say, — as the flowers are not allowed to blow out fully, as the otto, although it abounds in every part of the clove plant, is most plentiful and fragrant in the unexpanded flower. We were fortunate to be here at the right time in the season to witness this beautiful sight. The average annual crop of cloves from each tree is two, or two and a half pounds ; these two trees were expected to yield one hundred and twenty-five pounds each, of this spice, in this single season, and as five thousand cloves only weigh one pound, you can imagine how fine these trees appeared, it being reckoned that each tree had on itself at least six hundred and twenty-five thousand flowers.

The Otto of Cloves may be obtained by expression from the fresh flower buds, but the usual way of procuring it, is by distillation of the dried buds ; this was done on the grounds at the factory, which we visited. Few ottos have a more extensive use in perfumery than that of cloves ; it combines well with grease, soap and spirit, and has formed a leading feature in some of the most popular handkerchief extracts ; it has the property, which no other spice otto possesses, that, when it is mixed with other perfumes, of making a most refreshing and enlivening odor. The Otto of Nutmeg and the Otto of Mace were also distilled on the premises. The nutmeg tree, like many others, yields two distinct odorous substances, — that is, nutmeg and mace, from which are made otto of nutmeg and otto of mace. The Otto of Nutmeg is a beautiful white and transparent fluid, having an intense fragrance of the nut, and enters into the composition of numerous perfumery preparations, of which the Frangipanni series are samples. By expression, the nutmegs will also yield an unctuous oil, of an agreeable odor; this combined with an alkali, produces a pleasant soap, which sixty years ago was commonly sold by perfumers under the name of Bandanna or Banda Soap, but is now quite out of date. The nuts when ground are used advantageously as an ingredient of sachet powders for scent bags. The nutmegs are inclosed in four different covers; the first a thick husk, something like that of our walnuts, but larger; under this lies a thin reddish coat, which is the mace of commerce, and yields the otto by distillation, and when ground is used in the manufacture of sachet powders. The mace is an elastic network embracing the shell, and expands as the fruit or rather seed grows; the shell is hard and thin, and destitute of odor; under this a greenish film forms, no use as yet, having been found for it, but which is in truth the shirt of the seed or nutmeg. The odor of mace only resembles that of nutmeg in being spicy; but otherwise cannot be mistaken for nutmeg. Thus otto of mace and otto of nutmeg are produced by the same plant within a fraction of an inch of each other, and are totally different in their odor. What wonderful valves and taps have been formed by nature to keep them from intermingling. The otto of mace is seldom used in perfumes, but is excellent as a scent for soaps. Mace when first gathered is of a beautiful crimson color, is dried in the sun or artificial heat, if the weather is unfavorable, as it requires a clear heat, when it assumes a golden yellow color, but nutmegs on the contrary requiring a smothered heat, are smoked by slow fires of wood for three months before they are fit for exportation.

The cloves are gathered by hand, or by beating the tree with sticks, when the buds, from the jointed character of their stalks readily fall, and are received on sheets spread for the purpose. The buds are then dried in the sun. Their name is derived from the French word *clou*, a nail, in allusion to their shape. Procuring several nutmegs in various stages of growth, and some of the otto of nutmegs, the oil of nutmegs, otto of mace, also some of the fresh and dried clove buds, we finished our visit and were soon on our way back to the ship, which we reached just before dark. Brad informed us that John Gagler had made all his plans as far as possible, and as we had nothing to detain us, he would start immediately. In the forenoon of the next day we steamed out, navigating the waters among the many islands of this archipelago which presented to us many pleasing sights.

As we were sitting on deck conversing, John Gagler asked Jean, "Whom or what he meant when he spoke of Frangipanni, when he was telling us about the uses of otto of nutmeg, as he had a messmate by that name."

"It is a name of a perfume," answered Jean, "in common use even to this day, which derived its name from a Roman family, — perhaps your messmate descended from them, but it is doubtful —bearing the patronymic of Frangipanni, as famous in Italy, as the Plantagenets and the Tudors in England. The origin of the name of this family is traced to a certain office which an ancestor filled in a church, — that of supplying the holy bread, the wafer in one of the ceremonials. Frangipanni literally means 'broken bread,' and is derived from *frangi*, to break, and *panus*, bread. Hence we have Frangipane puddings which good house-wives know are made from broken bread. One member of this ancient family, Mutio Frangipani, served in France, in the Papal army during the reign of Charles IX. The grandson of this nobleman was the Marquis Frangipani, Maréchal des Armées of Louis XIV.; and he it was, who invented a method of perfuming gloves, which, when so perfumed, bore the name of Frangipanni gloves.

"You remember, Susie, at the West Indies the name is used to designate the fruit of the *Plumiera alba L.*, and the *Plumiera rubra L. Frangipanier* is the French name of the *Plumiera*. One Mer-cutio Frangipani, who lived in 1493, was a famous botanist and traveller, noted as being one of the Columbus expedition, when they visited the West Indies. He told the sailors that the delicious fragrance which they perceived in the air, as they ap-proached Antiqua, must be derived from sweet smelling flowers, and on landing they found vast quantities of the *Plumiera Alba* in full bloom, rendering the air redolent with rich odor; from this plant, which the present inhabitants call the Frangipanni flower, is procured that exquisite fragrance which is so popular in fashion-able circles."

After dinner we again returned to the deck, and whilst amus-ing ourselves by reading and conversing, John Gagler, who was walking towards us, turned as he went by, looking in the direction of the horizon as he did so, and drew our attention to a line of dark clouds abaft the stern. We had noticed the short and pecu-liar puffs of wind which every few minutes had been rustling the leaves of our books, and then was succeeded by a calm.

"I'm hafraid we'll 'ave rough weather," he observed; "the

wind pipes hup queer, I see Capt. Cole 'as every thing laid low; 'e was studying the barometer at eight bells han' I thought 'e looked hanxious."

Looking again at the clouds we noticed they had increased an hundred-fold. We picked up our seats, books and other loose articles, and went into the cabin, where we watched the progress of the storm from the windows. In the short time that it had taken us to change our position the whole aspect of the sky had altered; the black clouds covered half the heavens, and were gathering like a herd of wild horses, each mass crowding the others onward, rolling and noiselessly clashing against each other; just beneath the edge of the black clouds, the sea was white with foam, the wind came in stronger puffs and changed in turns to every point of the compass.

Anticipating the storm, Brad had prepared everything to receive the first burst of the gale. Desiring to witness a storm at sea I went on deck and clung to a ladder, prepared for the shock, and awaited till the storm should reach us. Far off in the depths of the clouds we could see the vivid lightning in its fantastic leapings, and could hear the dull boom and continuous roll of the thunder. The storm seemed to advance with redoubled speed and fury, struck the ship full astern and lifted it like a feather. We seemed for a moment to be sailing through the air. It was a regular typhoon, and the way it tore through the rigging and wrenched the masts was fearful. Everyone unprepared was thrown from their feet by the shock. We rode before the storm, which carried us along with irresistible fury. I made my way back to the cabin as well as possible, expecting every moment to be blown or washed from my hold, and when I reached the door I was shot into the cabin like an arrow. The ship pitched to such an extent that my wife and Susie, who were more helpless than the men, were much alarmed. The books and other unsecured articles were strewn in dire confusion around the cabin. The storm lasted through the whole night and howled incessantly; we could get no sleep; just as we would begin to dose, a sudden gust would cause us to rise up in our berths expecting the ship was torn apart.

Capt. Cole did not enter the cabin till morning, excepting once, soon after the gale broke, he came to assure us that the ship was all right, and that there was no danger as long as she kept clear of the numerous islands which abounded in these seas. He only had a nap of an hour, then returned on deck to watch our progress, and look out for our safety.

The storm still continued, and seemed increasing rather than diminishing. All amusement, and in fact every employment on our part was suspended. Susie seemed preoccupied, thinking perhaps of some one, and his exposed position; Jean's look as he watched her, showed he had a supicion for whom she felt concerned.

Two days, — three days passed, — no abatement; the ship had suffered, and I saw that Brad was feeling anxious, for if the storm continued much longer she would be dismantled, and if any accident happened to the machinery we should be at the mercy of the elements. The sailors were worn out with working and watching, and although we had nothing to do, anxiety and lack of sleep had told upon us. Brad was looking miserably, but nothing could induce him to leave his post until we were out of danger.

The fourth day, — the wailing and shrieking of the wind is not so uproarious, Brad is asleep in his cabin, my wife and Susie are

THE WAVES ARE YET RUNNING MOUNTAINS HIGH.

Page 118.

dozing in their seats, Jean and I are are looking out upon the
sea ; the waves are yet running mountains high, and as each one follows its predecessor, it looks as if it would overwhelm us.   This
day went as the others had, in anxiety and restlessness.   At
night the wind was still less fierce, and we all hoped and wished
the storm would cease.   By midnight we were considerably
refreshed, having had an opportunity to sleep during the frequent lulls.

In the morning the intense blackness of the sky was changed to
a dull leaden hue.   The wind having subsided we passed a more
agreeable day, although the ship still rolled and pitched heavily.
In the afternoon the clouds broke, and we joyfully hailed the sun,
which we had not seen for five long days.   Night came, the stars
shone brightly and beautifully, seemingly more brilliant in comparison with the appalling blackness of the preceding nights.

Brad had lost his reckoning, but thought as we had been tearing along so furiously, we were off the west coast of Australia.
After the storm broke, a storm jib had been set with much difficulty, and with it we had been driving before the wind during the
whole hurricane, it being our only chance of safety.   John Gagler could not tell whether we were, or were not, near the island
on which he was cast, not knowing what currents we had encountered in the storm ; but he thought the direction of the gale was
almost the same as that in which the " Godolpha " was wrecked.

At the break of day, land was descried off the port bow.
Captain Cole having taken observations and made his calculations, told us the land was probably New Zealand.   As we
approached, tall precipitous cliffs were discernible near the shore,
and volcanic mountains reared their heads in the interior ; running in a short distance further, we anchored.

CHAPTER XIV.

CAPTIVES.

WE were all restless, and wanted to go on shore, for after the rough weather we had experienced we felt it would be a respite ; and Susie, as usual, was very anxious to examine the flora of this country. Captain Cole, and Mr. Roscoe the first mate, joined us, to see what kind of a place we had anchored at, and if there was a chance to replenish the water, for one of the tanks being damaged, we had run short during the storm. We landed, and wandering a short distance, came upon a fine spring, and around it indications of a recent encampment. Approaching carefully we could see no signs of the former occupants, but Jean cautioned us to be very careful against surprise, as most of the native tribes were cannibals, or practised cannibalism to some extent, and if we fell into their power we should certainly fall victims to their horrible practice, as have many of the first visitors to this island. Susie was the only one who had brought anything from the ship, with the exception of the firearms carried by Brad, Mr. Roscoe, Jean and myself. Her clipping scissors she always wore fastened to her belt, and she also carried a small net for catching insects, and a bottle of ether for smothering them or reptiles which she caught, previous to immersing them in alcohol; the large bottle of alcohol Patsey carried for her, she having intrusted it to his care with much risk as to its safety, for he was continually either turning it over, balancing it on one finger, or on the end of his nose, and performing all sorts of jugglery tricks with it. She had managed to find some strange reptiles which she had put in the alcohol, and did not care to lose these, or the jar, as it was a valuable one, being made of heavy white glass, with a platinum screw top to make it air tight to prevent the evaporation of the alcohol; seeing his carelessness she took the jar away, but he promising to carry it carefully she again intrusted it to him. It was fortunate, as we afterwards discovered, that he did take good care of it.

Sitting down around the spring we rested for awhile, all except Patsey; his restless disposition kept him rushing around into all the accessible places, frightening the birds, often coming in with some new flower or bush for Susie's or Jean's examination. Soon after this, Mr. Roscoe dispatched Patsey to tell the boatswain of the the boat that had landed us, to return to the ship and bring off two water casks and fill them at the spring. He soon returned and said they had gone to obey orders.

We were listening to his report, our attention directed to him, when noticing a peculiar subdued rustling we looked up. A sight met our eyes that made our hearts sink. Around us, above us, on every side stood a tribe of most ferocious looking savages. We grasped our guns to defend ourselves, but saw at once it was useless, for such were their numbers and the advantage of their position they would have soon overpowered us, then our treatment might be still worse. They had probably been in ambush during the whole time we were at the spring, and as we afterward ascertained, had been watching the ship, and seeing a boat put

AROUND US, ABOVE US, ON EVERY SIDE STOOD A TRIBE OF
THE MOST FEROCIOUS LOOKING SAVAGES.

Page 120.

off, had waited expecting some chance would throw a few captives into their hands; and had several times been on the point of capturing Patsey, but he was too spry for them, they being afraid to attack while the boat was at the landing, so had waited until they saw it returning, then completely surrounded us, rose, and surprised us.

Finding we were disposed to submit without resistance, one of the natives, principally noticeable for his tall form, broad chest and powerful limbs, advanced and by motions signed for us to lay down our arms, which we reluctantly did. Then four of the warriors stepped forward and took them up. The chief, was one of high rank, as could be seen by the delicate tattooing that striped his face and body. Two black spirals, starting from the nostrils of his aquiline nose, circled his piercing eyes, and meeting on his protruding and deeply furrowed brow, were lost in his abundant hair. His mouth, with a full set of perfect, shining teeth, and his peaked chin, were hidden beneath a network of varied colors, while graceful lines wound down to his breast. The sharp albatross bone used by Maori tattooers, had furrowed his face five times, in close and deep lines, showing that he had reached his fifth promotion. A large flaxen mat, ornamented with dog-skins, enveloped his person, while a girdle of violet wampum encircled his waist. From his ears dangled earrings of finely polished jade, and around his neck hung necklaces of "ponnamons," sacred stones, to which the New Zealanders attribute miraculous properties. He also carried a gun of American manufacture, and a patou-patou, or double-edged tomahawk. Motioning a detachment of his warriors to lead, he signified his wish for us to follow, and then ordering others to march on each side of us, and the rest of them to bring up the rear, we started. We knew not where we were going or what would be our fate.

How fervently and frequently, during that march did I wish I had never allowed my wife or her sister, to go on this search with us. We had not as yet been maltreated, neither had anything except our guns been taken from us. They inspected the jar containing the reptiles, but probably supposing that we were preserving them to eat, did not take possession of them. Knowing the habits of these savages, we could not but be seriously alarmed; they were very taciturn, and scarcely spoke to each other. However, from a few words exchanged, Brad perceived that they were slightly acquainted with the English language; he therefore questioned the chief in regard to our fate. After considerable haughty gazing, seeming not to notice what Brad said, the chief condescended to say we were to be exchanged for friends lost by them in a recent battle; if their enemies refused to make the exchange, we should be tortured to death.

Hope returned somewhat at the prospect of a transfer, as we had been expecting that at their first encampment some of us would fall victims to their appetites; but now, with this bright prospect of an exchange, even if we were not soon released by the sailors of our ship, when on their return they should discover our disappearance, there would still be hope left us of escape. If we kept on the march, there was a good chance of our rescue by the sailors, as they were devoted to Capt. Cole, and would follow, and do all in their power to liberate him and us. Our only fear now was that the savages had some rendezvous, where they had their canoes; then they could soon reach the interior, and be safe from pursuit.

We travelled for some hours, Brad and Mr. Roscoe ahead,

wife and I following, and Jean and Susie behind us, Patsey bringing up the rear, still carrying Susie's jar of reptiles, and he as
lively as ever, keeping up a continual fusilade of jokes and stories; it did not seem to make the least difference to him whether
he was a prisoner or not. Soon a distant murmur indicated our
approach to swiftly running waters, and not long after we came
to the junction of two streams, one uniting with the other in
resounding cascades. We were soon in sight of their canoes,
which were very large, nearly eight or ten feet broad and seventy
feet long, being made from the trunk of a pine, their lofty
prows resembling those of Venetian gondolas. Reaching them we
embarked; in the bow were seated eight oarsmen who propelled
the canoe; at the stern a native guided it by means of a movable
paddle. We ascended the river with swiftness, casting many
anxious looks towards the shores we had left, watching for signs
of rescuers; but alas, none appeared. Susie and my wife were
very much frightened, and shivered with terror; we could hardly
calm their fears. The sun was just sinking below the horizon as
the canoe ran upon a bank of pumice stones. Several trees grew
here, and the encampment was pitched for the night, we being
placed in the centre, and large fires built on the outer edge of the
circle, forming an impassable barrier.

The next day we ascended the river with the same speed; as
the day waned, we gave up all hopes of rescue, as we saw no
signs of our ship's crew. We encamped again at night, and embarked in the morning, other canoes joining us from various
affluents of the river as we reached them. During the day we
passed through a narrow gorge, thickly dotted with small islands,
and eddies breaking violently against them rendered navigation
extremely difficult and dangerous; also, at this point the river

flowed between warm springs; oxide of iron colored the muddy
ground a brilliant red, and not a square yard of firm earth could be
seen.   We were seriously annoyed by the noxious vapors exhaled
from the fissures of the soil, and the bubbles that burst and discharged their gaseous contents, filled the air with a heavy, penetrating, sulphurous odor.   If it had not been for some ammonia
I had with me, which I passed around for inhalation, I believe
we should have suffocated.   Patsey, of course, wanted to smell of
it.   I handed it to him, and after he had taken a mild sniff, seeing the steersman watching him, offered him a dose, Patsey showing him how to apply the bottle to his nose, and making believe
to take a long, strong breath; he then held it up to the savage,
who was probably congratulating himself that he was to have
something not to be shared with his comrades, who were facing
away from us.   The steersman stooped, and following Patsey's
directions as he understood them, took a long pull and a strong
pull.   You never saw such a surprised and demoralized savage
in your life; it took his breath away for a minute, and created so
much confusion by his losing control of the canoe, that we came
near being capsized.   He will probably never again smell from
a bottle in the hands of a stranger.   I did not see what Patsey
was doing, for if I had, I would have prevented it for fear of consequences.   Susie told me afterwards that she saw the whole
performance, but she would not stop it, as she said, " it was good
enough for the painted monkey."   I gave Patsey a lecturing, telling him, never to give ammonia to anyone to inhale, without first
cautioning them, and related to him many instances of people
being entirely deprived of their sense of smell by some foolish
person giving them a very strong and sudden inhalation of ammonia, thinking it a fine joke; and of others, who had been so

effected by it, as to be thrown into convulsions, and have their nervous system disarranged for years; and in the present instance, to think of the danger it put us in; for if we had been overturned, the banks would have afforded us no refuge, as whoever set foot on the porous crust would have perished.

For two miles after passing these hot springs the canoes glided within a vapory mass of white smoke, whose wreaths arose in gradually decreasing circles above the river. It came from geysers, hundreds of which lined the shore, making a magnificent spectacle, shooting forth their waters and vapors, which mingling in the air formed rainbows in the sunshine. We passed this region, and before the close of day ascended two more rapids, and at evening were a hundred miles from our place of capture.

At noon next day we entered a lake, and the natives hailed with frantic gestures a shred of cloth, their national flag, that waved from the roof of a hut. Here we were, helpless, at the mercy of these vengeful Maoris, in one of their strongest encampments, inside of a fortress. What hope had we? On our arrival, when passing into the fort, — the entrance of which was decorated with heads, belonging probably to hostile chiefs, whose bodies had been eaten by their conquerors, — we were so besieged by the fanatics of the tribe, that to secure our safety, for further use, we were transferred by the chief who captured us, to a sacred place on the edge of a precipice. Here we were temporarily sheltered from the fury of the natives, and we stretched ourselves on some flaxen mats to rest, for it had been a long and tiresome journey, especially for the ladies. Patsey climbed up the wall and looked out through an opening, left probably for ventilation.

When towards sunset the majority of the natives had retired to their huts, Patsey thinking that in the dusk he might get outside and perhaps escape and be of some help, asked Jean and Brad to lift the curtain that served as a door, when he had counted three.

The two guards at the door were drowsing, and no better opportunity could offer. Patsey going to the furthest part of the temple opposite the door, threw off his jacket and shoes, and prepared for a rush, and counted, —

" *One!*

" Two ! !

" THREE ! ! ! "

The curtain was raised.

He dashed past us like a flash of light, and turning around just as he reached it, he turned over and over from his hands to his feet, the same as we saw him do on shipboard. The guards jumped up, but so quickly did Patsey go, and such was their surprise at the novel manner of his exit, that they did not raise the alarm till he had got quite a distance. We saw at the first alarm the natives come out in swarms from their huts, and then we lost sight of Patsey. He did not return that night, and we were so worried about him that we censured ourselves many times for letting him try to gain his liberty, for perhaps the natives being provoked at him for his attempted escape, if they caught him would torture or kill him ; probably he was now furnishing some of them with a supper, though he would not be very tender ; for his muscles would chew like catgut. We saw nothing of him during the three days we were left to ourselves. At the end of that time an event happened which drove all hope from our hearts.

It seems we were held for exchange for one of their high priests, but now a messenger had come reporting his death. Uamuok Aik, our capturer, waited upon us, and told us that as our nation had killed their high priest, their revenge would fall on us.

"Our gods command it. Three days from now all of you shall die," he said.

He then left us.

The three days of grace were allowed to give them time for their mourning ceremonials.

What a night we passed! Who could depict our anguish or measure our sufferings!

As for escape, that was clearly impossible; neither could we rely on the sailors reaching here without a guide, and as for Patsey, — we were in a quandary, and knew not what to think. Ten warriors armed to the teeth, guarded us since his departure.

The first night after receiving our sentence had passed, and morning came, clear and beautiful. We were then removed from the temple, to a hut at the foot of an enormous kondi, where the guard was still further strengthened. The hut contained considerable food, which we scarcely touched. Hunger gave place to grief. The day passed without bringing a change or a ray of hope. The night was beautiful as the day had been, but it afforded us no pleasure; only two days more, and then we should never see the beautiful blue sky again.

That night, that livelong night, I paced the hut thinking of all manner of wild expedients to escape.

Towards morning, utterly exhausted, I laid down.

Was it a dream?

I awoke refreshed. The sun was high in the heavens. I raised myself on my elbow and looked around. Ah! yes, prisoners yet, — it was then all a dream! I had dreamed that I was following a star, and it led me and my friends through groves, filled with luscious fruits; and flowers of beauteous form and rich perfume bordered our paths; in the distance I saw home,

with all its well known surroundings, and hurrying to reach there
I awoke.

What was the meaning of it, — a star! Seeing me awake, my
wife, Susie, Brad, Jean, and Mr. Roscoe, came and sat down
around me. Many suggestions were offered for effecting our
escape, but all were abandoned as impracticable. I told them my
dream. They seemed to think it but a sign of our departure from
this life, instead of our return to our earthly home.

"In some way, we *must* and *will* escape," said Brad.

"In the dream of the star I seem to see a significance," spoke
my wife.

"If we only had certain chemicals we could produce effects
that would scare their wits from them," I soliloquized.

"I have it," said Jean, excitedly. "A star shall lead us!
Susie, where is your jar of reptiles? Bring it here, please."

"Patsey had it last," she replied; "we must have left it at the
temple. I never once thought of it."

"Then we can do nothing without it; on that I depended,"
said Jean, sorrowfully.

"Here it is," said Capt. Cole, "not a reptile lost. I looked
after it when we changed our quarters, and also brought Patsey's
jacket, which he threw off when he left us."

"How kind of you, Captain," said Susie, looking at him almost lovingly out of her beautiful, blue eyes.

"How fortunate," interrupted Jean, who of course did not like
to see such a scene prolonged; "on this jar and a dark night all
our success, if we escape, will depend."

"I do not see how a bottleful of reptiles is going to frighten
these savages," remarked Mr. Roscoe, "especially as they see
them so frequently."

"You shall see," answered Jean, pleasantly. "I suppose, Susie," said he to her, "you are willing to sacrifice your collection and jar, for the common safety, and you will also agree to all I ask of you, for perhaps upon your steadiness in this trial a great deal of our success will depend."

"Most willingly, dear friends," she replied, "anything in my power, I will do, if you but command me."

We had all gathered around Jean, wondering of what he had thought.

"If it is dark to-night, we will try to escape," Jean remarked; "if not, to-morrow night we must make the attempt, light or dark. Captain, will you take an observation and see how matters are outside?"

Brad raised the mat and counted twenty-five natives who were watching at the entrance.

"Rather dubious," said Brad, putting down the mat.

"Never mind," said Jean, "I think I can outwit them all."

"But how?" we all exclaimed.

"To commence," he responded, "I want the cork to your ammonia bottle, Mr. Montague; I have a knife, and I want to cut the cork up to make a float; and now, Susie, I want to use your scissors to destroy the top to your preserving jar. First the wire you use as a handle, then the cover. Mr. Roscoe, if you have a knife, I want to set you to work to make a lid for this jar; you will have to make it of wood. I see nothing better. Select a hard piece from the walls of the hut."

We were soon all busy under Jean's directions. Susie took the reptiles from the alcohol, and cleaned every speck of dirt from the inside and outside of the bottle. I was at work on another cover for the jar, making it out of hard wood; it was to fit over the one

9

that Mr. Roscoe was whittling out, for the cover was to be double, with holes cut in each one to make a draft to allow the entrance of air, or exclude it entirely. Jean was cutting a star from the platinum top, making it as large as it was possible from the size of the cover. I now knew what Jean was making, and on what his hopes rested.

We worked hard all day on the covers; it was slow cutting, and many times we were interrupted by the entrance of some one of the guard to see what we were doing, when we had to hide our work quickly, for fear they would take it from us. How quickly the time flew! The day did not seem but a few hours long. Occupation makes life pleasant, and time golden. Within an hour of dusk everything was ready; the jar almost full of alcohol, clear as crystal; in it the float, and pendent from it a large star of platina, the covers fitting rather roughly, but still well enough to accomplish what we wished.

"Now," said I, "gather up all the provisions; there is plenty for two or three days rations and we may need them."

We had eaten but little during our last three days' imprisonment, fortunately for us, as it now appeared.

"We will try our apparatus," said I to Jean; "carry it to the furthest corner where it is dark, so we can see the effect better, and not let the guards get a glimpse of it, for that would spoil all."

Jean carried the jar to the corner, took off the wooden covers, the star inside suspended just a hair's breadth over the cork which was floating on the alcohol, and applied a lighted match to the contents of the jar; a lurid flame sprang up, in a moment the star was red hot. Jean immediately put on the two covers, closed the drafts, almost smothered the flame for want of air,

then blew it entirely out. A moment of suspense — a moment
which was ages to Jean and I, knowing what ought to occur.
Then slowly the star turned a brilliant red, until it shone out in
the darkness like a natural star from heaven. A cry of joy could
scarcely be suppressed by either of us, and we heard exclamations
of surprise from Susie, Capt. Cole, and Mr. Roscoe. for even
they had never seen this really wonderful phenomenon. What
would be its effect on the uneducated savages, especially in the
manner in which Jean intended to present it, we could only sur-
mise. We looked on it, not only as a valuable discovery, a principle of a metal pertaining to no other known substance, but also
as a prime auxiliary in our proposed escape from the savages.

Jean explained that platina has the property, when once heated,
and exposed to the vapors of alcohol, or any perfume containing
absolute alcohol, of remaining red-hot. The heat of the platina
evolves hydrogen from the alcohol and the draft in the top letting
in the air, the supply being regulated by adjusting the draft, so as
to supply oxygen in proper quantity and make it burn more or
less brightly. No matter in what shape the platina is cut, it will
remain incandescent, as long as there is a drop of alcohol left in
the vessel in which it is put, without any flame being present,
being kept in that condition by the rising vapor only.

CHAPTER XV.

ESCAPE.

OUR situation for escape was more favorable in this hut, than it had been in the temple, as it faced the lake, on which rocked the canoes of the savages; if we reached them in safety, all would be well.

The night came and the moon rose early, shedding a light so bright and clear, one could almost read without the aid of artificial light; our star would be no guide, with the moon for a rival; we must wait another night and day. The night, how long! The day! Would it never end? Each one of us counted the interminable hours, but it did not shorten them. Everything was prepared for our flight; twilight came on, the sun disappeared behind a bank of dense clouds of threatening aspect, a few flashes of lightning illumined the horizon, and a distant peal of thunder announced a coming storm. Jean welcomed it as subsidiary to his scheme. About eight o'clock the sky looked like a black pall, forming an excellent background, as a contrast for our bright star. Before dusk we had studied our course and made our plans; all were cautioned to keep close together, and act well their part. Susie was to lead us; all her dark clothes were thrown aside; she was to wear nothing but her white clothing.

132

Her hair was unbound and hung loosely down her back and over her shoulders, and in her left hand she was to carry the jar, with its contents in full operation; the bright star only would show. Her right hand was rubbed with moistened phosphorus from matches, a plenty of which we always carried with us in our pockets. Brad, Mr. Roscoe, Jean, and myself, covered our faces with the same substance, so that in the intense darkness we looked like demons of fire.

At nine o'clock the time for action had arrived. The moment at which we had decided to go, a violent trembling of the earth was felt, and the action increased. Hollow rumblings and hissings, sounded in the air. Jean, all excitement exclaimed, —

" Do not be alarmed, the volcano of Maun Ganamu has broken forth in some new locality; it will help us. Now, Susie, take your position. Captain Cole, you and Mr. Roscoe simultaneously raise the curtain and grin like imps from Hades at the nearest guards; then, Susie, hold up your star, and every little while turn and beckon us on with your phosphorescent hand. Mrs. Montague will go between Mr. Montague and myself, and after we have passed out, drop the mat and bring up the rear, and do your best to make up the most horrible faces, and so, if possible, scare the savages out of their senses."

A glance to see that all was ready.

" Ready! Raise! Courage, Susie," said Jean in a subdued voice, for he saw she was trembling with nervous excitement.

The curtain was lifted.

Susie advanced.

The two principal guards nearest the entrance stepped before her to arrest her progress, when raising their eyes they saw the shining star; their dark faces turned a bluish livid color,

SUSIE ADVANCED.

Page 133.

The Golden Rule.

An Independent, Religious, Family Journal.

WHATSOEVER YE WOULD THAT MEN SHOULD DO TO YOU DO YE EVEN SO TO THEM.

$2.00 a year. Send for free sample; it will please you. Address, GOLDEN RULE, 25 Congress Street, Boston.

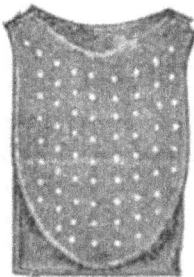

their herculean forms trembled, and their weapons fell to the ground at their feet. The others seeing what an effect it had produced on their comrades of higher rank, became themselves panic-stricken. Many fell to the ground, and covering their faces, tried to shut out the sight. We grinned and distorted our faces. The star still led us onward unmolested. The volcano poured forth its fire, smoke, and molten lava. The thunder rolled, and the vivid lightnings flashed, revealing to us for a moment the path we were to follow, and the terror-stricken savages we were fast leaving behind us. We approached nearer and nearer to the canoes, — a short distance further, a few moments more, and we are safe. Our hearts beating wildly, listening for any diminishing of the fear in our enemies. How eagerly we waited for the end. At last we reached a canoe, and stepping in, we pushed off.

"Free at last!" exclaimed Brad, with a deep sigh of relief, —"but — no — hear the noise; they have a suspicion that they are deceived."

"One more trial," I said. "All turn your faces towards the shore. Sing some weird chant, Susie, the moment the thunder stops; as soon as the lightning flashes, turn quickly all of you and pull for dear life, and then cover the star. Perhaps they may think we have arisen in a cloud."

An instant of calmness then Susie's voice broke the stillness, and a chant, the music of which penetrated the depths of the soul, hushed the noise on the shore, and all was still. Soon an intense flash of lightning, an overpowering burst of thunder and she paused, we quickly turned, and dipping the paddles we sped onwards over the lake to the river. No pursuers; the effect had been complete.

All night the thunder, lightning, and rain continued, but we worked steadily at the paddles; when day dawned there were many miles between us and our late captors. We carefully preserved our Magic Star, not knowing how soon we might require it. As soon as we felt satisfied there would be no pursuit, we washed the phosphorus from our faces, to avoid its producing any deleterious effect upon the skin. We went ashore at break of day, and concealed our boat and selves until near nightfall, then seeing as yet no signs of pursuers, we embarked and continued our way, cautiously at first, but soon exerting ourselves to our utmost, rapidly descended the river. Just as darkness began to settle on the river we passed the geyser region; then knowing we had nothing more to fear, pushed boldly forward, landing a little after midnight for rest. We were much troubled about Patsey's non-appearance, and could form no reason for his not being seen again, unless he had been recaptured. We finally determined that if he had not returned to the ship, we would come back with a well armed crew and rescue him from the savages, if he was yet alive.

CHAPTER XVI.

PATSEY'S ADVENTURES, ESCAPE, AND RETURN.

THE next morning we awoke with a start, caused by our hearing voices proceeding from parties in a boat turning a bend in the river below us. Keeping ourselves well out of sight, we anxiously watched the approach of the strangers.

" Probably they are another party of warriors returning," said Brad.

In a minute or two we saw a boat shoot around the curve, in the bow of which, like a figure-head, stood Patsey. Yes, Patsey, looking as jolly and hearty as ever. He was urging the crew to their utmost, and was keeping a sharp lookout on all sides for any appearance of an enemy. We saw each man had his cutlass and breech-loading rifle by his side ready for any emergency. They were probably going to our rescue. Patsey had by some means escaped, had got back to the ship, and was now directing them to the place of our supposed imprisonment, where he had left us.

How thankful we felt at once more seeing our friends can well be imagined. We went to the bank, and waved our hats and coats to attract their attention. They seemed struck dumb with surprise when they saw us, but in a moment they all rose, and with loud cheers greeted us.

John Gagler, — good old John, — sat in the stern holding the
rudder ropes; he headed the boat towards us, and embarking in
our canoe we were soon alongside of them.   Many were the hand
shakings and demonstrations of greeting and affection.   Six of
the sailors being transferred into the canoe, we entered the boat,
and both were headed down stream.

We related our escape, and told Patsey how anxious we were
about him.   We were now indebted to him for his exertions in
coming to our rescue, and thanked him a thousand times.   We
asked him how he succeeded in making his escape, and he told us,
that after making his exit from the temple, he kept turning his
flip-flaps until he had passed the guards, and he thought he was
going to make good his escape, when suddenly a tall and powerfully built savage rushed from one of the huts, — a stranger
chief he afterwards learned, who was visiting Uamuok Aik, —
and stood in his way to stop him; putting on more speed as he
came nearer to the visitor, just as he reached him he gave a leap
and went clear over the chief's head; landing on his feet he made
a dash for the river, but the natives had now become aroused, and
a number of them took up the pursuit.

There was only one savage in his course, an obese, short, wad-
dling fellow; thinking to frighten him Patsey said he turned
again, and doing his flip-flaps, as he called them, bore down upon
him with lightning-like rapidity.   Seeing the savage was determined not to move, Patsey became provoked and determined
to settle his account at once, so he kept on, and exerting all
his strength, which was not slight, struck the savage such a
powerful blow in the stomach, that it sent him rolling down the
embankment, over and over, emitting howls of pain, and Patsey
was thrown several feet in the opposite direction.   Springing to

his feet he started to run, but losing much time by the fall, and being almost out of breath with his exertions, they soon captured him. He was dragged back into the presence of Uamuok Aik and his friend.

They talked together for some time. Uamuok Aik seemed desirous to execute Patsey at once in punishment for his attempt to escape, and the indignity offered to the warrior whom Patsey had knocked down the hill, but the other chief seemed to be persuading him to sell Patsey to him, for he examined him closely, and felt of his arms, legs, and body, seemingly in admiration of their solidity, strength, and size. Some kind of a bargain was entered into, for Patsey was taken to the stranger chief's canoe, and they soon started off, heading the canoe towards the upper part of the lake. Patsey's hands and feet were tied, but having learned the *modus operandi* of extricating himself from ligatures when they were tied in various ways over his body, it was an easy task for him to slip his wrists and ankles from his bonds.

He was placed near the bow of the boat; the savages thinking him secure, were not watching him very closely. Slipping the binding from his ankles, and well loosening those around his wrists, he made a backward dive and went over the bow of the canoe. After the splash all was confusion; the guards looked into the water and all around to see Patsey as soon as he should rise.

The sun was fast sinking, and it would soon be dark. They knew if Patsey was not found at once, he would drown. They kept watch of the waters for a long time, and paddled back and forth, and in circles, still not a ripple except those made by themselves disturbed the surface of the lake.

What had become of him? His hands and feet being tied they

probably thought he must have gone to the bottom, — drowned himself rather than be a captive, for they gave up the search and paddled swiftly on their course.

The prow of the canoe, which was a very large one, extended some distance over the water, and cast a deep shadow, so anyone looking over the bow of the canoe, unless observing very closely, could not distinguish any object on the water's surface. Patsey said he noticed this, and being almost as much at home in the water as on land, when he plunged overboard, he passed directly under the canoe, and caught hold of the keel at the stern just as it was passing over his head, rose to the surface, and took a long breath. The attention of the savages, for the moment being diverted by the splash at the bow, they did not notice him at the stern. In a moment, having regained his breath, he sank, and swimming under the now stationary canoe, reached the prow. He said he always kept his eyes open under water, and could see just where he was going. Laying on his back, his head in the shadow of the prow, his nostrils just above water, and clinging with his toes and fingers to the bottom, he lay perfectly still until darkness commenced to settle over the lake, and the canoe was headed inland. Then filling his lungs with a long breath, he noiselessly sank, and swimming fast under the water till his breath was almost exhausted, he rose to the surface.

All was still save the dip of the paddles, and the song of the oarsmen. Sinking once more, he again swam until he was obliged to rise for air; still no signs of discovery. One more he went down, and rising to the surface floated on his back for a long time; then seeing he had really evaded his keepers, he struggled to the shore, and dragging himself to land, lay down and was soon in a sound sleep. Awakening about midnight,

RIDGWAY'S

4
SHAWMUT AV.

BOSTON,
MASS.

CALCIUM LIGHTS

FOR PUBLIC AND PRIVATE

ILLUMINATIONS,

THEATRICALS,

MILITARY PROCESSIONS, Etc.

STEREOPTICON EXHIBITIONS

OF ALL PARTS OF THE WORLD.

LECTURES ILLUSTRATED.

ALL ORDERS BY MAIL PROMPTLY ATTENDED TO.

cold and hungry, he commenced a brisk run, and was soon well warmed, but could find nothing to appease his hunger. He came within sight of the encampment of Uamuok Aik, and thought if he could get a small canoe, he could travel faster by going down the river, and in a short time reach the ship, after which he could return with a well armed crew to rescue us; so taking again to the water, he swam towards the canoes; reaching them he selected the smallest, and pushing it out into the lake, and with much difficulty getting into it, he paddled for life; had reached the ship only the morning before, and having told his story to the sailors, he took a short rest, and then, with the crew equipped as we saw them, was on the way to the lake again.

We applauded his pluck and skill, and expressed how gladly we felt at his escape. Feeling very much fatigued, though the excitement incident upon Patsey's narrative had for a time diverted us, we made ourselves as comfortable as possible, and were soon asleep. We slept soundly, and were aroused at night by the thump of the boat against our ship's side. We scrambled on board half awake and half asleep, received the congratulations of those who had been left to care for the ship, and retired to our cabins to complete our sleep. When we awoke and went on deck we found that the ship was under way and no land in sight. Brad had not retired, but immediately after we descended to our cabins, had the engineer get up steam and started as quickly as possible from these inhospitable shores. Although the vessel had been badly damaged by the late storm, yet with the repairs the ship's carpenters had made, we could reach Australia, and then finish the repairing in proper shape after our arrival there.

During the day Jean brought forth the jar containing the red-hot star, and putting into it some extract of roudeletia, which he changed later in the afternoon to extract of ylang ylang and sandalwood, he filled the ship with the odor of these delightful perfumes.

The sailors all wished to examine the apparatus, and one and all expressed their wonder and " Shiver my timbers," or " Hope I may die," if they could see how the " lubber" worked.

CHAPTER XVII.

WE soon reached Sydney, the voyage having passed without any unusual occurrence.

We staid here for a few days, during which all the damage that we suffered in the storm that drove us to the shores of New Zealand, was properly repaired.

We were delighted to be again among our own countrymen whom only a few days ago we never expected to see again. We visited the principal places of interest, and dined at a hotel for the first time since we had left La Union. In the evening we attended the principal theatre, the first we had entered since we left Boston. It seemed like being at home again. The next day we intended visiting the "Orangery," a few miles from Sydney, owned by Richard Hill, Esq.

We started early in the forenoon, the ladies in a caleche, with myself as driver, and the rest of our party on horseback. It was a beautiful day, and the ride was exhilarating. Reaching the Orangery, we asked permission to inspect the grounds, which was granted us by the foreman, who politely offered his services as guide, which we accepted.

The cultivation of the orange is entered into exclusively on this plantation. The indescribable odor of the orange blossoms, which greeted our senses when we were nearing the place, was exquisite. Groves of orange trees stretched for long distances before us. The sight of the blossoms, and the luscious fruit in all stages of development was pleasing to the eye. The orange tree is one of the most wonderful productions of nature, and the more we think of it, the more astonishing it seems, as four distinct odors are procurable from this tree. From the blossoms, by distillation, is procured the Otto of Neroli, the perfume of which is finer by far than that of otto of roses, and has not the cloying sweetness which belongs to the latter.

"The origin of the term 'neroli,' applied to the otto of orange-blossoms, is not very definite," I casually remarked.

"It may have been named after the celebrated Roman Emperor, Nero," answered Jean, "who was so fond of sweet odors that he caused the roof of his dining halls to represent the firmament, and to shower down, night and day all sorts of perfumes and sweet waters."

"Or it may be," observed Susie, "that neroli was first procured by the Sabines, who, to distinguish it from other perfumes of the period, named it neroli, from 'nero,' which signifies 'strong.' The Sabines, you know, inhabit Sabina, a province of Italy, where the orange trees are very abundant."

"The otto of neroli, produced from the flowers of the *Citrus Aurantium*, is considered to be the finest quality," said I, "and is called 'neroli petale.' The second quality is called 'neroli bigarade,' and is derived from the flowers of the *Citrus Bigaradia*, or Seville orange. The otto of neroli dissolved in alcohol forms the Essence of Neroli, which is used to an enormous extent in the manufacture of colognes, and although very agreeable, it has

no relation to the flowery odor of the extract of orange blossoms or extrait de fleur d'orange, which is the second distinct odor
derived by maceration from the same flowers; in fact it has as
different an odor as though obtained from a different plant.
Yet in theory, both these perfumes are but alcoholic solutions
of the otto of the flower. The Extract of Orange Blossoms as
a handkerchief perfume is surpassed by none and equalled by few.
This extract resembles the odor of the blossoms so perfectly, that
with closed eyes the best judge could not distinguish the scent
of the extract from that of the flower.

"Another otto, the third distinct odor from this same tree, called
Otto of Petitgrain, procured by distillation of the leaves, and the
young unripe fruit, is mainly consumed in scenting soaps." I
picked a leaf, and holding it in the line of vision between my
friends and the sun, pointed out the small globular sacs contain-
ng the otto. "From this fact the term petit grain, small grains,
is derived," I continued. "Look at these trees; here are blossoms, some of the fruit just forming, some very small, and some
almost fully ripe ready to be gathered."

"Yes," said the superintendent, coming up to us as I spoke,
"it is a strange freak of nature. Try this orange," picking one
from the tree as he spoke.

"It is very tough," I remarked, tasting it.

"Don't eat it," said he; "that orange was last year's growth;
we sometimes neglect to gather them all; that one was left and
the juice ran back into the tree, so that if you had picked it at
that period and opened it, you would have found it without juice,
the inner part appearing like a sponge; when the season came
round again this orange was again filled with its juices, but it is
not so tender nor so well flavored, as it was at its first develop-

WE STOPPED FOR SOME MINUTES IN SILENT ADMIRATION.

Page 147.

ment. We sometimes let them stay on the tree for several years, and in some varieties it does not seem to impair the flavor of the fruit in the least to allow them to remain for many seasons."

We each ate several oranges, and as we strolled along conversed about the orange trees. They were in fine condition, and heavily laden with fruit.

Jean told us that at Nice, where the tree may be considered naturalized, there was one tree which generally bore five thousand or six thousand oranges, and which was more than fifty feet high, with a trunk fifteen feet in circumference; and in Cordova, the noted seat of Moorish grandeur and luxury, in Spain, there are orange trees still remaining, which are said to be six hundred or seven hundred years old.

The produce of the tree is almost incredible, props always being used to prevent the weight of the fruit from breaking down the branches. One, an orange tree in the quinta or orange garden of Barao das Laranjeiras, the superintendent told us, produced twenty thousand oranges at one time. The "Orangery" we were now visiting contained some sixty acres, and was surrounded with high walls and tall growing trees to protect the orange trees from the cool sea breezes.

We walked a long distance through this perfume forest, and came at last to the operating house where the Otto of Neroli, petale, bigarade, and Otto of Petitgrain were distilled, and the Pomade Fleur d'Orange is prepared from which the extract of orange blossoms is taken. The water used for distillation in procuring otto of neroli, when well freed from the otto, is the eau de fleur d'orange or Orange Flower Water, useful and pleasant to bathe the skin, and as an eye lotion, as also a tonic for general debility or nervousness; and is finer in many respects than

13

rose-water. Here also is procured the Otto of Orange Peel, the fourth distinct odor derived from this prolific plant. This is the odoriferous principle of the rind of the orange fruit, and is procured by expression and distillation. The peel or flavedo is rasped, in order to crush the little vessels or sacs that imprison the otto, and it is then taken upon pieces of cotton, which are put into a press and subjected to a powerful pressure; this peel is afterwards put into a still with water, and an inferior quality of otto is procured. Its abundance in the peel is shown by pinching a piece near the flame of a candle; the otto that spurts out ignites with a brilliant illumination.

Having seen the principal features of this immense orange garden, we expressed our thanks to the superintendent for the instructive entertainment he had afforded us, and bidding him adieu, were soon on our way to Sydney.

"Why is it," said Jean to us, as he rode leisurely beside the carriage, "that parties in the United States do not ascertain the particular localities favorable to the production of certain plants valuable in perfumery, besides producing other commercial products, and make a specialty of raising them as they do here and in France and in many other countries?"

"I cannot tell," I answered, "but probably from ignorance of the profit accruing from such a course, though every year we find more and more business men are making specialties of some particular branch or article of trade, knowing that with a conscientious study of that one article or branch, and taking an interest in developing its worth and properties to their highest degree, they have a life's labor before them."

We reached the hotel on George Street, where we were to stop till the repairs on the ship were completed. Brad wanted to have everything in the best order, for he was determined to search all the islands in the neighborhood, and to follow any and every clew that turned up that he thought might help him in finding his father. He was with us at the hotel in the evening, and said he had planned a ride into the country for the morrow. We expressed our willingness to go, and he promised us a very pleasant trip.

This time we were all mounted on good horses. On our arrival at the top of the hill which we had been ascending, we stopped for some minutes in silent admiration of the beautiful scene displayed before us. A large plain lay below and in front of us in which the river that flowed around the base of this eminence, spread into a wide basin or lake, covered with white and blue water lilies, and here and there a head of pink nelumbium in the midst of them; its banks were adorned with reeds and flowering plants; the grass of the plain was five feet high and very silky, and small hillocks, and graceful shrubs some of which were in flower, and clumps of trees, were spread over the surface. Susie was in ecstacies at seeing so many new and beautiful flowers and plants, and the many brilliantly colored and curious insects that she sent Patsey to catch, kept her occupied, and made the excursion one of great pleasure to her.

Perceiving a musky odor in the air, we inquired of Brad the cause, but he could not tell us. In the woods through which we passed, Susie pointed out to us the myrtle tree, which rears its head a hundred feet high before it expands into its umbrageous canopy of foliage, and three kinds of the Eucalypti family. The *Eucalyptus amygdalina* or Tasmanian peppermint tree, the otto of which has a strange odor of peppermint combined with nutmegs. The *Eucalyptus odorata* or the peppermint tree, and the *Eucalyptus globulus* or blue-gum tree, a myall-wood tree, *Acacia pendula*, the wood of which has an intense and delightful odor of violets,— a very scarce perfume in nature. After having crossed the plain we came upon a scrub of the well known Gum Wattle, *Acacia decurrens*. Every year, as the season of blossoming returns, many of the valleys are redolent with their exquisite odor. This fragrance is, however, entirely in the blossoms, for the wood and leaves are wholly devoid of perfume. Extract of Cassie is procured from the blossoms of the plant, and is one of those fine odors which enters into the composition of the best handkerchief bouquets, imparting to them such a true flowery fragrance, that it is remarked by all who smell them. When the extract of cassie is inhaled alone, it has a powerful odor of violets, and is intensely sweet.

Jean and Patsey gathered a quantity of the blossoms, Jean telling us he would show us how to extract the perfume from them, in small quantities, so we would know how to do the same with a small number of almost any flowers.

" This odor," he said, " must not be confounded with cassia, which is derived from the cassia tree, that yields the common commercial cinnamon. Cassie is a contraction of acacia."

" From this same Gum Wattle," said Brad, " is procured gall-berries, of great utilization in many branches of commerce ; a gum similar to gum Arabic, and the bark is of much value to the tanner ; the gum is used as an article of food by the aborigines, and is said to be quite nutritious ; it would be well for some one to try naturalizing it in the United States."

We saw a few Sandal-wood trees, and some Linaloes from which is obtained a fragrant otto.

Here instead of plants of slight proportions, we found that

the products are procured from trees, which form the loftiest timber of Australia, and the animals here are like no others, seemingly to be combinations or cross-breeds of well known species.

After eating our luncheon, we took a long rest and then set out on our return. Whilst jogging leisurely along, we were startled by a large animal, apparently nine feet high, leaping across the road ahead of us. We soon saw that it was a kangaroo, and the leaps it made were so prodigious that it was soon out of sight. Capt. Cole related many anecdotes of these strange creatures, which interested us until we came in sight of the city. Spurring our horses we soon reached the hotel, quite weary with our long ride. After supper, the evening was whiled away in conversation, and as we were bidding Brad good night, he told us that the ship would be ready to start towards the evening of the next day, and if agreeable to us he would like to set sail then.

"If you would prefer to rest here for three or four months while I cruise among the islands, I would then return for you."

We, as with one voice, interrupted him and told him he ought to be ashamed to make such a proposition.

"The idea," said Susie, "of our wishing to leave you to make your search alone; but probably you consider us more of a drawback than a help, yet you must confess," and she smiled at him bewitchingly, "that we are company for you, and you know the old saying, — 'poor company is better than none.'"

"I'll be a martyr to your company awhile longer then," he merrily answered.

A pleasing martyrdom to him, I thought.

The next day we laid in a supply of necessaries for a long voyage, and saw them safely aboard the ship. Brad was resolved to make a careful and thorough search among the islands, and not to return unless inevitably obliged to do so.

CHAPTER XVIII.

WE had started from Sydney on the evening the *Cynthia* was ready, and for two months we have sailed among and examined many islands, but not the slightest trace of the wrecked "Godolpha," can we bring to light. We had first set out to the island where John Gagler had been a slave to the savages for two years, he knowing the exact latitude and longitude of it. From there we were to commence our search. Either John Gagler had forgotten to which point of the compass it lay, or else he had not ascertained it correctly, for not the least sign of it could we find. He was puzzled, or appeared to be. Brad was disappointed, and judging from present appearances, began to doubt John Gagler's story. We had used up our supply of coal, and had been obliged to have recourse to our sails, by which we made but slow progress; so Brad very reluctantly was obliged to put in here at Colombo, Ceylon, to get a supply of coal, and then we were to renew the search.

This island, in comparison to its limited area, is wonderfully endowed. Brad was not positive that he could be supplied here, but thought he would try as it would save the trouble of going to Calcutta. It offered to Susie, Jean, and I, a splendid opportunity

for the examination of many productions of this place, of which we
used large quantities. During the time Brad would be making
his contracts, we should have sufficient time to see all we wished.
On the estate of Mr. Winter, who cultivated large tracts of the
Citronella, Lemongrass, Cinnamon and Cassia plants, and distilled
from them their ottos, we saw all of these articles in their various stages of production. The Otto of Citronella is distilled
from the leaves of the *Andropogon Schoenanthus*, acres of which we
noticed growing on his grounds, almost wild, and in abundance,
requiring but little care in its cultivation. The otto possesses a
very sweet, overpowering odor; its color when taken from the
bottles, is a light brown; after being exposed to the light a
little while, it changes to a beautiful green, and after a great while,
if much air is allowed to come in contact with it, it again
changes to a dark brown color. The annual yield of this otto
in Ceylon, is a little more than five thousand pounds. It is
used extensively for perfuming soaps and oils. It is exported by Mr. Winter, in old English porter bottles, as is also
the Otto of Lemongrass. This last named otto is derived from a
species of grass, that Susie called *Andropogon Nardus*, and is
cultivated here to a great extent. The otto is a very powerful
perfume, well adapted for scenting soaps and grease, but its
principal consumption is in the manufacture of essence of verbena, and for this reason, and also on account of its similarity
of odor to the verbena plant, it is commonly called otto of verbena. From its comparatively low price, great strength, and
fine perfume, when diluted, it has almost completely driven
the true Otto of Verbena from the market. The annual yield of
otto of lemongrass in Ceylon, is nearly two thousand pounds.
The fresh leaves of the plant when bruised, emit a delightful odor,

and when roasted, are used for medicinal purposes. The double distilled otto of lemongrass has been used as an embrocation in cases of rheumatism, and found a most efficacious remedy, and also administered in cases of cholera with beneficial effect. The dose is from twelve to twenty drops, on a small lump of sugar, repeated till the symptoms abate, at the same time applying it externally to the hips, back, and stomach, to prevent cold and cramp so invariably accompanying the disorder. The otto when distilled, contains a large quantity of resin and is highly colored, and to remove these impurities, charcoal grits, which have been previously well washed and thoroughly dried, are saturated with the otto, thrown into the still with a requisite amount of water, made slightly sharp to the taste, and redistilled.

In his warehouse, Mr. Winter had many hundred pounds of Cinnamon bark, which he told us was yielded by the *Cinnamomum zeylanicum*, and is largely cultivated. The trees have beautiful white blossoms, and red tipped leaves. The bark is stripped off the branches, when it rolls into quills, the smaller of which are introduced into the larger, and then dried in the sun. As a general rule the thinner the bark, the finer its quality, and from this bark is distilled the Otto of Cinnamon. It is exceeding strong, and requires to be used sparingly; it is the warmest to the taste of all ottos. The ground bark enters into the composition of pastiles, tooth powder, and sachet powder.

"Its name," said Jean, "is derived from *China Amomum.*"

Otto of Cassia is often called otto of cinnamon, and is frequently sold for it, owing to its similar odor. This otto is procured, however, from the outer bark of the *Laurus Cassia*, and has a strong, coarse, and less delicate odor, and is much cheaper. One hundred weight of bark yields rather more than three-quar-

ters of a pound of otto; it has a pale yellow color, which is
changed by age to a brownish red, in smell much resembling cinnamon.   Otto of Cinnamon and Cassia are more aromatic or
spicy than flowery in their odor; they therefore find no place for
handkerchief use, but in compounds where the clove answers, so
will they.   The same tree, or a closely allied tree to the *Laurus
Cassia*, furnishes Cassia buds, used as a perfume for the breath,
which are something like cloves, and like them are the unexpanded flower buds.

Procuring samples of these articles, we set out upon our return,
and on our route we saw troops of monkeys of most comical appearance; and hanging heads downwards from a group of India
rubber trees, were a number of flying foxes, which were chattering and screaming, trying to outdo the monkeys.   Asking our
guide about some slender palm trees that attracted our attention,
he informed us they were the Areca Palm.

"From which is procured the areca-nut?" said Jean interroga-
tively.

"The same," he replied.   "The nut resembles a nutmeg in
shape, color, and internal structure, but is harder and larger."

"I understand," Jean remarked, "that it has astringent, sial-
agogue, stomachic, and narcotic properties.   That nut and husk are
employed in some form or other by all classes of the natives as a
masticatory.   So used, it sweetens the breath, preserves the
teeth, and gives the gums and lips an attractive red color.   It
carries these properties in a great degree into its charcoal, which
also possesses higher detersive and antiseptic qualities, than any
other vegetable charcoal.   Besides this, its peculiar hardness
without grittiness, peculiarly fits it for acting mechanically on the
teeth.   It is extensively used, and highly esteemed throughout

the East as a dentifrice. I believe it is recommended by the
most eminent surgeon dentists for whitening and preserving
the teeth, removing tartar, and sweetening the breath, and whilst
doing this, it medicates the mouth, and gradually removes soreness, scurvy and bleeding of the gums. By its regular use, loose
teeth are said to become firm again, and the whole set preserved
to a late period of life."

"I remember," observed Susie, "that a Dr. Lind, an eminent
physician of Bengal, stated that by its means he preserved all his
teeth perfectly sound to the age of eighty."

"I have heard old residents of the East Indies assert," said
our guide, "that they found it a great preservative of their teeth,
and an infallible preventative of toothache."

"Prof. Hertz, the celebrated Prussian dentist," said Jean,
"says that those who regularly use areca-nut charcoal as a dentifrice, will never require the assistance of himself or any of his
fraternity."

"I think that areca nut is too antiseptic for general use, as
well as any other drug or powerful preparation for the teeth," I
remarked, "for the teeth and gums are very delicate in their
organization; if injured, it is extremely difficult to restore them
to a healthy condition. There are no members of the human
body so sensitive, or that add more to personal beauty, than a set
of fine, natural teeth, and so should be well cared for and preserved."

"There is the *Convolvulus scoparius*," suddenly exclaimed
Susie.

"Be gorra, an' phats that? Is it thim thavin' nagur savidges
agin'?" asked Patsey, and he pulled up his horse with a jerk.

"No, Patsey, only a Rosewood tree," answered Jean.

"Och, botheration on yer Italeann," said Patsey, spurring his horse in disgust.

Jean explained that "when rosewood is distilled, a sweet smelling otto is procured, resembling in some slight degree the fragrance of the rose, hence its name, but it is also called Rhodium. Prior to the cultivation of the rose-leaf geranium, the distillates from rosewood, and from the root of *Genista canariensis* or Canary rosewood, were principally drawn for the adulteration of real otto of roses. One hundred weight of wood yields about three ounces of otto. Ground rosewood is valuable as a basis of sachet powders."

Huge dark masses ahead of us attracted our attention; coming nearer we perceived they were three very large elephants. We noticed with interest their movements, and watched them till out of sight, admiring their huge proportions.

Reaching the ship, Brad said he could not obtain a sufficient supply of coal, and so must sail immediately for Calcutta. Coming into the saloon after we had started, he said, —

"A native, with a friend of his from Calicut, the capital of the province of Malabar, was on board while you were away, and offered a kitten for sale, and I bought it."

"Oh! where is it?" asked Susie; "let me see the little darling."

"In the laboratory," said Brad. "Come, and you can see it."

We followed him in, but no kitten was in sight.

"Look in this box," said Capt. Cole.

We looked, but we did not see a kitten, or rather not what we generally term a kitten, but a large cat, about one foot high and three feet long; it had a pointed nose, and small ears, was of a brownish gray color, and its fur standing erect on the neck, and

WE LOOKED, BUT WE DID NOT SEE A KITTEN.

Page 156.

ridge of the back ; it had a long bushy tail, something like a grey
squirrel.

" The *Viverra Civetta*," said Jean, " or Civet Cat."

" Yes," said Capt. Cole. " I thought one would be interesting to you, so I took it. It is easily cared for, its favorite food
being boiled meat, eggs, birds, and small animals, and it is particularly fond of fish, which you can catch for it."

This animal secretes the substance known as Civet, which is
formed in a large, double glandular receptacle between the anus
and pudendum of the creature. Like many other substances of
Oriental origin, it was first brought to Europe by the Dutch, who
used to keep numbers of civets alive at Amsterdam, for the purpose of collecting the perfume when secreted. When a sufficient
time had been allowed for the process, the animal was put into a
long, wooden cage, so narrow that it could not turn itself around.
The cage being then opened by a door in the rear, a small spatula,
or spoon introduced through the orifice in the pouch, which was
carefully scraped, and its contents put into a vessel. This operation was performed twice or thrice a week, about a drachm at a
time is thus obtained, and the animal was said to produce more
civet when irritated. The quantity, however, depended chiefly
on the quality of the nourishment it took. Civet, in its natural
state, has a most disgusting appearance, and its smell, such is its
strength, is equally repulsive. But when properly diluted and
combined with sweet smelling odors, it produces a very pleasing
effect, and possesses a much more floral fragrance than musk ;
indeed it would be impossible to produce the perfume of some
flowers without it.

" It is difficult to ascertain," Jean musingly remarked, " the
reason why the same substance, modified only by the quantity of

matter presented to the nose, should produce such an opposite effect on the olfactory nerve; but such is the case with nearly all odorous bodies, especially ottos, which if smelled at in bulk, are far from nice, and in some cases nauseous, — such as otto of thyme, patchouly, and vetiver; but if diluted with a thousand times their volume of oil or spirit, then their fragrance is delightful."

"So the whirlwind and the hurricane become the gentle zephyr that makes the aspens quiver; so the fire-proof block of iron becomes, when divided, more combustible than gunpowder; so the silken fibre becomes a rope to stay the course of a ship; so the lightning flash becomes the electricity which makes ones hair stand on end. Quantity is equivalent to an allotropic condition of matter; quantity produces opposite physical effects upon the faculties."

After our examination of the civet cat, we returned to the saloon and awaited supper.

CHAPTER XIX.

WE had entered the roadstead of Calcutta and had dropped anchor. Brad had gone ashore to see what prospect there was of obtaining a supply of coal. He came back about noon, saying a famine had commenced, owing to the supply of rice failing, and a general drought. Workmen could not be obtained, and coal had been brought in only in small quantities, and was very expensive. Probably his contracts would not be filled for some days. "Meanwhile," he said, "if you wish to go ashore, I am at your service."

"Supposing, after the heat of the day is over, we take a short stroll about the city," I suggested.

Jean had been relating to us, how in this country perfumes had been used since the earliest records; a fact easily accounted for by the sensual temperament of its inhabitants, and the abundance of fragrant materials placed at their disposal by bountiful Nature. Perfumes were mentioned in the poetry of India more than two thousand years ago. From it, we learn they were then applied both for sacred and private purposes. The sacrifices were usually offered in the temples of the Indian Trinity, or Tremoortee, comprising Brahma, Vishnu, and Siva. They consisted of a

159

HENRY ALTON, Sec'y.   ISAAC H. WILLIAMSON, Pres.

THE
Promontory
Consolidated
MINING COMPANY.

PRINCIPAL OFFICES:

Nos. 40 and 42 BROADWAY,

—AND—

17 State Street, Boston, Mass.

ELEVATOR, 47 DEVONSHIRE STREET.

Organized under the laws of the State of New York.

Capital Stock · · $5,000,000

100,000 Shares.   Par Value, $50.00.

Stock Full Paid and Unassessable.

fire of fragrant woods lighted at each of the four cardinal points.
The flames were fed now and then with a consecrated ointment,
and around the fire was scattered a fragrant herb called *kusa*.
Jean said it was what is now known as ginger grass, and Susie
called it *Andropogon nardus*, from which an otto is distilled.
According to Hindoo mythology there are five heavens, a different
and superior god presiding over each.   That of Brahma, called
Brahma-loka, is situated on Mount Meru ; those of Vishnu, Siva,
Kuvera and Indra are on the summit of the Himalayas. In all these
eiysiums, perfumes and flowers are among the chief delights.
The principal ornament of Brahma's heaven is a blue flower,
which the Brahmins say blooms nowhere but in Paradise.   It is
the blue campac or champac flower, a great rarity.   The only
species known on this earth, *Michelia champaca*, has yellow blossoms, with which the Hindoo maidens are wont to ornament their
raven hair.

In Indra's paradise, called Swarga, is to be found the still more
attractive Camalata, whose rosy flowers not only enchant the
senses of all those who have the happiness of breathing their delicious fragrance, but have also the power of granting them all they
may desire.   This Indra, the *Jupiter Tonans* of the Hindoos, appears very partial to perfumes, for he is always represented with
his breast tinged with sandalwood.   Kama, the god of love,
or Indian Cupid, is armed with a bow made of sugar cane, the
string of which consists of.bees ; he has five arrows, each tipped
with the blossom of a flower, which pierce the heart through the
five senses, and his favorite dart is pointed with the chuta or
mango flower.

Entering the boat we were pulled ashore, and landing, we found
our way to the principal thoroughfares, and examined the strange

crowd of people surging around us. We noticed the Hindoo barber, like his Chinese brother, plying his trade in the open air, and handling with great dexterity his razor, a curious affair, mounted on hinges, and which is also a formidable looking instrument. Some of these razors are elaborately constructed, one which we saw being made of gilt metal, engraved, and studded with jewels.

Perceiving an odoriferous fragrance in the air, we looked around and saw, a short distance ahead, what Brad told us was a perfumer's establishment. Coming up to this Hindoo Perfumer, or gund'hee, we found he did not indulge, like his foreign *confreres*, in showy glass cases and a brilliant shop, but his whole *establishment* consisted of a few sacks, boxes, and trays, containing his various fragrant stores, in the midst of which he sat dispensing them to his beauty-seeking patrons. We examined his stock, and through an interpreter learned that he had Musk, Vetiver Root, or kus kus, the rhizome of an Indian grass, *Anatherum muricatum*, which grows in abundance here, and is used extensively in the manufacture of awnings, blinds, and sunshades, called Tatty. During the hot season an attendant sprinkles water over them; this operation cools the apartment by the evaporation of the water, and at the same time perfumes the atmosphere in a very agreeable manner with the odoriferous principle of the vetiver. Bundles of this vetiver he sold for perfuming linen and preventing moth. The Essence of Vetiver, made from the Otto of Vetiver, which is distilled from the root, is seldom used alone as a handkerchief perfume except by those who, perhaps, have learned to admire its odor by their previous residence in this "Eastern Clime." A hundred weight of vetiver root yields about fourteen ounces of otto, which in appearance greatly resembles otto of

11

sandal.   He showed us Patchouly leaves and Otto of Patchouly, which is distilled from the leaves and stems of the *Pogostemon patchouli.*

"One hundred weight of good herb will yield," he said, "about twenty eight ounces of otto of *puchaput*," as he called it.

It is of a dark brown color, and of a density about the same as otto of sandal, which it resembles in physical character.   Its odor is one of the most powerful derived from the botanical kingdom.   It is as agreeable to some, as it is offensive to others, a most peculiar odor ; some say it smells musty.

"Why," said Susie, when examining the otto, "my India shawl when I first bought it had the same odor as this."

"True," said Jean, "and that is the way the perfume of patchouly became introduced.   Years ago real India shawls brought an extravagant price, and purchasers could always distinguish them by their odor, they being always perfumed with patchouly.   The French manufacturers had for some time successfully imitated the India fabric, but could not impart the odor.   At length they discovered the secret, and began to import the plant to perfume articles of their own manufacture, and thus palm off homespun shawls as real India."

"Well, I hope mine is genuine," said Susie.

We purchased some Vetiver root, Otto of Vetiver, Otto of Patchouly and Patchouly leaves, then passing again among the throng, we wandered on until espying another dealer in perfumes, we stopped to examine his stock.   We noticed some Cardamom seeds, much used as a perfume for the breath, and some Gum Olibanum, which is used to a limited extent in the manufacture of pastils and incense.

"Gum Olibanum is chiefly interesting as being one of those

odoriferous bodies of which frequent mention is made in the Bible," Jean remarked. " It is believed to have been one of the ingredients in the sweet incense of the Jews, and is still burnt as incense in the Greek and Romish churches, where the diffusion of such odors around the altar forms a part of the prescribed religious service."

This last perfumer, who seemed to be of some relation to our interpreter, informed him that a party were going to the north to a depot, where was to be held the annual auction of sandalwood. It seemed it is the custom, at the end of the year, to fell the trees that have reached maturity. They are then stripped of their bark and conveyed to the various depots, where they are cut into billets, which are carefully dressed and sorted according to the quality of the wood. These billets are sold by weight at auction, native merchants congregating from all parts of India to make purchases. The pieces that are straight and have most heartwood obtain the highest price, as the fragrance for which they are so much prized depends on the presence of otto, which is chiefly situated in the dark central wood of the tree. The perfumer offering to buy for us a quantity of fresh otto at the auction, we respectfully declined, as we did not want it. Jean asked our interpreter if we could not induce the perfumer to allow Patsey, himself, and I, to accompany him to the auction. The perfumer said he had no objections to our company, for a consideration, to which we bowed.

" And perhaps," said the perfumer, "we may get a chance to participate in a hunt for the musk deer, for it is just the season now for them to come down low on the mountains."

This just suited us. We knew that in most of the hilly states, the musk deer is considered royal property. In some, the Rajahs keep men purposely to hunt it, and in Gurwhal a fine is imposed upon any Puharrie who is known to have sold a musk-pod to a stranger, — the Rajah receiving them in lieu of rent, and it might be dangerous for us to go ; but for another " consideration," it was understood that all necessary arrangements should be made, so that if an opportunity offered to bring down a deer we should be prepared ; and he said that if we would be ready and at the depot on time the next day, we could accompany the party.

We were elated at this, and hurrying back to the ship awaited with impatience the close of day. My wife and Susie did not like it because they could not go with us, but as it would be a rapid and rough journey, and no arrangements had been made for them to accompany us, they at last agreed it would hardly be enjoyable for them.

We were on time at the depot, as we were to take the cars to Raneegunge, that being the terminus of the route, and from there go on horseback the rest of the journey. We met our interpreter, the perfumer, and four others. We all entered the cars and were soon rushing on toward our destination, feeling as though we were again in New York, this being the first railroad ride we had been able to take since leaving that city. Reaching the railroad terminus we engaged horses, and waiting till the noon heat had subsided, we mounted and rode towards the mountains. This little persecuted animal which we wished to have a shot at, the Musk deer, (*Moschus moschatus*), would probably have been left unmolested to pass a life of peace and quietness in its native forest, but for the celebrated perfume with which Nature has provided it. Its skin being worthless from its small size, the flesh alone would hold out no inducement for the villagers to hunt it while larger game was more easily procurable, and its comparative insignificance would also have protected it from the pursuit of the travelling sportsman. As the musk, however, renders it to the Puharries, the most valuable of all game, no animal is so universally sought after in places it is known to inhabit.

If not walking leisurely along, they always go in bounds, all fours leaving and alighting on the ground together. Our guide told us they eat but little, compared with other ruminating animals; he judged from the small quantity of food found in their stomachs, the contents of which were always in such a pulpy state, that it was impossible to tell what food they preferred. If shot while feeding, various kinds of shrubs and grasses, and often portions of the long white moss that hangs so luxuriantly from the trees in these higher forests, have been found in their mouth and throat. The Puharries believe that the adult males kill and eat snakes, and feed upon the leaves of the "kedar patta," a small and very fragrant smelling laurel, and that the musk is produced by this food. It is in the adult males only that the musk is found; the females have none, neither has any portion of their bodies the slightest odor of musk. The excrement of the males has a strong odor of musk, but singularly enough, neither in the contents of the stomach, nor bladder, nor in any other part of the body is there any perceptible scent of musk. The young are born either in June or July, and almost every female brings forth one yearly, and often twins, and if two are born at one time they always deposit the fawns in separate places some distance from each other, the dam herself keeping as much as possible away from both, only visiting them to give them suck.

"Should you succeed in catching a young one," said the Hindoo Perfumer, "its bleating may bring the old one to the spot, but I never knew an instance of one being seen abroad with its dam, or of two young ones being seen together. Their solitary habits are innate, for if a fawn is taken young and nursed by a sheep or goat, it will not for some time associate with its foster-dam, but as soon as its hunger is satisfied, seeks some spot for concealment. It is amusing to see them nursing, as all the while they keep leaping up and crossing their fore-legs rapidly over each other. They are rather difficult to rear, as many, soon after they are caught, go blind and die."

"How do they generally hunt them?" I asked.

"In some districts," he answered, "they are hunted down with dogs, but snaring is by far the most common method practised for their capture. A few are occasionally shot by the village shikaries when in pursuit of other animals, but the match-lock is seldom taken out purposely to hunt them, for a hill shikarie does not carry the match lighted, so almost every one would get away before he could strike a light and apply the match. If they had such rifles as you carry, the task would be easy."

"What is the method of snaring them?" Jean inquired.

"A fence is built about three feet high," he replied, "composed of bushes and branches of trees, in the forest, generally along some ridge, as towards evening they begin to move, and during the night appear to wander a great deal from the top to the bottom of the hill, or from one side to another. Their nocturnal rambles are apparently as much for recreation as in search of food, as they often visit regularly some steep ledge of rocks or precipice where there is little or no vegetation. The Puharries believe that they come to such places to play and dance with each other. The fences I spoke about are often upwards of a mile in length. Openings for the deer to pass through, are left every ten or fifteen yards, and in each a strong hempen snare is placed, tied to the smaller end of a long stick, the thick end of which is firmly fixed in the ground, and the upper end bent forward to the opening, so that the deer when passing through, treading upon some small sticks, which hold it down, sets the snare free, the stick springs back and tightens the cord around the animal's leg. Besides the musk deer, numbers of forest pheasants, moonals, corklas, and argus are caught in these snares; they are visited every third or fourth day, and it is seldom that the owners return without some kind of game. The polecats often find out the snares, and after once tasting the feast, if not destroyed, soon become a grievous annoyance, tracing the fence almost daily from end to end, and seizing on everything caught; they are often caught themselves, but immediately bite the snare in two and escape. The musk deer are frequently lost to the hunters in this manner, for when one is eaten by the polecats, the pod is torn to pieces, and the contents scattered on the ground. No animal swallows the musk, and when a deer has been killed and eaten by a leopard or other animal, if the ground be carefully examined, much musk may be picked up. Insects and maggots also leave it untouched."

"Excepting in one instance," interrupted Jean. "The case was this; Mr. G. W. Septimus Piesse, a very learned and celebrated perfumer of Europe, who understands his business thoroughly, in May, 1861, purchased six caddies of musk; they were examined and appeared to be all right; in the following August, on opening one of these caddies he was surprised to find every pod of musk perforated with maggot holes, and on opening the pods he found endless numbers of white maggots all alive and fat, enjoying the banquet."

" Whurrah ! an' were he mad at 'em ? " asked Patsey.

" I should think he would have been provoked," said Jean.   It
was a banquet that had cost him about fifteen dollars per ounce,
and as there were a hundred ounces in the caddy, it involved a
total loss of some fifteen hundred dollars.   Do you think you
would have been put out about it ? "

Patsey gave a long whistle, and mumbled something about he'd
put them out.

" The creature being new to him," Jean continued, " he called
it the *Musk Grub*."

" That is something unusual," said the Hindoo perfumer ;· " for
I once found what I thought to be a newly killed musk deer, but
on examination I discovered it was merely the skin and skeleton
of one, which, from its dry and withered state, must have been
dead some months ; the flesh had been completely eaten away by
maggots, but the musk-pod was entire."

We camped for the night, and again mounting early in the
morning, we became aware by the roughness of the way that we
were ascending some of the spurs of the Vindhya mountains.
The toil of getting up and down these immense eminences is very
great, and the pursuit of the musk deer is attended with many
dangers, hardships, and privations.   The time expended and distance traversed, render the occupation very expensive from the
necessity of being accompanied by various grades of servants,
some to hunt up and look out for game, others to carry provisions
and camping equipments ; consequently genuine musk must
always maintain a high price.   We, however, were only watching for a chance shot, so we dispensed with all but one servant.
We were now at quite a height, and it being within about two
hours of dark, the guide informed us if any deer were about it was

time now to look for them. The others of the party were armed
with bows and arrows. Jean, Patsey, and I, each carried a rifle;
we had practised considerably with them since our adventure
with the bear, so that now we were good marksmen.

We were riding slowly along, when directly in front of us stood
an animal about the size of a full grown English greyhound, almost three feet long, and standing nearly two feet high at the
shoulder. It was looking inquiringly at us. It had a small horn-
less head, ears long and erect, and two tusks about three inches
long, the thickness of a goose quill, sharp-pointed and curving
slightly backwards, depending from the upper jaw. Its legs were
long and slender, the toes pointed, the hind heels long, and resting on the ground as well as the toes; its color of a red-brown
with two white stripes down the neck and breast.

"The musk deer," exclaimed our guide, excitedly.

At the sound of his voice the deer started down the gentle
slope, making most astonishing bounds, clearing a space of more
than sixty feet at each bound, and springing over bushes of considerable height.

"They are very sure footed," said our guide, "and although
a forest animal, have, perhaps, no equal in travelling over rocky
and precipitous ground. Where even the burrell is obliged to
move slowly and carefully, these deer bound quickly and fear-
lessly, and although often driven on rocks, which are thought
impassable, they invariably find a way in some direction, and
never miss a footing, or fall unless wounded."

This one, after making two or three bounds, passed around
some bushes, and again came out in our pathway and faced us.
Patsey, who was standing on the back of his horse, the better to
see the deer, the horse keeping quiet for a wonder, when the

RISING IN EVER DECREASING SPIRALS ABOVE THE HEAD
OF THE HORSE.

Page 170.

deer showed himself again, discharged his rifle.   The sound of
the first shot of the hunt!   We see the smoke wreathe up!   Above
the smoke we see, rising in ever decreasing spirals above the
head of the horse, a young man about the size of Patsey, and a
rifle going in an oblique manner towards the neighboring trees.
The shot from the back of the horse was too much for the animal's good nature, so he gave Patsey some help up in the world.
Patsey came down astride the neck of his horse, hugging him
affectionately as if he had just returned from a long journey, and
was glad to see him.   The horse tried to shake Patsey off, not
being used to such displays of affection, but Patsey got control
of him, and fastening him to a tree, went in search of his rifle,
which took him a long while to find, for it had lodged up in one
of the highest branches of a tree.

" Do not try any more Tartar riding on a green horse," I cautioned him.

" Shure, an' he's a foine hoss," he replied, " but he's niver been
in th' sarvace ; he's afraid of a moite of goonpowdther."

Cautioning him to be more careful another time, we started
again.

CHAPTER XX.

"THESE deer seem to like the cold," observed the Hindoo Perfumer, "and the nearer we get to the snow line, the more likely we are to find them. They seldom, if ever, lie in the sun, even in the coldest weather; their forms are always made where there is something to shelter them from its rays. In many respects they are not unlike hares in habits and economy. Each individual selects some particular spot for its favorite retreat, about which it remains quietly throughout the day. They occasionally rest during the day in any place where they may happen to be in in the morning, but in general they return to near the same spot almost every evening, making forms in different quarters of their retreat, a short distance from each other, visiting them in turn. Sometimes they will lie under the same tree or bush for weeks together. They make forms in the same manner as hares, where the ground is sloping levelling with their feet a spot large enough for their purpose."

We were now entering a birch forest where the underwood consisted chiefly of white rhododendron and juniper. This being the kind of forest in which are their favorite resorts, we were not surprised when one arose directly in front of Jean; it looked

171

curiously at him, and before it could prepare to bound off, Jean brought it down with a shot from his rifle. We rushed to the spot, and found it had been sport for us, but death for the deer.

We carefully examined the animal and found that the general color was a dark, speckled, brownish gray, deepening nearly to black on the hindquarters, and edged down the inside of the thighs with reddish yellow. The throat, belly, and legs were of a lighter gray. The fur seemed to be composed of thick, spiral hairs, not unlike miniature porcupine quills, and were very brittle, breaking with a slight pull, and so thickly set that numbers could be pulled out without altering the outward appearance of the fur; it was white from the roots to nearly the tips, where it gradually became dark. The fur is much longer and thicker on the hind parts than on the fore, and gives the animal the appearance of being much larger in the hindquarters than in the shoulders, a fact we had remarked about the one Patsey fired at.

We looked for the pod, which we found near the navel, between the flesh and the skin. The pod is composed of several layers of thin skin, within the innermost of which the musk is confined, and has much the appearance of the craw or stomach of a partridge, or other small gallinaceous bird when full of food. We found an orifice outwards through the skin, into which with a slight pressure we could pass a stick about the size of the little finger, but found it had no connection with the body.

"I have heard said," remarked Jean, "that it is probable that musk is at times discharged through this orifice, as the pod is often found not half full, and sometimes nearly void. From this orifice the dishonest dealers extract the grain musk, and then insert in its place the pieces of lead, brass, copper, skin, dried blood, clay, tobacco, and other adulterations sometimes found in pods when opened by perfumers; from the size of these orifices it can be pretty fairly judged how the pods have been tampered with."

We heard the voices of the Bengalese approaching; after a short chase they had shot a smaller deer with their arrows, and two of them were bringing the deer between them to where we were. They threw it down when they reached us, and began to cut around the pod, and to skin the whole stomach. Meanwhile one of them built a fire, and put in it some flat stones to heat; when they were ready, the skin was laid with the fleshy side on the hot stones, and thus dried without singeing the hair. The skin shrank up from the heat into a small compass, and was then stitched round the pod, and hung up to dry until quite hard. This is the general method of preparing them, but some put the pod into hot oil, instead of laying it on hot stones; but either method must deteriorate the quality of the musk, as it gets completely baked or fried. It is best if the pod is at once cut from the skin and allowed to dry of itself. The musk is in grains, from the size of a small bullet to small shot, of irregular shape, but generally round or oblong, together with more or less in coarse powder. When fresh, it is of a reddish brown color, but when taken out of the pod and kept for any length of time, becomes nearly black. In autumn and winter the grains are hard, firm, and nearly dry, but in summer they become damp and soft, probably from the green food then eaten by the animal. The musk is formed with the animal, as the pod of a young deer taken out of the womb is plainly distinguishable, and indeed is much larger in proportion than in an adult animal, and for two years the contents of the pod is a soft, milky substance, with a disagreeable smell.

When it first becomes musk, there is not much more than an

eighth of an ounce ; as the animal grows it increases in quantity, and in some instances as much as two ounces have been found. An ounce may be considered as the average from a full grown animal, but as the greater proportion of the deer are killed young, the pods in the market do not contain, on an average, more than half an ounce. The pod from our deer yielded one and one quarter ounces, that from the Bengalese contained only an ounce. The musk of young animals, though not so strong, has a much pleasanter smell than that of old ones ; difference of food, climate, or situation does not seem to effect the quality.

Before we cut the pod from our deer, we bound around our mouths and noses several folds of linen, as otherwise, so pungent is the smell, it might cause hemorrhage. As, however, the Puharries take good care to adulterate the musk before it is exported, we are not exposed to such accidents at home. It is scarcely possible to detect the imposture of adulteration at the time of purchase, as the pods are generally sold without being cut open.

" I have often seen offered for sale," remarked the Hindoo perfumer, " pods which were merely a piece of musk deer skin, filled with some substance, and tied up to resemble a musk-pod, with a little musk rubbed over it to give it the proper odor. These are easy to detect, there being no navel on the skin as it is cut from any part of the body. But the musk is also sometimes taken out of the pod, and its place filled by some other substance ; these are difficult to detect even if cut open, as whatever is put in, is made to resemble musk in appearance, and only a small quantity of genuine musk added to give it the requisite odor.

" Some have a portion of the musk taken out and its place supplied ; others have all the musk left in, and something added to increase the weight. The substances commonly used for adulteration, or to fill the counterfeit pods, are blood boiled or baked on the fire, then dried, beaten to powder, kneaded into a paste, and made into grains and coarse powder, to resemble genuine musk; a piece of liver or spleen prepared in the same manner; dried gall, and a particular part of the bark of the apricot tree, pounded or kneaded. The dried paste from which common oil has been extracted, called "peena," is also used, and lumps of this without further preparation are thrust into a pod. Sometimes no care is taken to give the material employed in filling a counterfeit pod even the appearance of musk. A gentleman once showed me a pod he had bought from a Puharrie. On my telling him it was counterfeit, he cut it open, and found it filled with hookah tobacco."

The original extract of musk is principally used for a fixing ingredient in other perfumes, to give a permanancy to a volatile odor; customers requiring in a general way that which is incompatible — namely, that a perfume shall be strong to the smell, very volatile, and that it shall remain upon the handkerchief for a long period, *ergo*, not volatile!

"Small portions of extract of musk, mixed with essence of roses, extract of violet, and tuberose, and similar solutions, do in a measure attain this object; after the violet, which is the most delicate, has evaporated, and is followed in its turn by the other odors according to their volatility, the handkerchief still retains an odor, which, although not the original, yet gives satisfaction, because it is pleasant to the olfactory nerves."

It is the fashion of the present day for people to say, "I do not like musk," but nevertheless, from great experience in the sale of perfumery, we are of the opinion that the public taste fo:

musk is as great as any perfumer need desire. The Empress
Josephine was very fond of perfumes, and particularly of musk.
Her boudoir was filled with it, in spite of Napoleon's frequent
remonstrances. Sixty years have elapsed since her death, and
the present owner of Malmaison has had the walls of that dressing room repeatedly washed and painted, but neither scrubbing,
aquafortis, nor paint, has been able to remove the smell of the
good Empress's musk, which continues as strong as if the bottle
which contained it had been but yesterday removed.

We encamped for the night, and in the morning descended the
mountains on the opposite side to that which we had ascended.
On our way to Benares, we saw some trees of very graceful form
the trunks about nine inches in diameter, and the tree about
twenty feet high, growing out of masses of naked marble rocks
on the brink of precipices, presenting a very picturesque appearance. These, our guide informed us, were the *luban meyeti*,
which produce the luban or frankincense, the same as the gum
olibanum of commerce. On making a deep incision into the
trunk, the resin exudes profusely, of the color and consistency
of milk, but hardening into a mass by exposure to the air. The
young trees produce the best and most valuable gum, the older
trees merely yielding a clear glutinous fluid resembling copal, and
exhaling a strong resinous odor.

Olibanum was formerly in high repute as a sovereign remedy
against inflamation of the eyes, and as an efficacious remedy in
consumption, but for these purposes it has long gone out of use,
and is chiefly bought up by the Greek merchants for the use of
the Church. It is also produced by the *luban bedowi*, but not of
so good a quality. It is partially soluble in alcohol, and like
most of the balsams, probably owes its fragrance to a peculiar

odoriferous body, associated with the benzoic acid it contains. It is not much used in perfumery at the present time.

We reached Benares in time to attend the auction, and purchased a small lot of the sandalwood, and the otto.

The next morning, after we reached Benares, we took a boat and sailed swiftly down the Ganges. We saw on the river banks many fine gardens, and estates on which were growing patchouly plants. These plants resemble somewhat our garden sage in their growth and form, but the leaves are not so fleshy.

We entered Calcutta in the afternoon, and went directly on board the *Cynthia*, and were gladly welcomed back by all our friends. After relating our adventures to my wife, Susie, Brad, and John Gagler, we retired, feeling pretty well exhausted. Brad was not ready to sail as yet, and doubted if he would be for two or three days. Some gum olibanum, that we bought at Benares, Jean found was obtained from various species of *Boswellia, serrata, thurifera,* and *glabra*. It is the frankincense of the ancients, and the luban of the Arabs.

12

CHAPTER XXI.

WE were up bright and early, when Brad congratulated us on our success of the previous day, and informed us he had received an invitation to a Hindoo wedding, and asked us if we would like to attend.

"Certainly," we replied. "Can we all go?"

"It will be celebrated in the open air, so there will be room enough," he answered. "It is an old acquaintance of mine who is to be married, one with whom I traded when sailing with my uncle. They are quite wealthy, so it will be a grand affair."

Immediately after breakfast, we prepared ourselves and set out for the house of Brad's friend, where we arrived early enough to allow us sufficient time to observe that the house was arranged in half Hindoo, and half English style.

As they make a lavish use of perfumes in Hindoo private life, the number of presents made to the bride elect, by the bridegroom, were rich and numerous. They were displayed on a table in the room into which we were ushered. The *Singardan*, or toilet bag, which was one of them, contained among other things, a *pandan*, or box to hold betel, an aromatic mixture for chewing, to perfume the breath ; a vial containing otto of roses, a *goolabpash* or

178

bottle to sprinkle rosewater on visitors, a box or casket, richly carved, made of sandalwood, for containing spices, and one of ebony, inlaid with gold, for holding *meese*, a powder made of gall-nuts and vitriol, for *blackening* the teeth, — women blacken their teeth when they marry, and keep them so as long their husbands are alive. Another box for *soorma* to blacken the eyelids, and another for *kajul* to darken the eyelashes. These boxes were elegantly inlaid and incrusted with jewels.

The time for the ceremony having arrived, we proceed to the garden. Here, under a sort of canopy, called *peudal*, which was richly ornamented and brilliantly lighted with lamps, the bride and bridegroom sat, or rather squatted at one end, and at the other burned the sacred fire or *oman*, which was constantly kept alight by throwing into it sandalwood, incense, scented oils, and other ingredients, which shed aromatic fumes. The bride was good looking, with regular features and bright black eyes ; her hair was of a beautiful glossy black, almost jet, and quite long. It was anointed with a highly perfumed oil, and a profusion of jewels adorned it. She would have laid still more claim to beauty, but for the nose-ring, which, though very costly and elegant, must have been decidedly inconvenient.

One of the bridesmaids had her hair embellished with the blossoms of the silvery jasmine, and the hair of the other with the flowers of the golden champac, which set off admirably their raven tresses. Above their ears were placed blossoms of a sort of acacia, called *Sirisha*.

The Brahmins, after having recited a variety of prayers, consecrated the union of the couple by throwing a handful of saffron mixed with rice flour on their shoulders, and the ceremony was ended by the husband presenting his wife with a little golden

image, called *talee*, which is worn around the neck by married women as a substitute for the wedding ring. After the ceremony we
presented our gifts, and among other things gave them perfumes
as we understood that was the custom, a scented powder, called
abeer, which is sprinkled on the clothes, or rubbed on the face
and body, and is made of sandalwood, aloes, tumeric, roses, camphor, and civet; *Uggur-kee-buttees*, or pastils, made of gum
benzoin, and other odoriferous substances; *Urgujja*, a sweet
ointment, composed of sandalwood, aloes, otto of roses, and extract of jasmine; also *Munjun*, a tooth powder, which was a mixture of burnt almond-shells, tobacco ashes, black pepper, and
salt, all of which we bought of our friend, the Hindoo perfumer
for this occasion, as we should not care to use them ourselves.

Paying our respects, we made our salutations, and then, as we
had some spare time, proceeded to the Botanical Gardens for a
promenade. These gardens are very beautiful, and contain an
immense variety of plants, growing in the most luxuriant manner.
Susie pointed out to us a group of *Styrax benzoin* trees, from
which is procured that substance most in use by perfumers, and
is considered the best of all the balsams, with the exception, perhaps of the genuine balsam of Mecca — *Gum amyris opobalsam*,
which is so scarce and expensive it is not used. The kings of
Judah cultivated the shrub, but only to a very small extent.
What is generally sold by the name of Balsam of Mecca is merely
the oil, obtained by boiling the seeds, stones, and branches of
the tree. It is too rare to be purchased at any price, as it is generally supposed to be.

A bottle of this extraordinary balsam is kept at the botanical
garden at Paris, as an object of the rarest and highest value.
Josephus informs us that the Queen of Sheba brought it first to

Judea, where balsam. myrrh, and incense, in the days of old were to be seen used by the populace in abundance, almost daily. This is one of the many things we "mourn for" in the "days gone by." The reason of its excessive scarcity is supposed to be owing to the destruction of Jerusalem; the Jews, actuated by despair and hatred, destroyed all the balsam plants. There are none now to be found in Palestine. Only one plantation is now known to furnish it, and that is in Arabia Petrea. The whole plantation only yields about three pounds annually, and it is monopolized by the Grand Seignior. This, of course, we can scarcely refrain from noticing, without an expression of regret.

The Gum Benzoin, or Gum Benjamin, as some call it, used to be called Amygdaloides, because of its being interspersed with several white spots which resemble broken almonds. When heated, these white specks rise as smoke, which is easily condensed upon paper. The material thus separated from the benzoin is known in commerce as the flowers of benzoin, and chemically as benzoic acid. The best gum benzoin is obtained from Siam, but we could not possibly visit there, as we did not wish to waste any more of Brad's time; but we obtained a small quantity from the chief florist, which he had gathered from the trees growing in the garden. It is generally obtained by making incisions in the trunk of the tree, after it has attained the age of five or six years. The resin is white and transparent at first, then drying, becomes a hard gum resin. The benzoin usually brought into the market is dark, with the white spots only showing slightly, and when put with alcohol there is a great deal that does not dissolve, and is useless; but the specimen we obtained was in small lumps, all white, with a very slight transparent brownish tint on the surface, the lumps, however, when broken, showing perfectly white inside, and when put in alcohol they dissolved completely.

From the Gardens we proceeded to the Strand, the principal promenade of the Europeans and wealthy natives, and after a short stroll as it was getting late, and wishing to reach the ship before dark, we turned our steps towards the vessel.

During our absence the ship's bunkers had been stowed with coal, but owing to some delay we were not ready to start till after nine o'clock the next morning. Jean had gone on shore again to purchase some joss sticks, and some coconut oil, an opaque, unctuous oil obtained from the coconut, and having a delicate odor of the nut, much used by the Germans in making soap. He also showed us some balls of opium, scented with the essence of roses, which he had bought of the Hindoo perfumer, such as the wretched, cadaverous, idiotic, opium smokers consume, many of whom we had seen in our wanderings. They looked not unlike, and reminded us of the tobacco consumers of our own nation.

Opium is smoked at all hours by men and women in this country, as well as in the Celestial Empire. The English merchants sell every year of this miserable drug to the amount of one million five hundred thousand pounds — millions of dollars devoted to one of the most despicable of vices which afflict humanity; but yet how small is the sum compared to that wasted upon the slower, but no less certain brain-destroyers, liquor and tobacco.

Towards the cool of the evening Jean invited us into the laboratory, or "Perfumatory" as he sometimes called it.

"I will now show you how to prepare cassie pomade, or floral pomade of any odor you wish, when you have the flowers with which to work," he said to us, after we had assembled. "It is called maceration. You remember I promised sometime ago to instruct you in the art, but have not had the time since we left Australia. Patsey, bring me the new glue pot."

" I will that, sir."

" This glue pot, you see," continued Jean, " melts the material by the boiling of water; it is in fact a water-bath, in chemical parlance, on a small scale. I use beef suet or any grease in preference to lard, as pomades of lard body are more heating, causing dandruff and falling of the hair, especially where the system is scrofulous. I have prepared some beef suet which has been purified by melting and straining it through a close hair sieve, allowing the liquid suet to drop into cold water, thereby granulating, and washing the blood and membrane from it. In order to start with a perfectly inodorous grease I repeated the process three times, using a pinch of salt and a pinch of alum, to each water, then I washed it six times in plain water, and finally remelted the fat to free it from adhering water, and added a small quantity of powdered benzoin.

" Now, Patsey, put the clarified suet into this macerating pot, and we will proceed."

Patsey did so, and Jean went to one of the lockers and took out the dried cassie flowers, and putting as many in the fat as it would cover, let it simmer slowly on the fire of a small gas stove.

" I shall leave this to cook during the night; in the morning I shall strain off the fat and add more flowers till I obtain the strength of perfume I wish."

" Oh!" exclaimed Susie.

" What is the matter?" asked Jean.

" Some of that hot grease spattered all over the back of my hand, and has burnt me."

Her hand was indeed quite badly burned

"Wait a moment, Miss Susie," said Jean, and he hurried to his collection of ottos, and selecting his sample of otto of cloves, applied some of the otto with a small piece of cloth to the burn, a small place at a time being covered so the pain would not be so great as if the whole place was covered at once. "In a very little while your hand will not feel painful in the least, Miss Susie," said Jean. "Otto of cloves takes out the fire from a burn the quickest and best of anything I know."

It was true, for Susie felt no pain after a few minutes.

CHAPTER XXII.

A BEWITCHED SHIP AND CREW.

"WHAT is in that glass tunnel?" asked my wife, who having bound up Susie's hand, was now watching Jean at work among his collections; she pointed at the same time to a percolator in which Jean had some article from which he was obtaining an extract by displacement or percolation, the most approved method of obtaining extracts in small quantities, of uniform strength and in a short space of time.

The article being powdered, a diaphragm put in the tunnel to allow the liquid to pass slowly through the material from which the extract is made, then after the material has stood twenty-four hours in absolute alcohol, it is put into the percolator and the liquid, generally absolute alcohol, sometimes only proof spirit, is put in the percolator on the material, and as each portion of it displaces that before it, it gathers the virtues of the material which are found in the liquid in the receiver; the spirit left in the article is displaced by an equal quantity of water, and thus nothing is lost.

"That is the opium I showed you this morning," replied Jean. "I am preparing an extract from it."

"You did not soak it long in the alcohol?" I asked.

"No, sir. I thought it would not matter, as by having it per-colate very slowly I could obtain such an extract as I wished, merely for an experiment."

In the morning Jean repaired to the laboratory and strained off the fat from the cassie flowers and added fresh ones.

We were steaming south'ard now as fast as possible, for Brad wanted to visit every island in the vicinity of Australia, before giving up his quest.

The next evening we were almost opposite the Island of Cey-lon, and soon we should be far out in the Indian Ocean. We were sitting around the tables in the saloon. My wife and Susie at one ; their table covered with sewing, tatting work, and tidies ; John Gagler, Brad, and I were at the other — John Gagler and myself conversing, and Brad studying a chart of the islands near Australia. Jean was in the laboratory at work experimenting, as usual. Soon Patsey came and announced supper, also calling Jean from the laboratory.

After supper we again repaired to the saloon. The night being somewhat chilly and very cloudy we did not care to go on deck. About nine o'clock a peculiar, uncertain motion of the ship at-tracted Brad's attention, and he went on deck to ascertain the cause ; after sometime he returned, and we inquired, —

"What was the trouble?"

"The man at the wheel was overtaken with a sudden drowsi-ness, and had actually fallen asleep at his post ; that was the rea-son the ship staggered so," he replied. "We could only arouse him a little, and could not obtain anything intelligible from him. I ordered him to be taken to his berth, and when he awakes I will have an investigation."

Scarcely half an hour had elapsed before Mr. Roscoe sum-

VICK'S

FLORAL GUIDE

FOR 1882

IS AN ELEGANT BOOK OF 150 PAGES,
A COLORED FRONTISPIECE OF FLOWERS,
And 1,000 ILLUSTRATIONS of the CHOICEST
FLOWERS, PLANTS, AND VEGETABLES,

And Directions for Growing

It is Handsome enough for the Centre-Table or a Holiday Present.

Send on your name and post-office address, with 10 cents, and I will send you a copy, postage paid. This is not a quarter of its cost. I publish both an English and German Edition. Paper and printing and matter are not surpassed for excellence by anything in the country, and the illustrations are in the highest style of art.

VICK'S SEEDS ARE THE BEST IN THE WORLD.

The FLORAL GUIDE will tell you how to get and grow them.

VICK'S FLOWER AND VEGETABLE GARDEN.

175 pages, a colored plate, 500 engravings. For 50 cents in paper covers; $1.00 in elegant cloth. In German or English.

VICK'S ILLUSTRATED MONTHLY MAGAZINE.

32 pages, a colored plate in every number, and many fine engravings. Price, $1.25 a year; Five copies for $5.00. Specimen numbers sent for 10 cents; 3 trial copies for 25 cents.

ADDRESS - - - JAMES VICK, ROCHESTER, N.Y.

moned Brad, and he went on deck again. Jean having com-
plained of being tired had gone into his cabin. After Brad went
out my wife and Susie soon showed unmistakable signs of sleepiness by nodding over their work and suddenly recovering themselves, and trying to continue where they left off. I told them
they had better retire, and they did so. Brad soon after came in
looking somewhat perplexed. He saw my questioning glance.

"It is strange," he mused; "we have changed the man at the
wheel three times since I went out, and each and every one after
standing there less than fifteen minutes, has been overcome by
sleep and had to be taken to his berth. The fifth man is at the
helm now, and if they keep on at this rate another hour, we shall
not have enough left to carry us through the night."

"Th-at's a fa-a-ct," I answered, trying hard to suppress a
gape. "I—believe I'm getting sleepy myself," and I hurried
through the last part of the sentence, fearing I should gape again
before I could finish it.

"I shall be obliged to put you to bed also," said Brad, laughing. "Come out on deck and get the fresh air," and he pulled
me up by the shoulder; shaking myself, I was about to accompany Brad up stairs, when I noticed John Gagler, who was resting his arms on the table and his head upon them, almost
asleep.

"Come, John, you are sleepy too," I said. "Better go to
bed."

"Aye, aye, sir;" he muttered, but did not stir till I shook
him pretty hard.

"Aye, aye, sir;" he again said, rousing himself and rising.

"Halmost doused my top lights, didn't I? I guess its habout

time to turn hin. I feel h-awfully slee-slee-py," and he gaped himself into his cabin.

Rubbing my eyes and stretching my limbs, I followed Brad, who had preceded me, on deck. On coming into the fresh air it revived me somewhat, and finding Brad, who was watching the man in the wheel-house, — not the fifth one, but the seventh, the fifth and another had succumbed to that strange drowsiness. What could it be? I confess I felt a little uneasy myself, and cast furtive glances around, expecting to see some enemy.

The man now at the helm, Robert Hannaburn, was a powerfully built and strongly constitutioned Englishman, who had lived on the seas from boyhood, and feared neither visible nor invisible adver-sary ; even he, however, looked often with sidelong glance over his shoulder, and with questioning eyes sought courage from his Captain's face. Brad watched him closely, and the man strug-gled hard to control himself.

Sailors have their superstitions and fears, and many a brave fellow who in broad daylight, would fight till the last breath while their enemy was before them, yet when something inexpli-cable surrounds them, and the winds moan, and the dark clouds flit by full of mocking faces, their imagination conjures up all sort of hideous beings.

Hannaburn stood firm as a rock, but his fingers would some-how seem to lose their power for a moment, and the wheel slip almost from his grasp, yet he strove to keep his post. Slowly, but surely, the influence overpowered him, his strength left him, his head dropped forward ; again he started up, shook himself like a huge dog, threw out his broad chest, drew in a long, deep breath, and looked defiance at his unseen antagonist.

How long we sat watching him I know not. I felt a hand laid on my shoulder and awaking with. a start, saw Mr. Roscoe standing by me. Brad was still watching the wheel-house, but not the man at the wheel, for no one was there. Mr. Roscoe approached Brad and spoke to him, but receiving no answer, looked at his face, and saw by the light from the wheel-house that he was asleep. Mr. Roscoe took hold of his arm, and Brad suddenly opened his eyes. Looking towards the wheel, the man he expected to see was not there ; he went to the door and opened it and found Hannaburn lying beside the wheel sleeping soundly ; we drew him out of the wheel-house on to the deck, but no effort could rouse him, so we conveyed him to his berth, putting another man in his place.

This last man seemed loth to take the position, and when we went into the forecastle we found the night-watch, and some others who had not as yet retired, huddled together in groups, conversing in low tones ; and when they saw Hannaburn brought in, their faces assumed a queer, half-frightened expression, yet they said not a word, but tried hard to make believe they were employed about something ; we placed Hannaburn in his berth. Brad turned to his men and simply said, —

" I hope every man is ready for duty to-night."

They touched their caps, and their " Aye, aye, sir," though audible, was feebly given.

The sailor who succeeded Hannaburn was soon as fast asleep as his predecessors, and when Mr. Roscoe and I took him to his bunk the other men were thunderstruck, and endeavored to get behind each other, fearing to be the next one ordered to the mysterious wheel-house. After selecting another man, Mr. Roscoe commanded a young fellow, named Burndom, who had always shown himself possessed of considerable courage and daring, to

WE DREW HIM OUT OF THE WHEEL-HOUSE.

come on deck and be ready to take the wheel if this last man should succumb to that insiduous influence.

He followed us with faltering steps, and stopped a short distance from the gangway. But when he saw the man sinking down, overcome by that inexplicable, mysterious opponent, he sank to the deck, and crawled with shaking limbs to the gangway, and almost threw himself headlong down.

We heard the sailors jump up in fear, and a second after, the scuttle was closed with a bang, and with all our entreaties, commands, and threats, we could not induce them to open it. Brad had the wheel; he and Mr. Roscoe were nonplussed.

Surrounded by some enemy whom they could not see, ten of the men sick, asleep, or dying, they knew not which, the rest in mutiny, the ship in the middle of a vast ocean with only three or five at most to run her through the night, and they too liable to be overpowered! What accidents might happen! Where might they not be driven?

The engines still worked, the engineer stood to his post. He had not, however, ascertained what had occurred above him, or he perhaps would desert us. Anyway we decided not to call him, or let him get an inkling of what had happened.

We were still heading south, a little to the east of south, and going at a good speed. Mr. Roscoe now took the wheel, telling Brad to retire and rest an hour, and then he might relieve him. Brad would not, however, listen to any such arrangement.

"I am afraid you too will be asleep if I leave you five or ten minutes," said Brad, jokingly.

"Never fear," replied Mr. Roscoe. "The men are only frightened, and it is their imagination perhaps, that puts them under the spell; imagination will do almost anything with a man. You can stay here and watch me awhile, and if I show any signs of faltering, you can then relieve me; but I must first open one of these windows and get some fresh air in here, even if it does almost blow my head off," and he lowered one of the small windows as he spoke.

We watched Mr. Roscoe for half an hour and as he showed no signs of drowsiness, we began to think he was right, and that it was only the imagination of the sailors which had overcome them. Brad went to the cabin, and I sat on deck to watch an hour, and then I was to call him to relieve Mr. Roscoe.

The hour passed, and I was just falling into a refreshing slumber, when the voice of Mr. Roscoe aroused me, and he told me to call Capt. Cole. The wind had now increased to a gale, and as I arose, almost blew me from my feet; my eyes were half closed, and I staggered and stumbled about trying to reach the cabin; as I was going down the stairs to the saloon, I glanced toward the wheel-house and noticed Mr. Roscoe had closed the window again, within a couple of inches, the driving rain was so disagreeable, and I also perceived that he was unaccountably uncertain on his feet, or else I was, I could not tell which. Going to Brad's cabin I shook him and he said, —

"All right! I'm coming in a moment — be there in a minute."

I was too sleepy to wait till he went out, so telling him I was going to retire, as it was past midnight, I bid him "good-night," and entering my cabin, with difficulty divested myself of my clothing. I could never remember the time when I had ever felt so drowsy. Looking at my wife, I saw she was sleeping soundly. My entrance did not wake her. Putting out the light, I tumbled into my berth and dropped to sleep instantly.

I WAS STANDING AT THE ENTRANCE OF A HUGE EGYPTIAN
TEMPLE.

Page 192.

I felt as if I was borne on the winds, was drifted about from place to place, uncertainly, faintly heard thumpings and noise as of a commotion of the elements. It must have been dreamland, for shortly after a strange scene was spread before me.

I was standing at the entrance of a huge Egyptian Temple, one of those built when Egypt was in its glory, and the world was young. It was a pile of granite so stupendous that the mind could hardly conceive of such grandeur and vastness. On the side walls were sculptured statues of former sovereigns, in size ten times as large as life. In the centre of the Temple was a golden statue of their god, as large as a man, and on an altar, which was also of massive gold, burned a thousand talents worth of pure incense. Masses of swarthy Egyptians thronged the streets and byways. Some grand festival seemed preparing.

Faintly wafted by the breeze music presently reached my ears. Shortly after, in front of me moved a magnificent procession; clouds of incense, and bursts of harmony burdened the air. First came a long array of priests dressed in gorgeous robes, preceded, accompanied, followed, by five hundred of Egypt's finest formed youth, their hair profusely powdered with gold and diamond dust, which glittered and sparkled in the sun, producing a most brilliant effect. The air was filled with the smell of odoriferous substances diffused by the censers which each one carried firmly in his right hand, and into it cast with his left hand, balls of perfume. Behind these marched one hundred and twenty children, bearing incense, myrrh, and saffron in golden basins, followed by a number of camels ladened with frankincense, crocus, cassia, cinnamon, orris and other precious aromatics, each bearing three hundred pounds weight of the different articles.

Then came two hundred of Egypt's fairest women, sprinkling every one with perfume from golden watering pots; then a host of boys in rich purple tunics; following them two incense burners made of ivy wood, covered with burnished gold, and a large square altar between them. These were borne by stalwart men, whose muscles seemed playing under their burden.

The huge altar was placed in the centre of the square opposite the entrance of the temple, and the vast procession formed itself around about. An ox was brought forth for the sacrifice and filled with frankincense, myrrh, and other aromatic substances which the camels bore; the remainder was put into the large incense burners. They placed the ox upon the altar, and as he burned, fragrant oils were poured over him.

From the Temple were now brought forth four sepulchral vases; the first, surmounted with a human head, was consecrated to Am-set, the genius presiding over the South; the second vase, covered with a cynocephalus, was dedicated to Ha-pin, the genius of the North; the third, decorated with a jackal's head, in honor of Trant-mutf, the genius of the East; and the fourth, ornamented with a hawk's head, was put under the protection of Krebsnif, the genius of the West. After these ceremonies the viscera of some recently deceased and embalmed king were divided; in the first vase were put the large intestines, in the second one, the small viscera, in the third, the heart and lungs, and in the fourth, the liver and gall-bladder. This being done, the vases were filled with perfumes to ensure the preservation of their contents. The music then burst forth anew, and the procession was commencing to form; I turned to go into the Temple, when one of the Egyptians standing on the robe that had concealed me, pulled it off, and instantly a great

13

cry arose.   Seeing a being in the civilized costume of the year
eighteen hundred and seventy-four, among them of the early centuries, no wonder they thought I was what they called me.

" Satan ! "

" The Evil One ! "

" Seize him ! " they exclaimed in their language.

I was seized and conveyed before the head priest, thinking to
themselves, probably, that they had really caught the devil, and
that they would now dispose of him for all time.

The council of priests decided to seal me up in a sepulchral
vase, and have me thrown from the top of the Temple.   I struggled, but in vain ; the odds against me were too great.   The vase
was brought forth, one whose cover was ornamented with a cynocephalus, whether as a compliment to me or not, or it being the
first one convenient, I was unable to conjecture.   I was thrust in
and the cover hermetically sealed.   I felt the vase lifted from the
ground.

I knew they were carrying me up to some great height.   At
last the vase containing me was set down, and I felt it sway to
and fro, then after a short while I felt myself turning over as
though thrown from one side of the vase to the other — felt myself going down, down ; losing all control of myself, my head
went thumping and banging against the sides of the jar ; suddenly
the vase was shivered into atoms and I shot out into space and
became unconscious.

THE VASE WAS SHIVERED INTO ATOMS AND I SHOT OUT
INTO SPACE.

Page 194.

CHAPTER XXIII.

A STRANGE SAIL.

EARLY on a misty morning, within a few miles of the city of Aden, in the Gulf of Aden, there might have been seen a steam screw propeller yacht, of about three hundred and twenty tons burthen, with a ragged and torn foresail set, and the mainsail reefed and close-hauled, struggling hard, and swaying and drifting about uncertainly in the heavy waves. Either an inexperienced hand held the wheel, or else he was wearied by the recent storm that had only just exhausted itself. Her actions were extremely strange; those on board the various vessels passing her, remarked how unskillfully she was handled.

No sailor aloft, no sailors on the deck, no sign of life in any visible part of her. She still struggled on, or rather drifted with the tide, and her sails fluttered in the wind; her engines were not working. No smoke issued from her smoke-stack. The sun rose higher and higher, and the mist wholly cleared away, showing a beautifully clear sky. The yacht still rode tipsily along, presently attracting the attention of a group of officers of an English man-of-war lying at anchor in the harbor. So singular were her movements, every moment seeming as she floundered in the trough of the sea as though she would be capsized, that even the idlers on shore were disturbed from their lazy attitudes to watch her manœuvres.

Where were her crew? Her passengers? Her commander?

She showed no indication to heave to. No signals were given, and she blindly drove on, seemingly not knowing whither she went. Soon a boat pushed off from the man-of-war, and was rowed hastily towards the strange ship.

The officer hailed "Ship ahoy!" but no answer being returned he hauled alongside, boarded amidships, and standing upon the bulwarks looked around him.

The deck was deserted. No living thing in sight. Two other officers following the first, the three proceeded to the wheel-house. As soon as they reached the deck, the odd actions of the ship were more clearly perceptible.

Here in the wheel-house, as they opened the door, they saw stretched, almost at full length beside the wheel, a man, — a finely formed, well built man; his head, from which his cap had fallen, showing a mass of beautiful, wavy, chestnut hair, rested upon his arm; he breathed easily and naturally, so their fears that he was dead, and that some foul tragedy had been enacted on the high seas, were dispelled.

"Worn out at his post by over exertion in the storm," remarked the officer, who first scaled the ship's side.

They placed him in a sitting posture, and tried to arouse him. His arms, however, hung loosely, and his head sagged to one side. Lifting him out into the air they renewed their exertions and ordered those in the boat to make fast and come on board to drop the anchor, for the ship was fast drifting towards the shore; after a short time they revived the man somewhat. He looked vacantly around and tried to rise to his feet, but sank back, and

BOARDED AMIDSHIPS, AND STANDING UPON THE BUL-
WARKS, LOOKED AROUND HIM.

Page 196.

would have again dropped to sleep, but for the clear, fresh air
which he inhaled.

Leaving one of the officers in charge of this man, the other two
ordering two of their men to follow them, proceeded to the cabin;
but it appeared deserted; looking closer they noticed that the
door of the first stateroom leading from the large cabin was ajar.
Entering, they saw a man dressed as a ship's captain, asleep in
his berth, and after much difficulty, partially aroused him, so that
he gained his feet and tried to walk out into the large saloon, but
would have fallen had not one of the sailors from the boat caught
him.   Having had some experience with the other man, they had
the captain taken on deck immediately.

The noise made in resuscitating the captain, disturbed an oc-
cupant of one of the other staterooms, and soon a door opened,
and a man, evidently a foreigner, went stumbling along towards
the rear of the large saloon, as if bent upon accomplishing some
design, but soon he pitched headlong into one of the large easy-
chairs near, and was carried by the sailors to the deck.   The
officers followed, and going to where they had left the man discovered in the wheel-house, they were somewhat surprised to see
him suddenly arouse himself as if from napping, and salute them
with the question and request of, —

"Mr. Montague, have you spoken to Captain Cole to relieve
me?   Please tell him to hurry, as I feel a little sleepy, an unaccountable feeling of drowsinesss is coming over me."

Yes, it is the same *Cynthia* which we left in the Indian Ocean,
now in the Gulf of Aden, hundreds of miles out of her course.

A moment later the scuttle of the forecastle was thrown off and
up on the deck poured such a cadaverous, half-stupefied, hungry
looking set of men as one would seldom wish to see.   Their cloth-

ing was rumpled, their hair dishevelled, and their gait, as each
one tottered to some place to rest, was as uncertain as that of
some drunken idiot.

The fresh air very quickly revived them.   A stout little fellow
emerged from the crowd, in whom will be recognized Patsey ; he
advanced to the group surrounding Brad, Mr. Roscoe, and Jean,
and asked, —

"Shure, sir, an' have Misthur and Misthress Montague aris
yit?"

Jean, when he heard the question, having now recovered his
senses, jumped up and went down hurriedly into the cabin and began
to pound on my door and then on Susie's.   It broke up my dreams,
and it was probably the concussion of the knocking that made me
dream I was receiving blows on the head within that vase.   I was
glad, however, to find I was not really in a sepulchral vase.
Arousing myself with an effort, and wondering why I was called
so early, and what the hurry was, I dressed as quickly as possible.

I felt as if I had not slept half long enough.   It was as much
as I could do to awake my wife.   She would sink off to sleep
again as fast as I could arouse her.   I felt weak, as if I had not
eaten any supper, so I hastened as much as I could, for I thought
a breakfast would taste good.   I looked in the mirror while dressing, and could hardly recognize myself, so haggard, sickly, and
wasted I appeared, and I noticed my wife looked rather pale.

"Are you feeling well this morning?" I asked her.

"Oh, yes, well enough, only a little faint and hungry," she
replied.

I opened my stateroom door, and was surprised to find such a
number of people in the cabin, and strange faces too.   I saw

Capt. Cole helping Susie up the companion-way, and Jean was supporting John Gagler, and following Capt. Cole. I had rather a dizzy feeling come over me then, and I thought I would sit down a moment and think it over ; but I did not get far before I felt myself taken hold of and my steps directed towards the stairs leading to the deck. I made no resistance as I felt rather queer. Reaching the deck and recovering my senses somewhat, I inquired, —

"What is the matter? What is going to be done?" and gazing around, saw all our sailors, and noticed the strange manner in which they looked, as also did John Gagler, Brad, Jean, my wife, and Susie.

"It is all my fault, I —" said Jean.

"Beef-soup, ladies and gentlemen," announced the steward interrupting him.

"I had the steward prepare for us and the crew a light breakfast," continued Jean ; "it is as much as our stomachs can bear at present."

"I do feel somewhat hungry," I remarked, and taking a dish of soup which was handed me, ate it with relish.

"Do you know how long it is since you had your supper, Mr. Montague?" asked Jean.

"It is now about nine o'clock, I should judge by the sun, for my watch has run down," I replied, "and we had supper about seven last evening, so it is about fourteen hours."

Jean laughed at my answer, and said, —

"It is *six days* and *fourteen hours!*"

I stared at him, as did my wife and Susie.

"What do you mean?" I asked, surprised.

"Why, do you not know where we are?" he queried, and

without waiting for a reply said, "this is the Gulf of Aden, and
that is the city of Aden, and February third, eighteen hundred
and seventy-four, we were in the Indian Ocean abreast Ceylon."
We looked incredulously at him.   "And now, February tenth,
we are in the harbor of Aden."

"How did it happen," I asked.

"You remember how sleepy and tired I felt that evening," responded Jean, "and how early I went to bed. Well, I had been
working in the laboratory, experimenting with that opium I
bought in Calcutta. Having made a very strong extract of it, I
thought I would see what would be the effect, or if it would dif-
fuse any odor, if burned in the Magic Perfumer, the red-hot star
apparatus; so I filled the jar and set it going. Patsey calling
me, I thought I would let it burn during supper and then stop it
afterwards; but after eating, probably being somewhat overcome
by the narcotic powers of the opium, working over it so long, I
forgot about the burning star, and retired. You know what
effect it had upon the men and upon us. Capt. Cole has been
telling me what occurred after I retired. The laboratory, you
know, is directly under the wheel-house, and the ventilator opens
into it; so the house becoming filled with the fumes of the opium,
the men were immediately affected by the narcotic, and could not
help falling asleep. Thus the watch asleep in their berths, thus
Susie and Mrs. Montague, thus John Gagler, yourself, Capt.
Cole, and Mr. Roscoe, the engineer and the firemen were overcome by the fumes of the opium permeating the ship. That
magic perfumer within fifteen minutes after being set to work,
will perfume a room thirty by forty feet with the odor of any extract put in it, so you can see that it did not take long to fill the
ship. There was a quart of the extract of opium in the jar, and

as it burns very slowly, the liquid must have lasted till within a day or two, a very little coming out at a time, just sufficient to keep us asleep; even now there is a taint of the fumes about the cabins."

"We may thank Heaven that we came out of it so well," said Brad, "for we have been driving along without a guide or help, at the mercy of wind and water, for we have passed through a storm, as you can see by the condition of the ship, — have been driven in exactly the opposite direction to that in which I wished to go, and have been starved almost to death. I feel as weak as a baby."

"I cannot express to you my regrets for my carelessness," said Jean, sorrowfully, "for endangering the lives of so many, and of my best friends."

We told him not to mention it, and that we were all liable to mistakes, and as he was confused by the narcotic, we could not censure him.

"You are very kind," he answered, "and as there are still some of the fumes of the opium about the ship, allow me to do my best to relieve you of it as far as lies in my power. Patsey, bring me all the matches that can be found in the ship, to spare, with Capt. Cole's permission."

"Certainly," replied Brad, "but no more experiments, if you please."

"Don't be alarmed, Captain," Jean answered, laughing.

Patsey brought a considerable number of matches, which Jean wet, and leaving some in a saucer on the table in the laboratory, and in the large cabin, opened the doors of the smaller cabins, and took some into the forecastle. The ozone coming from the wet matches soon purified the air. Capt. Cole meanwhile set his

men to work about the ship to repair what had been damaged
during the storm, and arrange everything "ship-shape." We
thanked the officers of the English ship for their assistance, and
excused ourselves for not inviting them to dine with us, nor ac-
cepting their invitation to dine with them, as we felt so miserable.

Admitting that we must be physically demoralized after passing through the ordeal we had, they bowed their adieus, and went
over the ship's side to their boat, and we saw them shortly after on
board their own vessel.   Brad had mattresses brought on deck,
and awnings raised, and the sailors and ourselves laid on deck
to inhale all the fresh air we could.   Little was done that was
not necessary; beef-soup was served three or four times during
the day; no hearty food was eaten.

The question was, "What course shall we now take?   Shall
we go back over the route we have just been driven, along the
eastern coast of Africa, or — "

"If I might propose a plan," spoke up Jean, "I would say
that as we are all weak and almost sick, a short delay might be
beneficial to us, and might relieve your mind, Capt. Cole, from the
strain it is under, while you are cruising for your father; it is, that
you will favor my father with a visit, at Grasse, France.   It is not
far from here, and in that beautiful climate and among the enchanting scenes of my boyhood home, we should soon recover
our sprightliness, and then with renewed vigor continue the
search."

We looked at Brad to see what his answer would be.

"I confess I feel as if all the energy and life were taken from
me," he said, "but whether the feeling will wear off in a day or
two, I do not know; but I see by your looks, Jean, that you
would like to see your father and home once more, and as noth-

ing would so fill my heart with joy as to see my father, I would certainly be selfish not to go out of my way a little to give you the same pleasure."

"How can I thank you, sir?" said Jean, feelingly.

Brad gave orders to have everything prepared to set sail in the evening. We sent a message of thanks to the officers of the man-of-war, "Gulnare," and about six o'clock steamed from the harbor of Aden towards the Red Sea.

CHAPTER XXIV.

IN a week from the time we left Aden, we reached Suez, steamed through the Suez Canal, and thence into the Mediterranean Sea. Our health had improved, but we had not wholly recovered from the anæsthetic effects of our narcotic. All we did, was to sit on deck and watch the passing scenes. The ship was headed towards Nice, the port at which we were to enter to reach Grasse, Jean's native place.

We should liked very much to have stopped at Messina, but concluded, as we had seen so many hundreds of lemon trees in our travels, that it would be only a repetition, consequently needless. There are hundreds of acres of them at Messina. The fine perfume of the lemon is abstracted by expression, and also by distillation of the rind of the fruit. The Otto of Lemon, which is procured by expression, has a much finer odor, and a more intense smell of the fruit, than the distilled product. As a distinction the expressed otto is called Otto of Citron Zest, and the distilled is known as the Otto of Lemon.

Otto of lemon, like all the ottos of the Citrus family, is prone to rapid oxidation when in contact with air and exposure to light; a high temperature is also detrimental, and as such is the case, it should be preserved in a cool, dark cellar. Rancid otto of lemon may in a great measure be purified by agitation with warm water, leaving the water in the bottle, and letting it stand until a mucilaginous preparation forms on the top of the water and acquires a certain tenacity, so that the otto may be poured off nearly to the last without disturbing the impurities.

The Otto of Bergamot, that most useful and delightful of ottos, is also manufactured in Messina, in large quantities, by expression from the peel of the fruit of the *Citrus bergamia*, of which there are numerous and large groves in and about the city. One hundred medium sized fruit will yield about three ounces of the otto. It has a soft, sweet odor, too well known to need a description. When new and good, it has a greenish yellow tint, but loses its viridity by age, especially if kept in imperfectly corked bottles. It then becomes cloudy from the deposit of resinous matter, produced by contact with the air, and acquires the odor of turpentine. It is best preserved, like otto of lemon, in a cool, dark cellar; light, especially the direct sunshine, quickly deteriorates its odor. This observation may be applied, indeed, to all perfumes, except rose, which is not so affected. When bergamot is mixed with other ottos it greatly adds to their richness, and gives a sweet and mellow tone to spice ottos, attainable by no other means, and such compounds are much used in the most highly-scented soaps.

The next day we were expecting to sight Nice, and at eight bells (four o'clock), we steamed into its beautiful harbor.

The perfume from the Flower Farms of the World, — this ever flowering Eden, whose products are the sources whence flow the streams of sweet odors, — was so balmy, so delightful, gave to the senses such a feeling of pure enjoyment, that could be gratified

without stint or danger, such unalloyed pleasure, that one felt as
if they could float forever around such a spot, so blessed; and,
with half-awakened sense perceive the beauties before their vision, and filled to over-flowing with voluptuous feeling, so deep, so
refined, intense and powerful, that life or death, earth or heaven,
could supply no more.

Steam was shut off, and the vessel allowed to drift slowly into
port, each one seemingly wishing to prolong the pleasure, to go on,
yet not to move, seeking for more, yet fearing to lose one iota.
In the distance rose the Estrelle Mountains, enclosing this beautifully situated place, as if the gods had chosen this spot as their
own, and had shut it in from the sight of the outer world to look
down upon from the mountains, and drink in the nectar that arose
from the beauteous plain.

From this favored spot come those balmy treasures, which so
delight the senses, — the Violet, Mignonette, Orange, Tuberose,
and many others. Near the mountains of the Estrelle, at the
foot of the Alps, the violets are found sweeter than if grown in
warmer localities, where the orange-tree and tuberose bloom to
perfection.

The perfume exhaled by the *Viola odorata* is so universally admired, that to speak in its favor would be more than superfluous.
These violet farms, from whence the flowers are procured to make
this perfume, are very extensive here in Nice. The true smelling principle, or Otto of Violets, has been isolated by M. March,
of this place, a sample of which we saw, but its cost being enormous and exhorbitant, we only looked at it.

Were it not for the exquisite odor of the mignonette, that little flower would scarcely be known otherwise than as a weed.
Sweet as it is in its natural state, and prolific in odor, it is not

possible to maintain its characteristic smell as an extract. Like many other odors during separation from the plant, the fragrance is variously modified; though not perfect, it still reminds the sense of the odor of the flowers. Extract of mignonette is often sold under the name of Extract of Reseda.

The Extract of Tuberose is a most exquisite odor. It is, as it were, a nosegay in itself, and reminds one of that delightful perfume which pervades the atmosphere at the close of day, in a well stocked flower garden in full bloom.

As Grasse was the place we wished to visit, we cared not to delay, for Jean was anxious to be on the way; so making arrangements for an early start, we made everything ready for the journey. Reaching Grasse on the following day we found it picturesquely situated on a declivity, commanding fine views in all directions. Through the country which we had passed, the roads were bordered with gardens teeming with flowers, for the inhabitants of this country raise flowers which are bought by the manufacturing perfumers, who, although they produce such immense quantities, do not have enough to supply their wants. Groves of orange and olive trees, the latter yielding the finest olive oil that is enfleured in the many perfumery establishments of this neighborhood, surrounded the residences and flower-farms.

Jean was in advance, and quite hurriedly conducted us forward, up a short ascent, then around a sharp turn to the left, and halted before a small cottage embowered in orange and olive trees, and surrounded with a well cultivated flower and kitchen garden. He had written letters to his father apprising him of his intended visit, and the old gentleman was daily expecting us, — his mother was dead, — so we were not surprised that the noise of our arrival brought to the door an old man, who, before we

were able to get a good view of him, was enfolded in the arms of
the impetuous Jean.

We waited patiently until their greetings were over, then Jean
remembering us, we were introduced and cordially welcomed by his
father. We found him very affable and profuse in his hospitality.

He was short of stature, thin, but of wiry build, and very, we
must say, exceedingly nervous and quick in his movements, but
withal agreeable and pleasing in manner; his head was quite bald
on top, and the hair around the back part of his head was gray;
a well trimmed, iron-gray beard and moustache covered the
lower part of his full and pleasant face. He was overjoyed to
see his boy once again, and we were well paid, to see what pleasure we had afforded these kind-hearted Frenchmen by our accept-
ance of Jean's invitation.

The old gentleman took a great fancy to Susie, and lavished his
attentions upon her, which seemed to please Jean greatly. Mons.
Guillaume Souplesse, wanted of course to hear all about our adventures, and so we had an abundance of subjects to converse upon;
besides this, Mons. Souplesse was kept continually busy by the
many questions of Jean about his old friends and acquaintances
of this, his native place.

The night was beautiful, the stars shone with brilliancy, the
moon all resplendent illumined the groves and cottages, strollers
passed by the house wandering in the bright moonlight.

It must have been about half-past ten or eleven. Mons. Souplesse was closing the doors for the night, and we were about to
retire, when we heard such a sweet, full, rich voice break the
stillness of the night with song that caused us all to pause; the
sound came from the rear of the cottage; we also faintly dis-
cerned the light notes of a guitar.

Fuller and sweeter the voice rose. The effect on us was magical. It thrilled us through and through with delightful feeling.

Jean had risen to his feet at the first intonation, and seemed spellbound to the spot where he stood, with head bent and pale face, he appeared to drink in each note with almost exquisite pain. Could music so move one!

In a moment his manner changed, he threw open a door, and almost pitched headlong down a flight of stairs.

His father looked amazed, frightened, and it must be acknowledged we were surprised at his apparently insane conduct.

We went to the stairway to see what had become of him, when he came up again two steps at time, rushed by us, listened for a moment, then said, breathlessly, —

" Excusez moi."

He went out into the street, and running at full speed, was quickly passing from sight, when Brad, Patsey and I set out in pursuit of him.

We just got sight of him again as he turned a corner, overturning a couple of brigandish looking Frenchmen from among a group of idlers, who were quick with their tongues to berate him for his awkwardness.

We noticed some others had joined in the pursuit, and quite a number were running after us to see what was the rumpus. We heard them cry, —

" Lunatique ! " " Maniaque ! " the while tapping their foreheads significantly.

It increased the excitement as a matter of course, for we saw idlers, men, boys, and dogs, gathering from all directions. We were gaining somewhat on Jean, when he once more went around a corner ; as we reached it, we heard the fine voice of the singer

14

WITH FRIGHTENED AIR BOUNDED AWAY.

Page 210.

more distinctly.   The song, however, was quickly broken, as she noticed the commotion.

We saw she was a young girl of perhaps twenty-two or twenty-three years of age, of lithe and graceful form.   Perceiving Jean running swiftly towards her, and hearing the exclamations of the mob, she grasped her guitar tightly, and with frightened air bounded away ; she went swiftly as a deer.   Jean seemed to be directing his attention especially to her, and when she started to flee, called to her.   We did not hear what he said, neither I think did she, for she took no notice of him.

He increased his speed.

Was he really crazy ! — mad ! — or chasing an ignis fatuus?

For awhile he did not gain on her, but her strength at last failing, she faltered, and putting her hand to her heart, she gasped for breath, and would have fallen had not Jean at this moment reached her, caught her in his arms, and rained kisses on her cheeks and lips.   We wondered if it was the custom in Grasse to chase any pretty young lady, to whose face or voice you happened to take a fancy, frighten her almost to death, and then revive her by kissing.

The crowd coming up, and seeing that Jean did not harm her, as they supposed he would, looked on inquiringly and volubly commented on the occurrence.   The young girl recovering under Jean's fervent treatment, looked up in amazement, and seemed surprised to find a fine looking young man caressing her, instead of being in the grip of a maniac.

Jean kissed her two or three times more, but she resisted stoutly, stood away from him, and drew herself proudly up, while blushes suffused her cheeks, and fire came into her dark, lustrous eyes.   Jean looked at her, the moon shone directly on her, clothing her in a halo of light. For a moment he was thunderstruck. Then begging her pardon, he covered his face with his hands, and acted extremely dejected.

The young girl seeing his attitude, and that there had really been a mistake, touched Jean on the arm, and in a low, sweet voice, told him she forgave him.

Jean did not know what to say.

Drawing nearer to them, we told her we would vouch for Jean, and assured her, although we knew not the cause of his impetuous actions, that he would no doubt at once give us an explanation, if she wished.

She said in English, "None required, as I see he thought I was some one else."

"If you will allow us, we will accompany you to your destination, and give these inquisitive parties less cause for noticing us," said Brad to her.

"And I should be happy to explain," said Jean. "I suppose you were surprised at my sudden flight, but her voice reminded me so forcibly of my lost sweetheart, I thought no one else could possess the like — the mademoiselle that was lost on board the steamer when I went to America — that when I heard this young lady, it flashed on me like electricity; for a moment I reeled, then fearing if it was really my lost love and that I might again lose her, I started in pursuit, thinking the while that she, too, by some unaccountable means, might have escaped from the wreck like myself. I had no idea I should attract so much attention, or place a stranger in such an embarrassing position, for I see I am mistaken. Poor Lilla!"

"Lilla!" exclaimed the young girl, looking at Jean inquiringly. "Lilla —"

"Lilla Montrose was her professional name — Lilla Stanley her real name," interrupted Jean, he in his turn looking questioningly at the girl.

"And Millie Stanley is my name, sir. She was my sister!"

"You! Her sister? You do not resemble her in the least, now that the moonlight strikes on you, so I can see you better, but your voice is exactly like hers," said Jean.

"Yes, poor Lilla! when the news came that she was lost, I knew not what to do," she said. "I —"

"Come," interrupted Brad, "this crowd is getting too familiar, let us return."

We had not moved as yet in either direction, and the mob was pressing upon us to hear the conclusion of the adventure.

The young girl shrank timidly away at his remark, and was about to depart, but Jean took hold of her arm lightly and detained her.

"You must go with us, mademoiselle, and tell us your story," said Jean. "You don't suppose we intend to lose you so quickly. If only for love of your lost sister, you should consider me your friend."

We proceeded onward.

Arriving at the house again, we found my wife, Susie, John Gagler, and Mons. Souplesse at the gate awaiting us with anxious looks. The young girl was at first loth to go in, but Jean at last persuaded her, and she bashfully entered.

"Come and sit beside me," said my wife; "let me take your guitar?"

We had now an opportunity to observe her. We noticed she was neatly, but poorly clad, and revealed to us a handsome face. She had naturally a dark complection, with deep, liquid eyes, a

Grecian nose, black, rippling hair; but she was now slightly pale, excepting when the blushes mounted to her cheeks at thoughts of her momentary embarrassing position. We related the circumstances of the chase, with many merry jokes at Jean's expense, and his absurd position, yet not without due respect being given to the memory of the lost sister.

"Miss Stanley," said Brad, " we should like you to finish your story now, which you will please excuse me for so abruptly interrupting."

"You are very kind, sir," she replied. "I was about to say, after Lilla was lost, I had no one to take care of me. I was quite young then, and Lilla was having me educated for a singer. When all the money was gone that she had sent to me, I was obliged to go to work, and I struggled hard. By denying myself many luxuries, I finally had money enough to come to Europe to finish my musical education, — the dream of my life. My health failing after I had commenced my studies, I came here knowing what a reputation this place bears for restoring the health of invalids. My funds gradually diminishing, I had no option but to use my accomplishments, and so, in the evenings, when I thought I should not be recognized, I have taken my guitar and sung about the streets. With the few sous I thus earn, I have eked out a scant living; but it does not matter, I shall soon go to meet my sister, where there is no want or hunger."

She completely broke down, and cried as if her heart would break.

Mons. Souplesse, my wife, and Susie did all they could to console her, and succeeded after awhile in drying her tears; then the old gentleman showed my wife an apartment, to which she conducted Millie, and remained with her till she sank into a sound slumber, holding tightly to my wife's hand, as if fearing to lose her, or wake and find it all a dream.

The next morning at breakfast, we each greeted Millie cordially, and were pleased to see that she had recovered from her fright. She was reluctant to stay any longer with us, but both Jean and Mons. Souplesse insisted that she must make their house her home.

" Father will soon have no one for company," said Jean, " as I must shortly leave with my friends. You will cheer him, and be a pleasant companion for him, and —"

" I cannot so impose on your kindness," she quickly interrupted. " I shall be well in a little while, then I can obtain something to do, and in a short time be comfortably situated, — an opening at some theatre perhaps."

" I have no doubt you could soon get an engagement to sing, when you are strong enough, as you have a splendid voice," said Mons. Souplesse ; " but you must stay with us until that time. So please say no more, mademoiselle."

Millie could not of course refuse again such kind offers, so expressing her gratitude by her looks, she bowed her head, and two or three large, bright tears chased each other down her cheeks, showing how full of thanks was her heart.

CHAPTER XXV.

SOON after breakfast the next morning, we started out to visit one of the largest of the many perfumery establishments in this place, to witness the processes in use, of which there are four, — distillation, expression, maceration, and absorption, — for extracting the aroma from fragrant substances.

We selected the house of Messrs. Bertrand Fréres, and under the escort of Mr. Henry Fielding, their affable agent, with whom we became slightly acquainted in the United States, we commenced our tour of observation on the lower floor, where the steam apparatus and the raw materials were kept. As the process of distillation, maceration, and expression have been described in previous chapters, we will go on; first however stopping to view the process of purifying pomades for absorption, or as the French call it, *enfleurage*.

The suet is first melted by the heat of a steam bath, in an enamelled iron vessel, and adding to it gradually one ounce of powdered alum, and two ounces of pure table salt, to every fifty pounds of fat under treatment, the heat is continued above 212° Fahrenheit until scum ceases to rise to the surface, which contains all the organic and other impurities, and is skimmed off as

WE COMMENCED OUR TOUR OF OBSERVATION ON THE LOWER FLOOR.

Page 215.

fast as it forms. The fat is then strained through bolting cloth into clean stone jars, and left to cool. It is next spread upon a circular and slightly conical stone slab, upon which rests a conical stone roller, the smaller end at the centre of the slab, and the larger end towards the circumference, which is turned by suitable gearing. As the roller or muller revolves over the fat, cold water is allowed to trickle upon the slab at its apex, and this as it passes to the margin, dissolves the saline impurities remaining in the pomade, and carries them off the outer edge. After this the fat is heated until all the water is expelled by evaporation.

During this last melting, about two and one-half ounces of powdered gum benzoin are added, and as the scum arises, it is removed. When cold, the fat is very white and pure, and may be kept for an indefinite period without changing or turning rancid; any one can judge from this, how much trouble is taken with pomades for the hair, and how little danger there is of their containing impurities deleterious to its growth and preservation. This pomade is then taken to the next floor above to be enfleured with some one of the flowers of this prolific place.

We ascended a flight of stairs and here we saw vast numbers of air-tight frames filled with pomades which were being enfleured. This process of procuring the perfumes of flowers is of all others the most important to perfumers.

"The odors of some flowers are so delicate and volatile, that the heat applied to them by distillation or maceration, would greatly modify, if not entirely destroy them," said Jean. "This process is therefore conducted cold."

We noticed that the frames were made square, about one inch deep, two feet wide and three feet long, with glass bottoms; over the glass a layer of the purified fat about a quarter of an inch thick is spread, with a plaster-knife or spatula; the flowers are distributed on a fine net mounted on a separate frame. This net is introduced between two of the glass frames. The whole series of frames are enclosed in an air-tight recess, and there left from twelve to twenty-four hours, and all that is required, is to draw out the frames every morning and renew the flowers, which give their aroma to the two surfaces of pomade with which they are in contact. This method was invented by Mons. D. Semiria, of Nice.

The same result is accomplished with oils. Coarse cotton cloths are soaked with the finest olive oil; these cloths are laid upon frames made of wire gauze, in lieu of glass, and a net with flowers is put between, the same as for the pomades. When the oil is sufficiently perfumed, — different flowers, according to their strength or delicacy, requiring a more or less number of renewals and time, — the cloths are subjected to a great pressure, to remove the perfumed oil.

A great variety of these pomades and oils are made here. Maceration and enfleurage are both founded on the affinity which fragrant molecules have for fatty bodies, — becoming fixed into them more readily than into any others. Thus the aroma of the flowers is first transferred to pomades and oils, which are made afterwards to yield it to absolute alcohol, whilst the latter, if placed in direct contact with the flowers, would not extract it from them.

The first attempt that was made in this way, some two hundred years ago, was to place almonds in alternate beds with fresh gathered flowers, renewing the flowers several days, and afterwards pounding the almonds in a mortar, and pressing out the oil which had absorbed the aroma. The same process we had seen used in India by natives for obtaining perfumed oils, they, however, using benne, gingelly, or sesamum seeds instead of almonds.

The next improvement was a plain, earthen pan, coated inside with a thin layer of grease, strewing the flowers on the grease, and covering it over with another pan similarly prepared. After renewing the flowers several times during a few days, the grease was found to have stolen their scent. This process was abandoned in France more than fifty years ago, but is still resorted to by Arabs, who were probably the inventors of it, the only difference being that they used white wax mixed with grease, on account of the heat of their climate.

"A very curious pneumatic apparatus for the same purpose has been invented by M. Piver, an eminent Parisian perfumer, who submitted a plan of it to the jury of the last Exhibition," said Mr. Fielding. "It consists of a series of perforated plates supporting flowers alternately with sheets of glass overlayed with pomade, in a chamber, through which a current of air is made to pass several times until all the scent of the flowers becomes fixed into the pomade.

"There is also a no less remarkable invention of a M. Millon, a French chemist, who found means to extract the aroma of flowers by placing them in a percolating apparatus, and pouring over them ether or sulphuret of carbon, which is drawn off a few minutes after, and carries with it all the fragrant molecules. It is afterwards distilled to dryness, and the result obtained is a solid, waxy mass, possessing the perfume of the flowers in its purest and most concentrated form. The process, although ingenious, has not received any practical application as yet, owing to the expense attending it, some of these concrete essences costing as much as two hundred and fifty dollars an ounce. It has, however, served to prove the total imponderability of fragrant molecules, for although this substance, from its high state of concentration, appears at first sight to be the solidified principle of scent, if it be treated several times successively with alcohol it gradually loses all its perfume, the alcohol receiving it, and yet the residue is found not to have lost one atom of its weight."

During the morning quite a number of cottagers had brought in their small lots of jasmin flowers, so we saw them placed between the two frames of pomade. The cultivation of the jasmin is very extensive here, and more so at Cannes du Départment du Var, a short distance from here, where is situated the well-known Laboratoire pour le Travail des Fleurs et des Ottos de Lubin, which we wished to visit, but thought we could not spare the time. The cultivated jasmin differs from the common jasmin, inasmuch as the blossoms are four times the size of the wild jasmin ; the plant also grows more like a small bush, and, not being a creeper, requires no support.

Susie called the cultivated jasmin, "*Jasminum Grandiflora.*"

Its growth and cultivation resemble very much that of English lavender. From the odors already known, we may produce, by uniting them in proper proportion, the smell of almost any flower, except jasmin.

The late, lamented Charles Dickens, seeing this statement, says in *Household Words*, July third, eighteen hundred and fifty-seven : " Is jasmin, then, the mystical Meru — the centre, the Delphi, the Omphalos of the Floral World? Is it the point of departure — the one unapproachable and indivisible unit of fragrance? Is jasmin the Isis of flowers, with veiled face and

covered feet, to be loved of all, yet discovered by none? Beautiful jasmin! If it be so, the rose ought to be dethroned, and
the inimitable enthroned queen in her stead.   Revolutions and
abdications are exciting sports; suppose we create a civil war
among the gardens, and crown the jasmin empress and queen of
all."

The jasmin is one of the flowers most prized by the perfumer.
Its odor is delicate and sweet, and so peculiar that it is without
comparison, and as such cannot be imitated.   When the jasmins
are distilled, repeatedly using the water of distillation over fresh
flowers, the Otto of Jasmin may be procured.   It is, however, exceedingly rare, on account of the enormous cost of production.
Mr. Fielding showed us a fine sample, but would not sell it, the
cost of it being fifty dollars per fluid ounce.   The plant is the
Yasmyn of the Arabs, from which the name we call it is derived.

We retraced our steps, and when we arrived at the house, we
found dinner awaiting us.   Having concluded to return to Nice
the next day, the afternoon and evening were spent at the home
of Jean's father.

In the morning, when we set out on our return, we bid Mons.
Souplesse and Millie Stanley good-bye, inducing Millie to promise, when she visited Boston, to come directly to us.   Jean held
her hand as if loth to relinquish it, when bidding her adieu, and
I am inclined to the belief, would like to have repeated that in-
troductory kissing operation, but she shyly drew her hand away,
and thanked us for the interest we exhibited in her welfare.

As we passed from sight, we raised our hats to them, and they
waved their handkerchiefs as a farewell to us.

We reached the *Cynthia* on the following morning, and steaming towards the open sea, proceeded leisurely on our way back to our lost course, stopping first at Constantinople on our passage to Adrianople, which place Jean and I expressed a wish to visit, to inspect the Rose Farms of the World.

CHAPTER XXVI.

THE QUEEN OF FLOWERS.

A T about six o'clock one morning soon after leaving Nice, we came to the guardian rocks of the Symplegades, the lighthouse, and the mouth of the Bosphorus, and then between the guns of the alternating fortresses, the lines of the Turkish men-of-war, the villas of the embassies, the palaces of the sultans, the terraced treillages, and the cypress groves, we ran rapidly down these famous straits of Europe and Asia, and shortly disembarked. Brad was to run around to Varna to take in coal while we were visiting.

Proceeding through the narrow, squalid, rugged, and steep streets, threading our way among mangy dogs, and no less so swarms of human kind, we sought conveyance to Adrianople.

Adrianople opened upon us in a most striking manner, and at every step of our approach, grew more attractive to us. Groves of plane and cypress, and terraces of vines and fig trees surrounded the white minarets. As we rode in, under a most glowing sunset in the customary sky of Asia Minor, while the vivid green of the trees of mulberry and the dark hue of the cypress were blending themselves under the radiant azure of the sky, and the cliffs growing rosier every moment beneath the partıng ray, the effect was very magical, thoroughly Eastern, and very beautiful.

We waited till morning to visit the places of note, and starting at sunrise, we made our way to the Rose Gardens, where we were greeted by such beauty and fragrance as no language can describe. What would you think of viewing a rose garden of twelve thousand acres? Yet such are the rose fields of Adrianople, extending over twelve to fourteen thousand acres, the chief source of wealth in this district. These beautiful flowers are not cultivated merely for the pleasure of looking at them, or inhaling their rare fragrance, but for the manufacture of the famous Otto of Roses. The vast plain was literally covered with flowers, and the whole air redolent with their odor.

Hundreds of Bulgarian boys and girls were gathering the sweet blooms in huge baskets or sacks, while they enlivened the scene with songs and laughter. These sacks of rose petals were taken to the manufactory, to which we betook ourselves; the rose petals were there put into a still with an equal quantity of water, then distilled, after which the roses are taken out of the boiler, and the product of the first distilling is put in and redistilled; this second product of the alembic gives the otto of roses, it rising and floating upon the water, whence it is separated; the water remaining is the pure rose-water of commerce.

After we had seen the above process, Susie turned, and looking through a window out upon the garden, thus soliloquized, quoting Byron : —

> " Know ye the land of the cedar and vine,
> Where the flowers ever blossom, the beams ever shine;
> Where the light wings of Zephyr, oppress'd with perfume,
> Wax faint o'er the gardens of Gul in her bloom !

Where the citron and olive are fairest of fruit,
And the voice of the nightingale never is mute.
*   *   *   *   *   *   *
'Tis the clime of the East, 'tis the land of the Sun."

"Luxuries are only sought and enjoyed by people living in a
high state of refinement," said Jean.   "When the Roman Empire
of the West crumbled beneath the attacks of a horde of barbari-
ans, who invaded its fertile plains, and laid waste its magnificent
cities, the arts of civilization, which they were unable to appreciate, took refuge in the Eastern metropolis, where they had been
cultivated since the days of Constantine the Great.   Perfumery
by them was ranked among the arts, and the Greek emperors and
their court showed for aromatics a fondness at least equal to that
which had been displayed by their Western predecessors, for having at their command all the fragrant treasures of the East, they
made a lavish use of them in private life, and in all their public
festivals perfumes were made to play an important part.

"Nor were they confined to unhallowed purposes, for the Oriental Church had likewise introduced them into all their religious
ceremonies, and their consumption was so great at one time that
the priests purchased in Syria a piece of ground, ten miles square,
and planted it with frankincense trees for their own special re-
quirements.   After several centuries of glory and splendor, the
Eastern Empire, torn by religious dissentions, was doomed in its
turn to fall under the aggressions of its enemies, and although it
struggled many years against the followers of Mahomet, the
Crescent succeeded at last in displacing the Cross on the proud
domes of Constantinople.   In this instance, however, the conquerors were nearly as polished as the vanquished.   If their religion, by forbidding them to delineate the form of man in any

way, had checked their progress in art, it offered no impediment
to the pursuit of science, and they had already attained considerable proficiency in many of its important branches. We are indeed indebted to the Arabs for many valuable discoveries in the
field of knowledge, and these children of the desert may well be
called the connecting link between ancient and modern civilization."

"Avicenna, an Arabian doctor who flourished in the tenth century, was the first to study and apply the principles of chemistry,
which were but imperfectly known to the ancients, was he not,
Jean?" I asked.

"Yes, sir. He was an extraordinary man. In a wandering
life of fifty-eight years, he found time to write nearly one hundred
volumes, twenty of which were Encyclopediæ of general information. He is said to have invented the art of extracting the aromatic or medicinal principles of plants and flowers by means of
distillation. Perfumes had for many years been known and used
by his countrymen, and long before Mahomet's time, Musa, one
of the chief cities of Arabia Felix, was a celebrated emporium for
frankincense, myrrh, and other aromatic gums; but hitherto the
far-famed 'perfumes of Araby the blest' had merely consisted in
scented resins and spices. The floral world, so rich and fragrant
in these favored climes, had not yet been made to yield its sweet,
but evanescent treasures.

"To Doctor Avicenna belongs the merit of saving their volatile
aroma from destruction, and rendering it permanent by means of
distillation. The Orientals always exhibited for the rose a par-
tiality almost equal to that of the nightingale, which dwells constantly among its sweet bowers. It was, therefore, on that flower
that Doctor Avicenna made his first experiments, selecting the

15

most fragrant of the species, the same that you now see so extensively cultivated."

"The *Rosa centifolia*," said Susie.

"Or, as the Arabs call it, *Gul sad berk*," said Jean. "This queen of the garden loses not its diadem in the perfuming world, but the rose-bearing *shrubs* of our colder climate, cannot compare with these huge rose-trees of the East."

Jean spoke truly, for the roses in this garden grew not on bushes, but on trees, which were from twelve to twenty feet high, and the wide spreading branches were loaded with thousands of buds and blossoms in all degrees of advancement, while sweet singing birds hopped from bough to bough, and uttered their melodious notes. We scarce knew which to admire, the fragrance of the thousand flowers, or the merry carols of the dainty, many-tinted songsters.

"We do not have quite so large rose gardens in Grasse or Nice, if you remember," said Jean, "but still they are quite extensive. The otto of roses which they manufacture there by distillation of the Provence rose, has a very characteristic fragrance, imparted to it, I believe, by the bees, which carry the pollen of the orange blossoms, so numerous there, into the rosebuds. The French otto is richer in stereopten than this Turkish otto; an ounce and a half will crystallize in a gallon of alcohol, at the same temperature that it requires for three ounces of the best Turkish otto to do the same."

Our guide informed us that "otto from different districts slightly varies in odor, and that many places furnish an otto which solidifies more readily than others, and therefore it is not a sure test of purity, though many consider it such."

"If I have any otto of rose that I think is adulterated, I place the suspected otto in watch-glasses, under a bell glass, along with a capsule of iodine," said Jean. "The vapors of iodine, after some hours, condense, and form a brown areola upon the otto if it is adulterated, but does not change its color if the otto is pure. On exposure to the air, the iodine volatilizes, but the color in either case remains fixed."

Our interpreter told us, that "the cultivators of the rose in Turkey, are principally the Christian inhabitants of the low counties of the Balkan, between Selimno and Carloya as far as Phillippopolis in Bulgaria, about two hundred miles from Constantinople. If the spring is cool, and the fall of dew plentiful, the crops prosper, and an abundant yield of otto is secured. In good seasons this district yields seventy-five thousand ounces, but in bad seasons only twenty thousand to thirty thousand ounces of otto are obtained. The important thing is to collect the roses at daybreak, before the sun strikes on them; otherwise they will not yield so much. It is estimated that it requires at least sixteen thousand of these large rose blooms to yield one ounce of otto. There are also very extensive rose farms at Broussa and at Uslak, in Turkey in Asia, and also at Ghazepore in India, as I suppose you know."

"Yes," Jean replied, and then said that, "roses were also cultivated to a large extent in England, near Mitcham, for perfumers to use in making rosewater. In the season when successive crops can be obtained, which is about the end of June, or the early part of July, they are gathered as soon as the dew is off, and sent to London in sacks. When they arrive, they are immediately spread out upon a cool floor, otherwise if left in bulk, they would heat to such an extent in two or three hours as to be useless. There is no organic matter which so rapidly absorbs oxygen, and becomes heated spontaneously, as a mass of freshly gathered rose leaves. To preserve, the London perfumers immediately pickle them; to every bushel of leaves, weighing about six pounds, one pound of common salt is added, and thoroughly rubbed in. The salt absorbs the water existing in the petals, and rapidly becomes brine, reducing the whole to a pasty mass, which is finally packed in casks. In that way they can be kept any length of time without the fragrance being seriously injured. From these pickled roses, a good rosewater is made by distillation, but not like the residue product of the distillation of roses for the otto. This has a richness of aroma which appears to be inimitable with English grown roses."

"Of course Doctor Avicenna succeeded in his experiments?" asked my wife of Jean, "or else we should probably never had any otto of roses."

"Yes, madam," answered Jean. "He succeeded by his dexterous operations in producing this delicious liquid known as rosewater, the formula for which is to be found in his works, and in those of the succeeding Arabian writers on chemistry. It soon came into general use, and appears to have been manufactured in large quantities, if we are to believe the historians, who tell us, that when Saladin entered Jerusalem in 1187, he had the floor and walls of Omar's mosque entirely washed with it."

"I have heard of another authority stating," said Susie, "that otto of roses was first discovered by Noorjeehan Begum, Light of the World, the favorite wife of Jehan-Geer, who was once walking in her garden, through which ran a canal of rosewater, when she noticed some oily particles floating on the surface. These were collected, and their aroma found to be so delicious, that means were devised to produce the precious essence."

"So ancient is the custom of using fragrant waters," I remarked, "that one of the oldest authors repeatedly mentions it. In the Arabian Nights, written prior to the Christian era, in the story of Aboulhassan, the following passage appears : — ' when the prince of Persia visited the queen, and he had partaken of refreshments, the slaves brought him golden basins filled with odoriferous water to wash in, and that after the declaration of love by the queen and the prince, they both fainted, but were brought to themselves again by throwing odoriferous waters upon their faces, and by giving them things to smell.' "

"Rosewater is still held in high repute here," said Jean, "and when a stranger enters a house, the most grateful token of welcome which can be offered to him is to sprinkle him over with rosewater, which is done by means of a vessel with a narrow spout, called *gulabdan*. There is one over there on a bench, also an Arabian censer, — let us go and examine them."

We crossed to the place where they were. The "censer," and "gulabdan, or casting-bottle," — as it was called in England two or three centuries back, — are made either of glass or earthenware, for use by the medium classes living in ordinary houses ; but among the wealthy both this and censers are made of gold or silver, richly chased or ornamented. On the walls of every Temple in Egypt, from Meroe to Memphis, the censer is depicted smoking before the presiding deity of the place, on the walls of the tombs glow in bright colors the preparation of spices and perfumes.

"In the British Museum," remarked Jean, "there is a vase No. 2,595, the body of which is intended to contain a lamp, the sides being perforated to admit the heat from the flame to act upon the projecting tubes, which are viaducts of vases containing

ottos of flowers ; the heat volatilizes the ottos as fast as it reaches
the outer end, and quickly perfumes an apartment.   This vase or
censer is from an Egyptian catacomb.   Niebuhr, in his ' Description of Arabia,' makes mention of the habit of throwing rosewater on visitors as a mark of honor, and says, ' It is somewhat
amusing to witness the discomfited and even angry looks with
which foreigners are wont to receive these unexpected aspersions.
The censer is also generally brought in afterwards, and its fragrant smoke directed towards the beards and garments of the
visitors, this ceremony being considered as a gentle hint that it
is time to bring the visit to an end.' "

The censer as used in " holy places," is made either of brass,
German silver, or precious metals, the upper part being perforated to allow the escape of the perfume.   The word " perfume "
is derived from the Latin *per fumus*, by smoke, because the first
perfumes used were composed principally of vegetable matter, and
when set on fire, burned with a visible vapor.

In the outer vessel is placed an inner one of copper, which can
be taken out and filled with ignited charcoal.   When in use, the
ignited carbon is placed in the censer, and is then covered with
the incense ; this rapidly volatilizes it in visible fumes, the effect
being assisted by the incense-bearer swinging the censer, suspended from a handle by three long chains.   The manner of
swinging the censer varies slightly in Rome, in France, and in
England, some holding it above the head.   At La Madeleine,
the method is always to give the censer a full swing at the greatest length of the chains with the right hand, and catch it up short
with the left hand.

Censers of various styles and methods of operation have been
devised of late years, — the Magic Perfumer, or red-hot star

apparatus, described in a preceding chapter, which Jean had us construct to frighten the Maoris; another operates by having a covered dish perforated at the top, in which is placed an equal quantity each of any desired extract and water; underneath is a small lamp in which alcohol is burned; the heat of the burning alcohol makes steam of the water, which takes up the perfume and carries it through the perforated top out into the air. This censer gives a soft mellow tone to the perfume; and there is still another, operated in a similar manner, the steam being driven through an atomizing tube, drawing the extract from a small receptacle, and discharging it in the form of spray; these atomizing machines are also made smaller, and are operated by hand pressure on a rubber bulb arranged with suitable valves, and are, for all ordinary purposes, the best censers. The latest introduced censer, is one operated by a small bellows run by clock work, and consists of two bowls, one within the other, the inner one holding ground bark, pastilles or incense, which is lighted and the machinery set in motion; it draws the odoriferous fumes of the perfume, down through a tube and expels it into the outer bowl, and it arises into the air; this operation keeps the incense ignited, and uses up every atom.

Jean stated that, "Mahomet, who was a keen observer of human nature, founded his religion on the enjoyment of all material pleasures, well knowing that was the best means of securing the adhesion of his sensual countrymen; he had forbidden the use of wine, but simply because he feared the dangerous excesses to which it gave rise, and knew how many crimes were committed when people were under its influence. The indulgence in perfumes was one, on the contrary, he liked to encourage, for they assisted in producing in his adepts a state of religious ecstasy favorable to

his cause.   He professed, himself, a great fondness for them, saying that what his heart enjoyed most in this world, were women,
children, and perfumes, and among the many delights promised
to the true believers in the *Djennet Firdons*, or Garden of Paradise, perfumes formed a conspicuous part, as you see from these
quotations I remember to have seen, taken from the Koran : —
' When the day of judgment comes, all men will be obliged to
cross a bridge called Al Sirat, which is finer than a hair, and
sharper than the edge of a Damascus blade.   This bridge is laid
over the infernal regions, and however dangerous and difficult
this transit may appear, the righteous, upheld and guided by the
prophet, will easily accomplish it ; but the wicked, deprived of
all assistance, will slip and fall into the abyss below, which is
gaping to receive them.'

" After having passed this first stage, the ' right hand men,'
— as the Koran calls them, — ' will refresh themselves by drinking at the pond of Al Cawthar, the waters of which are whiter
than milk or silver, and more odoriferous than musk.   They will
find there, as many drinking cups as there are stars in the firmament, and their thirst will be quenched forever.

" ' They at last will penetrate into Paradise, which is situated
in the seventh heaven, under the throne of God.   The ground of
this enchanting place is composed of pure wheaten flour mixed
with musk and saffron ; its stones are pearl and hyacinth-zicon,
and its palaces built of gold and silver.   In the centre stands the
marvellous tree called *tuba*, which is so large that a man mounted
on the fleetest horse could not ride round its branches in one hundred years.   This tree not only affords the most grateful shade
over the whole extent of Paradise, but its boughs are loaded with
delicious fruit of a size and taste unknown to mortals, and bend

themselves at the wish of the blessed inhabitants of this happy abode.'"

"As an abundance of water is one of the greatest desiderata in the East, the Koran often speaks of the rivers of Paradise as one of its chief ornaments. All those rivers take their rise from the tree *tuba;* some flow with water, some with milk, some with honey, and others even with wine, this liquor not being forbidden to the blessed. 'Of all the attractions, however, of these realms of bliss, none will equal their fair inhabitants, — the blackeyed houris, — who will welcome the brave to their bowers, waving perfumed scarfs before them, and repaying with smiles and blandishments all their toils and fatigues. These beauteous nymphs will be perfection itself in every sense: they will not be created of our own mortal clay, but of *pure musk.*'"

I said that I doubted if the prospect of inhabiting a place with a soil of *musk*, peopled with ladies composed of the same material, would prove a great allurement to Americans or Europeans. But in the Oriental East, tastes are different; and it is a singular fact that the warmer a country is, the greater is the taste for strong perfumes, although one would suppose that the heat, developing to the utmost such powerful aromas, would render them actually unbearable.

As an instance of the fondness which the Orientals exhibit for musk, Evila Effendi relates that in Kara Amed, the capital of Diarbekr, there is a mosque called *Iparie,* built by a merchant, and so called because there was mixed with the mortar used in its construction seventy juks of musk, which constantly perfume the temple. The same author describes the mosque of Zobaide, at Tauris, as being constructed in a similar way; and as musk is the most durable of all perfumes, the walls still continue giving out the most powerful scent, especially when the rays of the sun strike upon them.   Many of Mahomet's prescriptions were of a sanitary nature, and in order to insure their observance by his superstitious followers he gave them, like Moses, the form of religious laws.   Such were the ablutions and purifications ordained by the Koran.   All true believers are strictly enjoined to wash their heads, their hands and arms as far as the elbows, and their feet and legs as far as the knees, before saying their prayers, and when water is not to be procured, fine sand is to be used as a substitute.

When the Turks settled themselves in the Greek Empire, they did not rest satisfied with these limited ablutions, but soon adopted the luxurious system of baths, which they found already established in the conquered cities.   These Turkish Baths have often been fully described, and have been introduced into all the large cities of America and Europe, and although what we are offered is but a poor imitation of the magnificence of the palaces devoted to the purpose in the East, yet the method of operation is the same.

As the rose is the favorite flower of the Orientals, the beauty of its aspect, and the sweetness of its perfume, are favorite themes for their poets.   The finest poem that ever was written in the Persian language, the "Gulistan," meaning the garden of roses, which Sadi, its author, with the *naive* conceit of Eastern writers thus explains his motives for giving that name to his work: "On the first day of the month of Urdabihisht (May), I resolved with a friend to pass the night in my garden.   The ground was enamelled with flowers, the sky was lighted with brilliant stars; the nightingale sang its sweet melodies perched on the highest branches; the dew-drops hung on the rose like tears on the cheek of an angry beauty; the parterre was covered with hyacinths of a thousand hues, among which meandered a limpid stream. When morning came my friend gathered roses, basilisks, and hyacinths, and placed them in the folds of his garments; but I said to him,

"'Throw these away, for I am going to compose a Gulistan (garden of roses), which will last for eternity, whilst your flowers will live but a day.'"

Hafiz, another renowned Persian poet, was also a great admirer of perfumes and flowers, which are constantly occurring in his verses, and furnish him with most charming similes. Addressing his mistress in one of his *Gazels*, he exclaims:

> "Like the bloom of the rose, when fresh pluck'd and full blown,
>   Sweetly soft is thy nature and air;
> Like the beautiful cypress in Paradise grown,
>   Thou art every way charming and fair.
>
> When my mind dwells on thee, what a lustre assume
>   All objects which fancy presents!
> On my memory, thy locks, leave a grateful perfume,
>   Far more fragrant than jasmin's sweet scents."

The taste for perfumes has in no wise diminished among modern Orientals; it has, on the contrary, been constantly increasing, and now pervades all classes, who seek to gratify it to their utmost, according to their means. It is principally cultivated among ladies who, caring little or nothing for mental acquirements, and debarred from society, are driven to resort to such sensual enjoyments as their secluded mode of life will afford. They love to be in an atmosphere redolent with fragrant odors, that keep them in a state of dreamy languor, which is for them the nearest approach to happiness. Sounini in his Travels in Egypt, says,

" There is no part of the world where the women pay a more rigid attention to cleanliness, than in Oriental countries. The frequent use of the bath, of perfumes, and of everything tending to soften and beautify the skin, and to preserve all their charms, employs their constant attention. Nothing, in short, is neglected, and the most minute details succeed each other with scrupulous exactness. So much care is not thrown away; nowhere are the women more uniformly beautiful, nowhere do they possess more the talent of assisting nature, nowhere, in a word, are they better skilled or more practised in the art of arresting or repairing the ravages of time, an art which has its principles and a great variety of recipes."

As it may interest some to know the composition of the far-famed Oriental cosmetics, I transcribe here a few recipes which were obtained from an Arabian perfumer, and can be vouched for as authentic.

The *kohl*, which has been in use for darkening the eyelids since the time of the ancient Egyptians, is made as follows: — They remove the inside of a lemon, fill the skin with plumbago and burnt copper, and place it over the fire until it becomes carbonized; then they pound it in a mortar with coral, sandalwood, pearls, ambergris, the wing of a bat, and a part of the body of a chameleon, the whole having been previously burnt to a cinder and moistened with rosewater while hot.

A complexion powder, called *batikha*, which is used in all the harems for whitening the skin, is made in the following manner: They pound in a mortar some cowrie shells, borax, rice, white marble, crystal, tomata, lemons, eggs, and helbas, — a bitter seed gathered in Egypt; mix them with the meal of beans, chick-peas and lentils, and place the whole inside a melon, mixing with it its pulp and seeds; it is then exposed to the sun until its complete dessication, after which it is reduced to a fine powder.

The preparation of a dye used for the hair and beard is no less curious. It is composed of gall nuts, fried in oil and rolled in salt, to which are added cloves, burnt copper, minium, aromatic herbs, pomegranate flowers, gum arabic, litharge, and henna. The whole of these ingredients are pulverized and diluted in the oil used for frying the nuts. This gives it a jet black color, but those who wish to impart a golden tint to their hair, employ simply henna for that purpose.

To conclude the list of Oriental cosmetics I will mention an almond paste, called *hemsia*, which is used as a substitute for soap; a tooth powder, named *souek*, made from the bark of the walnut tree, pastilles of musk and amber paste, *kourss*, for burning and also for forming chaplets of beads, which the fair odalisques roll for hours in their hands, thus combining a religious duty with a pleasant pastime; a depilatory called " termentina," which is nothing more than turpentine thickened into a paste; and last though not least, the celebrated *schnouda*, a perfectly white cream, composed of jasmin pomade and benzoin, by means of which a very natural, but transient bloom is imparted to the cheeks. The coloring principle of this sympathetic blush is known to chemists under the name of *Alloxan*, and was discovered by Liebig.

The Turks shave their heads, leaving a single tuft of hair on the top, by which they expect Azrael, the angel of death, to seize them when conveying them to their last abode. They preserve their beard with the greatest care, and make it a point of religion

to let it grow, because Mahomet never cut off his.   No greater in-
sult can be offered to a Mahometan, than to deprive him of this
hirsute ornament; it is a degradation reserved for slaves, or a
punishment inflicted on criminals.

The barber of the King of Persia is no insignificant personage;
he enjoys all the privileges and considerations naturally attached
to one who has in his charge such a venerated object as a royal
beard.   The *dellak*, or barber, of the great Schah Abbas amassed
such riches that he built a splendid bridge, which still bears his
name; and his modern successor erected, not long since, a magnificent palace for himself in the vicinity of the Royal Baths at
Teheran; but we are digressing, so let us return to the subject
of the rose.

There are six modifications of rose for the handkerchief, which
are the *ne plus ultra* of the *perfumer's art;* though I do not suppose many would acknowledge the justice of that expression,
and may say it sounds too ambitious.   Yet the first musician who
tried to echo with a pierced reed the songs of the birds of the
forests, the first painter who attempted to delineate on a polished
surface the gorgeous scenes which he beheld around him, were
both artists endeavoring to copy Nature; and so the perfumer,
with a limited number of materials at his command, combines
them as the artist does his colors on a palette, and strives to imi-
tate the fragrance of all flowers which are rebellious to his skill,
and refuse to yield up their aroma.   Is he not, then, entitled to
claim also the name of *artist*, if he approaches even faintly to the
perfections of his charming models?

> "The roses soon withered that hung o'er the wave,
>   But some blossoms were gathered while freshly they shone,

And a dew was distilled from their flowers that gave
All the fragrance of summer when summer was gone."

Thus the sweet, but evanescent aroma, which would otherwise
be scattered to the winds of heaven, assumes a durable and tan-
gible shape, and consoles us for the loss of flowers, when Nature
dons her mourning garb, and the icy blast howls around us.   To
minister to these wants of a refined mind — to revive the joys of
ethereal spring by carefully saving its balmy treasures — consti-
tutes the art of the perfumer.

"At Rome," said Jean, "the odor of the rose was in such request that Lucullus expended fabulous sums, in order to be able
to have it at all seasons."

But pure otto of roses from its cloying sweetness has not many
admirers; when diluted, and compounded into the six modifications, — such as Essence of Roses, Extracts of Twin Roses, Tea
Roses, White Roses, Yellow Roses, and Chinese Roses, — then
there is nothing to equal it in odor, and especially, if the otto is
mixed with soap to form rose soap.   The soap not allowing the
perfume to evaporate too fast, one cannot be surfeited with the
smell of the otto.   The finest preparation of rose as an odor, is
made in the south of France by maceration in pomade or oil,
and the extract afterwards taken from the pomade, it furnishes
another instance of the wonderful properties of flowers, two almost
distinct odors being derived from the same flower, the process
only, being different.

When Nero honored the house of a Roman noble with his impe-
rial presence at dinner, there was something more than flowers;
the host was put to an enormous expense by having — according
to royal custom — all his fountains flinging up rosewater.   While

the jets were pouring out fragrant liquid, while rose leaves were
on the ground, in the cushions on which the guests lay, hanging in
garlands on their brows and in wreaths around their necks, the
couleur de rose pervaded the dinner itself, and rose pudding chal-
lenged the appetites of the guests.   To encourage digestion, there
was rose-wine, which Heliogabalus not only drank, but was extravagant enough to bathe in.   He went even further, by having
the public swimming baths filled with wine of roses and absinthe.

After breathing, wearing, eating, drinking, lying on, walking
over, and sleeping upon roses, it is not to be wondered at that
the unhappy ancient grew sick.   His medical man touched his
liver, and immediately gave him a rose draught.   Whatever he
ailed, the rose was made in some fashion or another to enter into
the remedy for his recovery.   If the patient died, then of him
more than any other, it might be truly said that, " he died of a
rose, in aromatic pain."

Various authors say, that the sense of smell is the sense of
imagination.   There is no doubt that pleasant perfumes exercise
a cheering influence on the mind, and easily become associated
with our remembrances.   Sounds and scents share alike the property of refreshing the memory, and recalling vividly before us
scenes of our past life, — an effect which Thomas Moore beautifully illustrates in his " Lalla Rookh " : —

> " The young Arab, haunted by the smell
> Of her own mountain flowers as by a spell,
> The sweet Elcaya, and that courteous tree,
> Which bows to all who seek its canopy,
> Sees call'd up round her by those magic scents
> The well, the camels, and her father's tents,
> Sighs for the home she left with little pain,
> And wishes e'en its sorrows back again."

Tennyson expresses the same feeling in his " Dream of Fair Women : "—

> " The smells of violets hidden in the green,
>   Poured back into my empty soul and frame
> The times when I remember to have been
>   Joyful and free from blame."

Criton, Hippocrates, and other ancient doctors, classed perfumes among medicines, and prescribed them for many diseases, especially those of a nervous kind. Pliny also attributes therapeutic properties to various aromatic substances, and some perfumes are still used in modern medicines.

Who would think of depriving sick or well of flowers, or forbidding their use?

When perfumes are rightly and discriminatingly used, as one should, how do they differ, except in favor of the perfumes. For it is true that particular kinds of flowers, if left in a sleeping apartment all night, will sometimes cause headache and sickness; but this proceeds not from the diffusion of their aroma, but from the carbonic acid they evolve during the night. If a perfume extracted from the same kind of flowers were left open under the same circumstances, no evil effect would arise from it.

Discarding, however, all curative pretensions for perfumes, I think it right at the same time to combat the doctrines of certain medical men, who hold that they are injurious to health; however, " when doctors disagree, let a man of common sense decide." It can be proved that the use of perfumery in moderation, — and I never heard or knew of a case where any one was seriously harmed by their use in large quantities, or by continual use, — is more beneficial than otherwise; and in cases of epidemics they

16

have been known to render important service, both as curatives
and preventatives, were it only to the four thieves, who, by means
of their famous aromatic vinegar, were enabled to rob half the
population of Marseilles at the time of the great plague, without
any fear of infection.

We have also seen the benefits of the employment of perfumes
in our own times, when small-pox, cholera, and contagious diseases were prevalent in our land. As for health, we only ask
that those who are constantly engaged in handling and manufacturing perfumery be observed, and their physical condition
compared with that of any other class of manufacturers or professional men. The cultivation of flowers for the manufacture of
perfumes also gives out door employment to thousands.

One great benefit in the use of perfumes, is, that it tends to
cleanliness, and " Cleanliness is akin to Godliness," — almost
compelling one to notice when they are breathing a vitiated air,
or associated with filth ; the nose when well educated is a true
monitor. To the " unlearned " nose all odors are alike, but when
tutored, either for pleasure or profit, no member of the body is
more sensitive.

Perfumers, drug dealers, tea brokers, and general dealers in
odoriferous substances, have to go through a regular nasal education. A hop merchant buries his nose in a pocket, takes a sniff,
and then sets his price upon the bitter flower. The odors have
to be remembered, and it is noteworthy here to remark with what
persistency odors fix themselves upon the memory ; and were it
not for this remembrance of an odor, the merchants in the trades
above indicated would soon be at fault. An experienced perfumer having two hundred odors in his laboratory, can distinguish
every one by smell and call it by name. Could a musician with

an instrument of two hundred notes, distinguish and name every note as soon as struck, without his seeing the instrument?

It can be said that some delicate people may be affected by certain odors; but the same person to whom a musky scent would give a headache, might derive much relief and pleasure from a perfume with a citrine base. It would be like one who had eaten something which disagreed with them and saying: " This food makes me sick; I will never eat anything."

Besides imagination has a great deal to do with the supposed noxious effects of perfumes. Doctor Cloquet, who may be deemed an authority on this subject, of which he made a special study, says in his able Treatise on Olfaction: — " We must not forget that there are many effeminate men and women to be found in the world who *imagine* that perfumes are injurious to them, but their example cannot be adduced as a proof of the bad effects of odors. Thus, Doctor Capellini relates the story of a lady who *fancied* she could not bear the smell of the rose, and fainted on receiving the visit of a friend who carried one, and yet the fatal flower was only *artificial*."

We noticed many acres of green plants growing luxuriantly in the rear of the otto of rose establishment which we saw were *Pelargonium odoratissimum*, or Rose-leaf Geranium. We are sorry to say it is grown here in Turkey by the rose growers for the express purpose of adulterating the otto of roses, as from the leaves of this plant, by distillation, is procured a very agreeable rosy-smelling otto. One hundred weight of leaves will yield about two ounces of otto.

Used to adulterate otto of roses, it is in its turn adulterated with otto of ginger-grass, and thus was formerly very difficult to obtain genuine. On account of the increased cultivation of the

plant, it is now, however, easily procured pure. The genuine
otto of rose-leaf geranium is worth about four dollars per ounce,
whereas imitations of it, one an andropogon otto, sometimes called
geranium, is not worth more than that sum per pound.

We may observe here that the perfuming ottos as well as every
article pertaining to the perfumery trade, are best purchased
through the perfumers, as from the nature of their business they
have a better knowledge and means of obtaining the real article
than drug dealers; drug dealers have such strong, disagreeable
smells about them, and cannot therefore distinguish, appreciate or
compare the fine, delicate odors of perfumes.

On account of the pleasing odor of the true otto of rose-leaf
geranium, it is a valuable article for perfuming many materials,
and appears to give great satisfaction, especially as an essence
for the handkerchief.

We passed, on our return, many of the *Liquid ambar orientale*,
shrubby trees, common to this country, from which true storax,
a fragrant balsam, is procured. We had purchased some of this
balsam, as well as some otto of roses and rose geranium, of the
rose growers at their establishment.

After we had alighted from the cars, we were proceeding to the
ship, when Patsey espied a poster, with large wood-cuts, and glar-
ing type. It was an announcement of some European Barnum,
who was travelling in this country with his show. Patsey's spirit
was aroused; old remembrances crowded upon him. He was
beside himself to visit the circus, but we concluded we could not
spare the time; however, as we went a little further we heard the familiar music of such entertainments, and soon came upon the gypsy-
like scene. Patsey's eyes brightened, his chest heaved convul-
sively, his muscles seemed to leap for joy, throes of excitement

"THE YOUNG ARAB, HAUNTED BY THE SMELL."

Page 240.

shook him, and that fascination for the horse and sawdust, — so enthralling, which cannot be appreciated or understood, except by those who have been in the business, — possessed him He must see the entertainment.

To please him we went in and wandered among the cages of the wild animals, and examined the numerous curiosities. There were "bears, lions, tigers, leopards, camels, elephants and a variety of other animals ; an American Indian, an Esquimaux, a bushy-headed man and woman, and all the other interesting objects too numerous to mention," which are the "make up" of a first-class itinerant hippodrome.

But what is John Gagler doing? Has he parted with his wits?

He is roughly elbowing his way through a crowd that surrounds a tall, powerfully built, half-naked savage, a specimen of the natives of some of the South Sea Islands, we should judge. He at last reaches him, and grasps him by the arms. They are rubbing noses together like two mad apes, holding each other off every little while, then rubbing noses, and shaking hands the harder. John Gagler seems delighted. He and the savage are jabbering away in some outlandish tongue, and meanwhile the crowd is looking on with open-mouthed wonder, but none more surprised than ourselves.

At last John Gagler remembered us, and standing on tiptoe, beckoned to us over the heads of the people, who made way for us to come to him and his savage companion.

"Messmates, ladies, 'ere's han hold friend," he said ; "ha native of that island hon which I was kept ha slave for two years, by 'is tribe."

We looked at the savage, hardly knowing how to greet him, not caring to use the same salutation employed by John Gagler, as he was not only arrayed in gaudy dress, but his face was well painted in various colors.

"'E 's 'ad a 'ard pull," explained John Gagler. "Hall of the natives of 'is island have gone to Davy Jones's locker; the 'ole island was swallowed up by the sea, han' 'e han' ha native boy were the honly ones to 'is knowledge who hescaped. That's the reason I couldn't find the island; I thought my reckonings han' bearings were wrong, but hit seems they weren't. 'E 's told me the course to take to find the island hon which I was wrecked, han' says 'e can give me hexact directions to go to the island hon which the wrecked people were seen some four years afore they captured me."

·Brad, whom we had met at the depot, and who had accompanied us, was deeply agitated during this recital, and the color came and went in his face as his heart pulsated with hopes and fears.

"Oh! if it should prove to be my father and some of his sailors, my fondest hopes would be realized, and our search may not prove in vain," he exclaimed with emotion.

John Gagler and the savage were again chattering away, and the savage pointed with his finger to different parts of the compass, gesticulated with his hand in various directions, and it appeared as if he were recalling to John Gagler's mind the numerous landmarks of the now submerged island. After a while John Gagler turned to us again and said, —

"E's given me complete bearings, so I think I can sail directly to the place; but you remember, Captain Cole, that the parties, who hever they were, left the island hon which 'e says they were seen; left hin a boat, hand from there we shall 'ave to trace them; still it will be better than 'aving no port to start from, yout

THEY ARE RUBBING NOSES TOGETHER LIKE TWO MAD APES.

Page 245.

honor. What say you, me boy? Shall we slip hour cable to-morrow for the southern waters?"

"Are you ready, ladies, to accompany me on this as yet fruit-less quest, to again brave the dangers of the Southern Seas, now that you are so near civilization, so near home?" asked Brad.

"Aye, aye, sir," both my wife and Susie responded. "Always ready to follow our Captain; we shall stick to you through thick and thin; you cannot get rid of us so easily," said Susie.

"God bless you, ladies, you make my heart glad," said Brad, feelingly.

We wandered around for some little time, while John Gagler conversed with his friend, the savage, and made notes of what the savage told him, until Patsey coming out from the acrobatic part of the exhibition, we turned our steps towards the entrance, first, however, shaking hands with the savage, and from whom John Gagler took a farewell hand-shake and nose-rub.

On our way back we wandered through a Turkish perfume ba-zaar. As we passed along between the rows of booths, on the counters of which the Turkish perfumers were sitting cross-legged, their goods arranged in easy reaching distance about them, we saw many curious articles; among others the odd shaped otto of rose bottles, filled with that precious substance, and richly deco-rated with gold and colors; various styles of censers and casting bottles, amulets, that famous Turkish hair dye, called *Rastik-Yuzi*, which gives to the hair and beard such a fine black color and which almost every Turk uses; also a componnded perfume, *karsi*, used in the scralios.

After leaving this bazaar we went as quickly as possible towards the ship, conversing on our way upon the happy occurence of the

WE WANDERED THROUGH A TURKISH PERFUME BAZAAR.

Page 247.

day. Patsey exhibiting the greatest demonstrations of joy at thinking that his wilful desire to see the show had produced such propitious results.

CHAPTER XXVII.

AN ENCHANTED ISLAND.

IT was now just a month from the day we reached the latitude and longitude of the submerged island. From there we steered for, and soon came upon the island on which John Gagler had been landed, and where he had spent five years of his life. We went ashore and found his hut, and many signs left of his occupancy; the hut and its protections were overgrown with climbing plants, but completely worthless from decay.

He escorted us around the island, which he had named "Good Enough;" showed us the places in which he had passed his time, and took us to his lookouts and signal points.

We felt encouraged by finding this island so easily. From there we had directed our course a little to the south by west in the direction John Gagler understood the savage to have told him; it was also the direction in which the wind was blowing at the time of the gale when the "Godolpha" was wrecked, so we were almost sure we should soon find the island on which the shipwrecked people were seen; but we have been cruising since then, visiting many inhabited and uninhabited islands, and our explorations have as yet proved unsuccessful. The uninhabited islands we explored thoroughly, in hope of finding some signs of shipwrecked people, ever on the alert to discover some clew of Brad's father.

We saw hulls of wrecked ships, and broken timbers on many of the islands, that silently told their tale of disaster and suffering, but no castaway had we observed. When we came to an inhabited island we steamed along its shores, and when it was possible, by means of signs and by gifts to the natives, tried to get information if there were any white men among them, or living on the adjacent islands. Nothing of any importance had been gained from them. Their stories were without value, as on the islands we visited at their instigation we found no sign of white occupants.

We were now out of the course of all sailing craft, in almost unknown waters; we had not spoken or seen a sail for many days. A strict lookout was kept, and whenever the cry of "Land, O!" was heard, we were all immediately on deck, anxiously watching to see the slightest sign of a signal from some, perhaps, long imprisoned brother.

Brad was despondent, and we all felt as if it was beyond human power to determine what we wished. John Gagler, — good old John, — was firm and never despairing. If we lost hope after exploring an island, he would advance so many reasons for a still more thorough search, that we would at last be as eager as himself to try again. He knew full well, by his own experience, with what longing eyes a castaway watches the seas, year in and year out, for the slightest token of a rescuing hand. Having such experience he would not leave one stone unturned till something definite was known.

Brad was not the man to give up anything he attempted until he had accomplished it, and I knew, although he felt somewhat discouraged, that as long as our facilities lasted he would not turn back.

This beautiful morning, all nature seemed in sweet repose; the smoke from the smoke-stack sailed off in slow undulating motions; we listlessly lounged about the deck or on the rail, dreamily watching the placid waters, when we were suddenly aroused by the lookout's cry of —

" Land, O ! "

" Where away? "

" Starboard, two points."

The ship was headed in the direction indicated.

Every one was on deck, and took note of each outline as it became more distinct.

In about two hours we were sufficiently near the shore, and cast anchor. A beautiful beach extended to the right for about a mile, until checked by a rocky headland; to the left the beach seemed to continue around a densely wooded peninsula, in front of which were lines of reefs. Tangled woods above the beach covered the shore, presenting an almost impassable barrier to the interior.

We landed on the beach and made our way to the cliff. This cliff was broad and irregular, and in one of its cavities, a cascade of pure fresh water came sparkling and gushing down to the foot of the rock. Here we found by its continual dropping and washing it had formed a great basin which was now full of water, cool, deep, and transparent, reflecting in its depths with as much accuracy as a mirror the passing clouds, and the trees and plants which surrounded its borders. Susie named it " Mirror Lake."

We sat down beside it instinctively, so impressed were we with its refreshing beauty.

Birds of pure white, others gorgeously colored, flew in and out among the trees, and lit on the edge of this miniature lake to dip for a moment their tiny bills in the refreshing liquid, and a gentle breeze wafted odors sweet and aromatic, yet delicate, from unseen trees. We rested here for an hour, and then sent to the ship for our dinner, which we ate in this charming spot.

After dinner we strolled around, discovering new beauties at every turn. Then we decided to follow the beach, go around the point, and see what was on the other side of the island. We started, all but Brad, who had gone on board where his official services were required.

"I will wait han' tell 'im where you are bound," said John Gagler, "han' 'e can follow or hawait your return."

"Very good," I answered.

On the pink sand many shells were strewn, which we gathered, and like children, as often threw away for others which appeared more beautiful. Seeing an opening in the wood, we thought we could cross the point instead of going around. Pushing our way through a mass of tangled undergrowth we came into the woods. It was large and dense; except a very small portion, the trees were of the palm genus, containing several species, including the coconut tree.

We came upon some trees covered with small fruit, resembling quinces in every particular of look, taste, and smell, of which we ate, and felt refreshed.

We continued on till we reached a belt of shrubs that bounded the palm forest. Here our progress was not so easy, and it becoming more and more difficult, we made a detour and soon came out upon open ground. Some distance to the right we saw a cliff, and wondered if we had so quickly made a circuit of the is-

WAS BRAD, BUT HOW CHANGED.

Page 233.

.and. We were making our way towards this cliff, and saw at its foot the sparkle of waters in a basin; it looked the same, and yet it did not seem to be the same place at which we had rested and dined, but we were approaching it in an opposite direction, and of course it must appear a little different.

We came still nearer.

"Look! Look!!" I exclaimed.

Each one, almost simultaneously, put their hands to their eyes, rubbed them, tried to brush away the illusion, to ascertain if they were awake or asleep, and bent forward with an intense, awe-striken stare. We clung to each other, and turned our eyes in every direction, knowing not what next to fear.

Were we on an enchanted island?

Had we been wandering for years, or slept away a lifetime at the Lake?

Could we have changed like what we were looking upon, or had we eaten of something in this beautiful island which had distorted our imaginations, changed our perceptions and senses?

For rising from a recumbent position, which we had seen Brad take during our lunch in the morning, or perhaps for all we knew a morning fifty years ago, was Brad, but how changed.

A heavy, white beard adorned the lower part of his face, snow-white hair crowned his head in place of the dark jet locks we had so often admired. He was resting upon a stout cane which he had used to help him to his feet. His eyes were of as an intense black as ever, but had about them a strained, far-off look, almost wierd-like, and they stared at us and mesmerized our own. The face was wrinkled; the hands long and thin; the body emaciated; but the form as yet erect, with signs of strength to battle with death for many years

Could it be Brad? Had he come back to the tiny lake, and
looking too long into its crystal depths, been transformed by
some fair water nymph, or was it some trick he was perpe-
trating?

"Speak to him, Susie," I said.

"I cannot, oh, I cannot," she said, "I am so frightened. Why
does he stare at us in that wild way?"

"Speak to him," urged my wife. "He always thought so
much of you; if it is only a joke he will stop it if you beseech
him. Speak! Do speak, and break this horrid spell."

Susie shuddered, tried to speak, but no words passed her lips.
After a great effort she partially overcame her fears and feebly
called, —

"Captain Cole, Captain Cole, what —— "

We were surprised at the effect it caused. He dropped the
stick that supported him, fell on his knees, lifted his hands to
heaven, and with upturned eyes seemed to be pouring out thanks
in prayer. We could not hear distinctly what he said, but the
tones of his voice reached us, yet so feebly we could hardly say
we really heard them. It was Brad's voice that spoke, the last
sentence we caught, —

"My name, she speaks my name."

Rising, he was coming towards us, and we turned to flee from
him.

Why did we fear this old man? Some spell had been laid
upon him; we could see the thought in each other's eyes; we
were afraid if he but touched us, we too should awake to find ourselves old and wrinkled, and with snow-white hair.

We heard him feebly and hesitatingly call, as if he knew not
how to speak the words, or had forgotten how to place them.

"Do not afraid be, it are I, Captain Cole."

This however did not pacify our fears; they but seemed verified at this statement.

At this moment we heard a step behind us; looking in the direction of the sound we saw John Gagler. He was hurrying towards us, and it was with a puzzled look that he saw us huddled together as if in fear; but when he reached us, and looked to where we pointed, he too seemed transfixed with terror, but a moment after, he was running as fast as he could towards Brad; reaching him, he eagerly grasped his hand and said, —

"My hold friend, JACOB COLE, — my hold captain, so long lost, we 'ave found you hat last. Thank 'Eaven!"

What a change this produced in our actions, you can imagine. We hurried to the old man and greeted him warmly, assuring him of our friendship for him, and explaining our fears. When we were telling him of the striking resemblance which had so deceived us, he said, —

"My son, my boy, is he here? Praised be God. Where is he? Why not has he come to me? My darling boy, I want take him on my knee and pat his curly head. Why he does not come?"

We could not deceive him. He was thinking of Brad as he last saw him. We told him we would take him to him.

"He sick?" he asked.

"Oh, no," said Susie.

"Take me to him," he almost pleaded.

John Gagler told him where he was. He had left him at the lake. Brad told John Gagler he would wait till we returned, probably feeling a little piqued at our going away and leaving him; but we had gone by Susie's urging, as she seemed to be very anxious to wander along the beach; probably they had had some tiff, and both were trying to be as hateful and provoking as possible to each other.

Captain Jacob walked between Susie and John Gagler, leaning on John Gagler's arm, and keeping hold of Susie's hand; he was quite taken with her, and kept gazing into her face with a fond and pleased look. He talked slowly and feebly, and sometimes had to stop and think what to say; some words he had entirely forgotten, but he looked so happy it was a pleasure to watch him.

He conducted us a different way from the one we came; soon we were in sight of the bluff. We saw the cascade and the basin, but could see nothing of Brad. We sent Patsey along the beach to the ship to see if he was on board, and to bring him on shore, but not to tell him anything concerning our discovery.

Meanwhile we continued our way to the pool to await Brad's return. We sat down under the trees a short distance from its borders. Captain Jacob was, however, too nervous and anxious to remain sitting. He frequently got up, then came back and sat down again.

He unconsciously strolled towards the pool at one time, and appeared attracted by its brilliancy. In front of him were some plants growing luxuriantly, and forming a low hedge for a few feet. He stood looking over these into the water. A surprised look came into his eyes, then changed to one of gladness.

" Why !—Why ! !—How strange ! ! !" he said slowly. "Have —Have grown I again young? My gray hair is to jet black changed since I looked last into this pool; my eyes bright, like fifty years ago; no wrinkles; my beard —"

He raised his hand, and commenced slowly to pass it downward over his beard.

"Is black, too. But — but, not short as one I see — Friends ! — Friends ! ! — What is this? Why is this so?"

He called to us in an alarmed tone of voice.

At the first moment, when Captain Jacob began to speak, we saw the hedge in front of him move slightly, and changing my position a little to one side I looked around it.

There was Brad.

He had been sitting down looking into the water, and had probably fallen asleep; the sound of a voice so near had partially awakened him.

Jean was about to approach the lake to see what it was that Captain Jacob saw, but John Gagler restrained him, as I motioned him to do so.

Brad having now become almost fully awake, looked off into the pool; he saw the reflection of old Captain Jacob, and opened his eyes wider at the sight, but instead of jumping up, he said, —

"What — what is this? Have I slept for fifty years that my hair has turned so white, and my beard grown so long?"

At the sound of Brad's voice Captain Jacob stared in astonishment, but did not seem to have the power to move.

"My face wrinkled," continued Brad. "Have my friends left me alone upon this island to sleep so long?"

He put his hand to his beard, and seeing how much its shortness contrasted with that of the one reflected in the waters, I saw that he comprehended all.

His face turned white from suppressed emotion; his limbs shook as he tried to gain his feet; his strength failed him for a moment, then, with one bound he sprang over the hedge.

"Father !"

"My boy !"

17

They were in each other's arms.　We left them to their happiness, and walked in the woods till we heard the cheery voice of Brad calling us to come to them.

How happy they looked, and how like !　They well represented sprightly youth and hearty old age.

Seeing them standing together, we could not wonder at John Gagler's fright when first spoken to by Brad — of our own at first sight of Captain Jacob, or of their mistakes about their reflections.

Fondly leaning upon Brad, who almost carried him, so eager was he to help his father along, we all proceeded to the beach, and getting into the boat, were soon on board.

Captain Jacob was received with a burst of hearty cheers, and the pivot gun spoke loudly its welcome to the old captain.　He bowed low to the men as he passed, and Brad conducted him to the large saloon, where he ensconced him in the largest easy chair.

Captain Jacob admired the perfect arrangement of everything, but he could not long keep his eyes from Brad, and Susie must be at his side, or else, he said, he could not be content.

THEY WERE IN EACH OTHERS ARMS.

Page 258.

CHAPTER XXVIII.

CAPTAIN JACOB COLE'S STORY.

THE next day was a busy one for all of us, each was trying to outdo the other in bringing Captain Jacob Cole's mind back to civilization; it was difficult at first, but ere nightfall we had accomplished our herculean task, as he gave positive evidence by the rational manner in which he conversed.

The following morning we again went ashore. Brad had related the incidents of his search to his father, and told him of the many obstacles that had to be overcome. As we were being rowed ashore, Brad said, —

"Father, why did you not have some signals flying, to notify any passing vessel that you were an exile here?"

"My dear Bradford," he answered, "it is thirty and three years since I first landed on this island. The first year we were on the beach every day, and the first months ten and a dozen times a day we would go to our lookouts and watch with longing eyes the vast expanse of waters for some rescuing sail. After five long years, only two besides myself were left, and we made it a duty for each one to see to the lookouts alternately; then when I was left alone, every day I would spend hours at the signal-stations, and every night lighted fires on the bluffs. At last I gave up all hope. I felt doomed, — felt I should soon have to follow my comrades, and after awhile became resigned to my fate.

"My signals wore away, were blown down by the winds, and feeling as I did, I cared not to repair them.

"Of course friend John has told you all about the storm in which the 'Godolpha' was wrecked. Well, after he and his comrade, — whose name I have forgotten, it was so long ago, — were washed overboard, —"

"I never knew who hit was," interrupted John Gagler.

"Well," continued Capt. Jacob, "after they were washed overboard, we drove on until we were stranded on the rocks of the island you visited, where five besides myself succeeded in reaching the shore, constructed a boat from the broken timbers of the ship and left the island.

"There was Joe Broomer, the ship's carpenter, Matt Tolboth, the steward, Jim Maguire, Tom Carter, and Tom Dracut, mariners. Steering westerly from the island we kept on for two weeks, but ran across no sail, and passed only two islands, of volcanic formation, barren and desolate.

"Our boat becoming unseaworthy, one of us was obliged to keep bailing day and night. One day, thinking we saw land to the northwest of us, we headed our boat towards it, but even with the sails and oars we did not make headway enough to reach it before nightfall, and lay to to wait till morning to effect a landing. Unfortunately during the night we drove on a reef, and the boat being poorly built, soon parted, and we had to cling to the reef. At break of day we worked our way to the shore, helping each other as best we could, but only five of us reached it. Tom Carter was missing.

"We were pretty well tired out. Kitty Bright Eyes and her mate Jack clung to my back all night, and sent up piteous howls every little while."

"Who were they, Captain?" asked Susie.

"Two pretty kittens, my dear, who jumped into the sea and were washed ashore when the 'Godolpha' was wrecked, and who followed us aboard the boat when we left the island. They and their children have been my time-pieces during my exile here."

"Your what?" asked my wife, inquiringly.

"My clocks, ma'am!" he replied. "I tell time by their eyes, which dilate regularly from morning till night."

"How curious," she answered.

"After resting we searched for food and water, built us the best protection from the weather we could, having no tools, and then explored the island and set up our signals around it," Captain Jacob continued: "Joe Broomer and Matt Tolboth died fifteen years ago, by eating some game we had killed, which had probably fed on some of the poisonous berries on the island; they were strangers to the island and not acquainted with the character of its productions.

"We all came near following them, but finally recovered. Jim Maguire went next, about eight years ago, was drowned while trying a boat we had built to circumnavigate the island; the wind caught her aback, and she went down stern foremost like a piece of slate. Tom Dracut I buried two years after.

"Poor Tom! He gave out from sheer despondency, — lost all hope of ever being rescued. Our parting was sad. I was left alone, and oh! friends, it was truly alone. You can imagine what I suffered in the parting. But, thank Heaven, I am among those with whom I have so long wished to be, — those whom I should have sought, if I had been rescued or escaped before you found me."

He bowed his head and tears of thankfulness coursed over his wrinkled cheeks.

"But see!   There is my hut!"

We were at a place half way between the two bluffs, and just emerging from the palm forest, through which we had come by a well worn path. We came out upon a grassy down, a huge lawn, which stretched before us to the edge of a beautifully enclosed bay, the waters of which sparkled in the morning sun. The hut stood upon a knoll to the left of us, a short distance from a river, or rather rivulet, which, keeping its course for some distance along the edge of the forest, made a wide curve into the extensive lawn, then returned in a zigzag manner to the first line of its course, and crossing the wide smooth beach at the foot of the down, emptied itself into the sea.

Proceeding to the hut, which was surrounded with high palisades, outside of which, neatly arranged, were groups of banana, yam, and pineapple plants, hanging with fruit ready to drop with ripeness, we saw the strong smelling, but delicious durian, the fragrant and luscious mango, and the more delicious mangosteen ; while golden paroquets and beautiful green pigeons flew in and out among the foliage, making a picture long to be remembered.

Coming to a gate in the palisades, Captain Jacob was greeted from within by a parrot.

"Where have you been, me hearty. Come in, come in. See Pretty Poll, Pretty Polly."

A pair of monkeys scrambled up the door post to the roof and chattered at us. As Captain Jacob passed in at the door, one of them jumped down upon his shoulder, and grabbing Patsey's cap

AT IT THEY WENT, HELTER-SKELTER.

Page 263.

from his head, began to try it on, and stretch it as large as possible. Patsey did not like that, so he tried to get it away from him, and the monkey leaped down and ran up the door post and was on the roof in a jiffy. Patsey gave chase; at it they went, helter-skelter, from the roof to the ground, from the ground to the roof, from one side to the other, from ridge-pole to eaves, from one end of the hut to the other, dodging this way and that way, the monkey just within Patsey's grasp, when it would give a frightened scream and elude him, grimacing at him, in his peculiar, comical way, seemingly almost tickled to death at every failure of Patsey's attempts to regain his cap. We could not help laughing at their capers. At last Patsey got it, then the little monkey tried to make friends with him, so as to get the cap again, but Patsey thought too much of his cap, and the monkey was obliged to amuse himself by worrying one of Captain Jacob's cats.

In the hut we found plenty of chairs, stools and other furniture; although roughly hewn, they were neat and strong. Mats, curtains, twine, and many other useful and necessary articles Captain Jacob showed us, all made by himself and his companions, from products obtained from the coconut tree. The hut and furniture were made with only the help of an axe, a small hatchet, and two cutlasses, worked down to a suitable shape, which they fished up from the reef where their boat was dashed.

Half a dozen kittens, and three staid old cats, besides the watchful mother of the little ones, came around their master for recognition, and the parrot called loudly and lovingly when he caught sight of him, but seeing so many strangers was somewhat afraid to fly to him.

After having made a thorough examination of the many interesting things in and around the hut, we sat down and conversed until dinner was announced, which had been prepared by Captain Jacob and Brad, with the help of Patsey, who always acted as our steward when we were away from the ship. The table had been set outside of the palisades, where we could enjoy the enchanting view as well as refresh ourselves inwardly.

Captain Jacob would not allow of anything being furnished by the ship, but insisted on our dining from the productions of his farm, as he called it, and well satisfied we were. Breadfruit, yams, and bananas, prepared in various ways, and milk from coconuts, besides cold spring water, and the fruits of the various plants we had seen growing in his garden, served as a rich dessert. After dining, Captain Jacob fed his pets, and then gathered up a few relics of his island home, saying he would leave almost every thing for the use of some other unfortunate who might be cast upon the island. Then closing the door of his hut, after taking the cats and kittens out, he bid adieu to the place that had so long protected him, and we proceeded to the ship, Brad intending to leave the island and head for England, taking his father to London and settle there.

CHAPTER XXIX.

THE BEAUTY AND THE BEAST.

"COAL'S out, sir."

"All gone?"

"All gone, sir."

Such was the conversation that occurred between Brad and his engineer about a week ago.

From that time we had been relying wholly on our sails.

The weather had been good since we had left Captain Jacob's island, until after we left Cape Town at the Cape of Good Hope, at which place we had stopped a few days. But after leaving there, when about a day out, we experienced bad weather, encountered head winds, and had made but little headway, so that a great deal of fuel had been consumed.

We were coasting along the northwestern shores of Africa, and for the last two days had been sailing well in shore. The barometer indicated a change for the better, and at sundown there was scarcely a ripple on the water. During the night a few puffs of wind were caught, but it only served to keep our head on, as only a few knots were made.

The next day the calm continued, and all hands were feeling lazy and blue, for they were not used to being at rest, as we could always keep moving when steam was up. We were all wishing for a favorable wind.

We expressed a desire to go ashore if possible, but Brad thought it too far to row, so we gave up the idea. In the morning we went on deck, and found the shore only a short distance off, and that we had come to anchor.

"Any breeze last night, Brad?" I asked.

"No, but I had the engineer use up all the wood he could get, and we got up steam enough to bring us near the shore, so you can take a run on *terra firma* this morning if you wish," he answered.

"Thank you, we shall be glad to. I thought I heard the engines working last night," I remarked, "but I sleep so soundly I was not sure."

After a short time the boats were ordered, and we all being seated, the men pulled leisurely towards the shore. Brad, Jean, Patsey, and I, carried our rifles in hopes of a chance shot, or to protect ourselves if we met any hostile natives; several axes were in the boats, as also a tent in a boat that followed us.

Brad had concluded to let his men gather all the dry wood they could, and take it on board to use in place of coal, till we came to a coaling station. This they could do while we were examining the country.

The shore we were approaching was only accessible in a few places, owing to the tangled growth of vines and plants. Susie looked with delight upon the profuseness of the vegetable productions of the shores, and remarked the number and variety of insects, many of which she wished to add to her collection, and for which she had come prepared, —pins, ether, and all the rest of her paraphernalia.

After landing, the men erected the tent, in which were placed eatables for a noon repast. Then, after making things as comfortable as possible, Brad, Jean, and I, set out for a short tramp along the shores, leaving Patsey to look after the ladies, and the men engaged in collecting wood and transporting it to the ship.

Susie had already commenced examining the flowers and plants, and as we passed out of sight she was chasing a brilliant-hued insect, eager to capture and examine it.

We wandered for some time and made one or two shots, but met with no large game, then wishing to get back to the camp, before the heat of the day became intense, we retraced our steps, and at ten o'clock, or a few minutes after, came in sight of the tent. My wife was sitting in the door reading, and Patsey was at work with the men.

"Where is Susie?" asked Brad.

"She is near by," answered my wife.

"Shall I call her?" said Jean.

"She will come back in a few minutes," answered my wife. "She said she was going over there"—and my wife pointed as she spoke to a small clump of undergrowth back of us, to the right,—"to get some new species of grass she thought she observed. You had better lay down in the shade of the tent and rest yourself till dinner-time."

We stretched ourselves on the ground, and watched the men at their work, and the ship resting so calmly on the water. The drowsy droning of the insects and the heat and quietness, combined with the fatigue of our walk, overcame us, and one and all must have dropped to sleep. I was aroused by my wife touching me on the arm.

I opened my eyes with a start.

"You had better get up and see where Susie is," she said, speaking concernedly.

"Has she not returned?" I asked.

"No, and I am anxious, for I fear she may have wandered and lost her way."

I noticed the side of the tent had been raised, and extended out over us to protect us from the sun, and looking at my watch I saw we had really been asleep, for it was half-past two o'clock.

Brad and Jean awaking, Jean asked me where I was going.

"We had better have dinner now," I said, so as not to arouse any fears in his mind about Susie.

So they arose, and calling Patsey he soon had a lunch spread for us.

We had hardly commenced eating when Brad again inquired,—

"Where is Susie?"

"She will probably be here in a minute. Patsey, please call her," said my wife.

"Yes, ma'am."

Patsey called but she did not come, and Brad asked Patsey if he had seen her.

"Faith I hevn't, sir, not for some hours, as I hev been a working wid the min."

Still she did not come, and Brad, hastily taking a few mouthfuls, arose and said, —

"I am going out to look for her."

"I will go too," I said.

"And I," said my wife.

"And I," chimed in Jean.

"I'm wid yees," said Patsey.

Picking up our guns, we went towards the place where my wife said she last saw Susie.

Brad sent word to the men to await our return, and if Susie came back to discharge three guns successively, as a signal.

We found where she had broken off flowers and grasses, gathering them for future study.

"We must follow these tracks," said Brad, "and hurry too, for we have not much time, as it will soon be dark. If we do not find her before then, she will be exposed to all the dangers and horrors of a night in an African forest, perhaps death from some wild beast."

We shuddered at the thought and hurriedly pushed along, though it was warm work, for the traces led us over a most circuitous and meandering route, as Susie seemed to have strayed about in the most eccentric manner, attracted probably by some new growth in the flora, or some curious insect.

Our hearts beating between hope and fear, our heads almost splitting with the heat, we struggled on through dust and vines, and tanglewood. If anything had happened to her how could we excuse our carelessness? Why had she wandered so far?

At last we came to a large tree, under which were some broken and clipped flower stems, appearing that she had rested here probably for a few minutes, arranging what she had collected, and had then resumed her rambling.

We found where she had stopped again and started off once more, and her foot-marks showed she was uncertain which way to go, but probably thought she was retracing her steps back to the tent, for she had not stopped to pick any flowers or to gather grasses.

We went for some distance, when an exclamation from Jean,

who was ahead, attracted our attention, and we hastened to him. He pointed out to us, further on, a spot where the grass was pressed down, and flowers were scattered over the ground as if there had been a struggle. Then our worst fears were aroused. Susie had been attacked by some wild beast, perhaps carried off or killed.

We rushed to the spot.

No signs of blood, and only a few shreds of her dress, which had caught on the neighboring bushes, showed of any damage done. Patsey discovered prints of feet with long claws, which ran far into the ground.

All hope was now lost, for the imprint of the foot, its size and the length of the claws, convinced us that it was an African lion by whom she had been attacked. We expected as we went further on to witness a heart-rending sight.

My wife was almost inconsolable at the loss of her sister, and implored us to hasten to her rescue. Brad called our attention to a spot where it appeared as if something heavy had been dragged along, and we followed this trail for some time.

Jean said the lion was probably dragging her to his lair, and perhaps she had not been hurt as yet, but had fainted, and as long as she made no resistance the lion would not kill her.

This revived a last hope, and we pushed on with renewed vigor, but ever on the watch for fear we should come suddenly upon the brute.

"His lair is probably in some cave in the high land we can just discern ahead," said Brad, "so we must approach carefully."

We all now moved along slowly and cautiously, each one instinctively having the same feeling, not of fear, but heart sickness, that every step would bring us face to face to all that remained of her whom we had learned to respect and love. Patsey, who had run ahead, came to a coppice, and was pushing through when he suddenly came to a halt, and stood motionless; then he turned and beckoned for us to come, at the same time putting his finger to his lips as a sign for us to do so cautiously.

We did so, and when we were at his side, he carefully pulled aside the boughs as if they were a curtain.

What a sight was revealed to our gaze!

Had the millennium come?

Was this Paradise?

Ten feet beyond was an open spot covered with thick moss, a kind of grotto formed by an overhanging rock projecting from the hill-side.

There lay Susie, her left hand at her side, her right hand on her bosom, still grasping a few of the flowers and grasses she had gathered. Her face was upturned, her eyes closed, and her hair having become loosened made a fitting drapery for so beautiful a picture.

She looked pale, breathed easily and naturally, and we could not discover that she was harmed in the least.

Beside her, separated from her only by a few inches of ground, lay a monster lion, with heavy mane and huge head, a fierce and powerful looking beast; he was as motionless as though carved in stone; one huge paw was stretched at full length, upon which rested his great head, and the other was drawn up under him; he took no notice of her or us.

This King of Beasts looked as peaceful and protecting as a great Newfoundland dog.

What could it mean?

"They are dead!" cried Jean excitedly.

"They are not dead, but sleeping," said Brad calmly.

He stepped boldly forward.

We called to him to come back, but he did not heed us.

He carried his rifle in his left hand, and in his right a huge bowie knife, ready at a moment's notice to strike if the lion moved; but it did not stir. He reached Susie, and lifted her in his arms, yet the lion showed no signs of life.

What was the reason?

Ah! the mystery is solved.

When Brad raised Susie an indescribable odor filled the air.

" Ether," said Jean.

"Yes," said I, "that is the cause of their sleepiness; in dragging Susie along, the bottle of ether which she carries with her for smothering insects, probably struck against that stone you see there just at the hind feet of the lion, which broke it or cracked it, saturating her garments with its contents, the fumes overpowering both of them, and we find them sweetly sleeping, — The Beauty and the Beast."

CHAPTER XXX

AS Brad started to bring Susie to us, she opened her eyes with a half-frightened, askant look, like a child awakened from a horrid dream, peopled with monsters and demons.

Turning her head, she saw the lion, and it flashed across her mind, in what real peril she had been, and seeing who her deliverer was, looked thankfully up into his face, put her arms around his neck, and nestled her head trustfully on his shoulder; then she either fainted or fell asleep from the effects of the ether.

Brad strained her to him, while his broad chest rose and fell under the strength of his emotions, and his eyes filled with grateful tears. Imprinting an adoring and loving kiss on her forehead, he carefully brought her to us beyond the coppice, we not having dared to approach too near this King of Beasts. Brad laid Susie down, and we did all we could to restore her to consciousness.

My wife took the bottle of ether from Susie's pocket and found it still half full. Patsey asked for it.

" Och plaze ma'am give it to me. I wants it to make th' ould fellow drame of his grantmuthers, an' while he's convarsing wid her, I'll pull out his tathes an' toe nails, and train him up for a circus."

He went cautiously towards the lion, held it under his nose.

The huge brute gave half a dozen kicks, clawed the air, and soon showed by his looks that he might be "draming moighty hard," and soon succumbed. Patsey saying that "he would bet considerable that the ould feller died in the belief that a flash from Miss Susie's bright eyes killed him;" but we would not oblige him, as we thought it would be hard to decide who won.

We soon succeeded in reviving Susie. She was very thankful for her miraculous escape.

While we were restoring Susie, Patsey had taken the skin from off the lion, with the neatness and dispatch of an experienced hunter; it was a beautiful one.

It was as we supposed. Susie had kept wandering, drawn on by new beauties, until getting turned around she lost her way; directing her steps towards a point which she thought would at last lead her to the camp, she at one time stooped to pick some flowers, when she espied underneath some small shrubs a lion watching her. She screamed and turned to run, when he sprang upon her, knocking her down; then he took her up in his jaws and dragged her along towards his den.

She kept perfectly still, knowing it would only cause more violence, and be useless if she resisted. Oh! how earnestly she prayed for help. After some distance had been passed over, she felt herself overcome by drowsiness, and fell asleep, wondering all the time what was the cause, and knew nothing more till Brad awoke her.

Brad picked up the flowers which Susie had kept in her hand through it all, and preserved them with the greatest care.

Reaching the camp we proceeded immediately on board, very much exhausted by the hunt and the excitement.

As we went up the outside gangway steps, to go on board, Brad ahead, assisting Susie, my wife and I heard him say to her, —

"Darling, how did you come to let me know you loved me? It makes me feel conceited to think you do, for I supposed Jean was the favored one."

"Oh! don't ask me, Bradford," replied Susie shyly, looking up into his face, with a half bashful, half pleased expression. "Probably I was so thankful that someone came to rescue me; perhaps if it had been any one else, Jean for example, I might have acted the same. I don't see how you did dare to think it was you in particular I was so glad to see," and from the corners of those snapping blue eyes of hers, a mischievous expression darted to watch the effect on Brad.

"I hope I was not mistaken, but if I was I shall be most unhappy to give place to anyone else," replied Brad, a tinge of disappointment in his voice. The honest fellow, he could not bear deception in anything. "But I thought actions spoke louder then words."

"Oh, no! of course I could not allow you to withdraw now. What would they think?" and she turned away her head, acting as if she were making a great sacrifice.

That mischievousness, so innate in woman could not help showing itself; that wish to test their best friends in the most trying situations, which has caused so many quarrels by being misunderstood, and when so received the perpetrator feels too piqued to explain, and lets it go on till time widens the breach, unless moved by a generous impulse to acknowledge their fault; then when all is made clear, they look back and see how much unnecessary pain they have caused, and how much valuable time they have wasted, or like Susie, their second and better thoughts show them at once the folly of their remarks.

"But there, Bradford!" she exclaimed, "I won't try to plague you," — now she spoke like her own true self, — "in my half consciousness, either moved by a feeling of gratitude for my miraculous escape, and having the one of all others come to save me, or having it brought so forcibly to my mind that life was full of dangers, and too short for deceptions, and seeing happiness within my reach, I should be foolish not to possess it. I am glad, more than glad, that I let you see I loved you, for I really and truly do love you, Bradford."

The mischievous expression had left her eyes, and they were filled with a soft, loving look, that is so expressive, beautiful and womanly; then the noise made by the sailors coming on board, the rattling and creaking of the sheaves in the davits drowned their further conversation, but we saw they were happy, and we too were glad.

At the foot of the companion stairs, Captain Jacob and John Gagler were awaiting us, to whom we related our day's adventures, and the dangerous situation Susie had been placed in; in fact, it formed the subject of conversation until we retired.

The next forenoon, with steam up, we were fast lessening the distance between us and Europe. We were all on deck, and we were a happy party, although Susie was somewhat unstrung and weak from the shock to her nerves, and looked slightly paler than usual, yet she said she felt nicely, and the happy light in her eyes showed us she was contented.

Old Captain Cole, who as well as John Gagler had been informed as to how matters stood between Susie and Brad; as they sat together talking about old times, they would every little while look up to watch Susie and Brad as they strolled fore and aft the deck, arm in arm, as lovingly as a pair of turtle doves; perhaps it was because Susie was so weak yet, that she leaned so heavily on Brad's arm, — but who can tell?

Wife and I were sitting near the rail, she at work upon some kind of delicate embroidery, and I reading or watching the distant shores of receding Africa. Wife too would cast a loving look at Susie, full of joy to see her happy.

Jean was reading a letter, in which he was deeply absorbed; he did not seem to be as much affected by the preference shown by Susie for Brad as we expected, but perhaps he found consolation in his letters, which he seemed to find awaiting him at almost every port we entered, and which we supposed came from his father, until one day a gust of wind blew a couple of pages from his hand; one of them fell at my feet, and as I stooped to pick it up I could not help seeing the signature, which was in a small, clear hand, — *yours in gratitude, Millie.*

Susie and Brad stopped as they were walking towards us, and Brad asked, —

"How would you like to visit Paris?"

"Oh! ever so much!" answered my wife.

"I should be delighted, Brad," said I.

"Will you stop at Paris, Captain?" questioned **Jean**. "I wanted to ask you to so much, but I hardly dared."

"I see you are all anxious to go, and I am pleased to hear it. What do you say, father?" said Brad.

"Anywhere, Bradford. John and I only care to be with you, so heave ahead, my lad, we will follow in your wake," answered the old gentleman.

"Thank you, father," said Brad. "This little girl will not promise to be my wife until we arrive in Boston, but as Paris is the headquarters for bridal outfits, I have persuaded her to go there and select all that is requisite, and as you are all in favor of it, we will drop anchor in Havre instead of London. There is the dinner-gong, let's go below. Come father, friend John, Jean, —— "

Brad took his father's arm on one side, and Susie on the other, and the rest of us followed them. It was a pretty picture. Brad guided his father's steps as if he were an infant, although old Captain Jacob was as strong and hearty as many a man twenty years younger, but Brad's solicitude could not help showing itself. Susie had hold of Captain Jacob's left arm, and her left hand was clasped in his, she would look admiringly up into his face and glance lovingly across to Brad, while old Captain Jacob's face gleamed with joy, as he looked from one to the other, and thanked Heaven that in his old age he had found two such good children —had found a true son and a kind daughter.

During the dinner we talked over our prospective visit to Paris, and congratulated Brad upon the happiness in store for him.

Having wood enough to last us until reaching a coaling station, we were relieved from all anxiety concerning our speed, which continued at a good rate.

I am afraid Brad did not care to go leisurely, and I had not much doubt, but what our engineer had standing orders to keep up steam and make the best possible time; for night and day we bowled along at a lively rate.

CHAPTER XXXI.

SELECTING A TROUSSEAU.

HAVING stopped at the Cape de Verde Islands to put in a supply of coal and other necessaries we soon arrived at Havre, and from thence here to Paris, putting up at the Hotel Meurice.

With what wondering eyes Captain Jacob regarded all the bustle, growth, and advance of the civilized world, no one could imagine who did not see him, or who has not been placed in a like position.

To visit the sights of the city was our first object. Brad seemed a little impatient, and was continually urging Susie and my wife to purchase, and have made as quickly as possible the trousseau. It was not a great while before the large parlor in the suite was filled with bundles and packages.

Every day and evening we were asked to admire some new addition to the collection. The ladies were in their glory, but remonstrated with Brad, and at last positively refused to receive any more articles, and said they would return them to the dealers, and tell them he was crazy if he persisted in buying. The great want was the wedding dress, which was not permitted to be seen, —

"Until the grand occasion," said Susie, laughingly, and blushing a little withal.

We were conducted by Jean about the city, with which he had once been so familiar. I was not much surprised, after we had seen almost everything of note, at his asking permission to absent himself from us for a short time to visit his father.

On our arriving here he had immediately repaired to the Post Office, and returned with radiant face, so I supposed he had received good news.

Meanwhile Brad and Susie, with the help of my wife, still kept purchasing little nick-nacks for the coming occasion. Jean returned, but we could not get him to confess to anything. He answered to our inquiries that, "father is in good health, and Millie is still with him, ' the joy of his old age, and the life of the house,'" as his father called her, he said. "They wanted me to stay with them, but I had thought of a better plan, and that was the reason I wanted to see father personally, that is, that he should dispose of his estates and come to America and live with me.

"Did he agree?" we asked.

"Offer him, for me, a passage in the *Cynthia*, that is if he is willing to stop at London on the way," said Brad, "and Millie, too; don't forget Millie," and Brad looked at Jean somewhat quizzingly.

"Oh, thank you, Captain! you are too kind. He would be delighted, and so would I," said Jean.

"Write to him immediately, Jean," said I, "and have them join us here."

While here in Paris, Jean and I improved the opportunity and visited the most extensive and popular perfumery establishments, Lubin's, Coudray's, Rimmel's, Violet's, Piver's and others. The

wonderful variety and immense quantity of perfumes, put up in every conceivable manner, and the beautiful and exquisite toilet articles, which we examined, showed what a centre of luxury, beauty and fashion, is Paris, and what an immense trade this city enjoys from the refined nations of the world.

Millie Stanley and Mons. Souplesse arrived a few days after Jean wrote to them. Millie was charming, and more womanly than when we first saw her, — a regal brunette, all beauty.

Mons. Souplesse was as nervous and excitable as ever, overflowing with congratulations and good wishes, and delighted with the prospect of a trip to the United States with us.

We were but awaiting their arrival to end our visit, so the day after, we took the cars for Havre, and reaching in safety the *Cynthia*, started for London.

Brad had apprised his aunt and uncle of the success of his search, and of the time he expected to meet them; we were not surprised, therefore, when we put in at the wharf to have Brad point them out to us, also two of his cousins, their son and daughter.

We received a cordial welcome, and old Captain Jacob was overwhelmed with congratulations and looked upon with almost awe as one raised from the dead. Brad and his father entered his uncle's carriage, and the rest of us followed them in a carryall, and after an hour's ride arrived at their residence.

After dining, to the numerous questions asked Brad, he gave an account of his journeyings since he left them.

Late in the afternoon he and his father visited his mother's grave, and sought out all the friends of his father whom they knew were living, which were but few. They came back looking sad and thoughtful, but quickly livened up after a short conversation, with Brad's aunt and uncle, who were a very cheer ful couple.

Mr. Danforth had given up the sea, and settled down to enjoy the rest of his life in cultivating his land and studying upon inventions, to make the life of poor Jack more enjoyable and safe — less like that of a slave.

Brad would probably have made quite a stay here, but when a man is going to be married he becomes impatient, and time hangs heavily, so we were shortly apprised of the fact that he was ready to start. We were perhaps as anxious to see home and friends once more, as he was to get to America; with our long voyage and many adventures we were quite fatigued, and quietness and rest we felt would be pleasurable, for a short time at least.

Having leisure we visited the Lavender Farms at Mitcham, in Surrey, and at Hitchin, in Herts, where lavender is grown to an enormous extent; in fact, the above mentioned towns are the principal places of its production, in a commercial point of view.

The climate of England appears to be better adapted to the perfect development of this fine old perfume, than any other on the globe.

"The ancients," said Jean, "employed the flowers and the leaves to aromatize their baths, and to give a sweet scent to the water in which they washed."

"Hence the generic name of the plant, *Lavandula*," observed Susie, "from *lavare*, to wash."

"Very large quantities are also grown in France," said Jean, "producing a very fair quality of otto."

"Yes," I remarked, "what is called Alpine lavender is very good; but the fine odor of the British produce, realizes in the market four times the price of that of continental growth."

"*Lavandula vera* is a native of Persia, the Canaries, Barbary, and the south of Europe," said Susie.

"It is said to have been first been brought here to England from the south of Europe," said Jean, "where, finding a congenial soil and being carefully cultivated, it was found to yield a much superior otto to that produced from it in its original places of growth."

"The peculiar qualities of most plants are susceptible of change," said Susie, "and in many instances of improvement, by cultivation, but none, perhaps, more so than this. It is not even in all parts of this country that it can be grown with success."

"Inferior ottos of lavender are distilled from the stalks, leaves and flowers of the plant," I said, "but the finest is produced from the flowers alone, and is used in making lavender water of the most refreshing fragrance."

CHAPTER XXXII

JEAN'S HIDDEN TREASURES.

ABOUT a week after being out from London, Brad had gone below, and Jean and I were walking to and fro on deck, when Jean said, —

"How would you like to accompany me in a search for treasures, Mr. Montague?"

"Treasures, Jean!" I exclaimed, "surely you are not serious."

"Never more so, sir," he answered. "I do not mean gold and silver, though this that I expect to find can be easily turned into gold."

"Have you been studying alchemy lately, going to search for the philosopher's stone?" I asked.

"No, sir," he replied, laughing. "But will you agree to go with me? I have obtained a promise from Captain Cole to steam around to the place, as it is not far out of our course, and assist me in my operations. I think it will be interesting to you also."

"Certainly, I will help you," I said. "When shall we reach the place?"

"To-morrow afternoon, sir," he answered.

I wondered what could have got into Jean's head; then forgot all about the subject until Jean at dinner reminded me of it.

"Where are we heading, Brad?" I asked.

"Galway Bay," he answered.

Coming on deck during the forenoon of the day we anchored off the Arran Islands, I was surprised to see a man standing at the bow, clad in full diving armor. He also had a Rumkorff apparatus to furnish light by electricity while under water, and attached to his helmet was a new kind of conversational tube, so as to be able to talk with those above water, making it less lonesome and safer for the diver. He also had a small pickaxe. Going up to the man, he took off his helmet.

It was Jean.

"How do you like my new uniform?" he asked. "I am ready for my search for treasures," and he laughed gleefully.

The boat was being lowered, and soon was reported ready. We went over the ship's side, and the boat was headed in the direction indicated by Jean.

There were two men detailed to assist Jean, and I took the speaking tube and stationed myself so as to converse with Jean while he was on the bottom of the sea. Brad was in the coxswain's seat and guided the boat.

Coming to the spot designated, Jean prepared to descend, and soon disappeared beneath the waves. Shortly after he reached bottom, his voice came through the tube, telling me, —

"Order the boat a little to the north, more in shore. I see what appears to be a long, low hill; I should like to examine it."

The boat was moved slowly towards the shore, when an exclamation and signal from Jean caused the men to suddenly cease.

"It is a large sperm whale," came his voice from below; "back slowly, he has not seen me as yet; he is an ugly looking fellow, the largest I ever saw, —"

We anxiously watched the signal-line.

Suddenly came a quick signal to pull up.

"Be quick! he has seen my light, and is heading for me. I am afraid he is going to attack me."

The men exerted all their strength; the rope spun through the water.

Should we be in time? It was a moment of suspense.

Just as Jean's head rose above the water, a commotion ensued only a few feet away, and in a second — almost before we could pull Jean over the gunwale — a monster spermaceti whale broke water, and with open mouth charged upon us.

"Pull, my lads!" cried Brad. "Hearty now!"

The boat almost leaped from the water and away we went, but the huge cetacean did not follow far. He blew forth a small water-spout as a vent for his rage, then plunged beneath his element; we saw him rise again, but a long distance away.

We were resting on our oars watching this one, when we were surprised by a disturbance behind us; turning we saw another monster whale heading for us, we barely had time to pull out of the reach of his huge jaws.

He also soon disappeared in the distance.

"Guardians to the treasures I seek," said Jean, coolly. "I shall try another descent. The presence of the monsters is one of the best indications I could have."

This time we went in still nearer the shore.

Once more the water closed over Jean's head.

"How does it appear now?" I asked through the tube.

"All right," answered Jean; "lower the pickaxe and the bag." We did so.

Had Jean discovered his treasures so quickly?

For some minutes Jean did not speak, but we felt slight vibra
tions of the ropes, as if he was digging. Then came a faint. —
" Hurrah ! "

" Pull up your treasures," 'came the call from below."

If we felt any excitement at the word " treasures" we did not
show it, but pulled till the bag appeared above the surface.

" Examine the contents," said Jean from the deep, like some
King of the Sea.

We took the lump from the bag. It was not heavy, comparatively to its size, and by that I knew it was not gold or silver. I could not understand it, and Brad looked at me inquiringly.

Why did Jean call it " treasure" I wondered.

The substance was of a deep gray externally, and light gray on
the edges, darker near the top layers. I broke a small piece off;
it seemed to have a waxy fracture with yellow, and a few black
streaks within.

" Could it be ? " I asked myself.

This lump which I held in my hand, whose weight was not less
than ten pounds — could it be?

I smelt of it. Yes, there was no doubt.

" It is Ambergris, Brad," I exclaimed, excitedly.

" You may well call it treasure, Jean," I called back to him
through the tube. " This piece you have sent up is worth more
than three thousand dollars, as the best ambergris you know is
never worth less than twenty dollars per ounce, and you have sent
up a lump containing more than one hundred and sixty ounces.
You had better come up now."

" Not yet," came back the answer. " Send down the bag
again."

A COMMOTION ENSUED.

Page 236.

"Is there any more left?" I asked in astonishment.

"Lower and I will convince you, sir," he replied.

We did so, and soon pulled it up full to the brim. In a few minutes Jean rose to the surface, and was pulled into the boat to receive our congratulations.

"For the ship," said Jean, "and I will explain to you as soon as I become rested."

We had taken off his helmet as soon as he got into the boat; after awhile he said, —

"You know, sir, for a long time it has puzzed *savans* to account for the origin of ambergris, and that there have been many volumes written to explain it, but the question respecting it is still at issue. It is discovered in the stomachs of the most voracious fishes, these animals swallowing at particular times, everything they happen to meet. It has been particularly found in the intestines of the spermaceti whale, *Physeter Macrocephalus*. As we have just seen, there is not a more appalling spectacle than to look down into the capacious maws of these ferocious cetaceans. They are almost all mouth and teeth, and are sometimes seventy-five feet long, their enormous heads occupying one-third of their entire body. Their jaws are supplied with twenty-five large tusks, each weighing as much as two pounds, and are eight inches in length.

"It is found most commonly in sickly fish, whence it is supposed to be the cause or effect of disease. It is probably the cause and not the effect.

"Some suppose it to be a vegetable production of the same nature as yellow amber, whence it derives its name, *grey amber*, — ambre-gris.

"It would, however, take a week to tell you all the theories I have read about its production, which could probably be satisfactorily explained if our modern appliances were brought to bear upon the subject. The field is open to any scientific enthusiast; all recent authors who mention it, merely quote facts known a century ago, nay more, for in the sixth voyage of Sinbad the Sailor, he says: —

" 'Instead of taking my way to the Persian Gulf, I travelled once more through several provinces of Persia and the Indies, and arrived at a seaport, where I embarked on board a ship, the captain of which was resolved on a long voyage.'

" Shortly after they were wrecked, and then describing the place, Sinbad says: —

" 'Here is also a fountain of pitch and bitumen that runs into the sea, which the fishes swallow, and then vomit it up again, turned into *ambergris*.'"

" No doubt," remarked Brad, " the writer was wrecked somewhere on the coast of Pegu, near Rangoon, where there are natural petroleum springs to this day."

" Yes, and it is something to say of science," I said to him, " that in our day beautiful white, wax-like, or true paraffine candles are made from this Rangoon tar, but which in Sinbad's time, ' was swallowed by fishes, and turned into ambergris.'"

" What is ambergris used for?" asked Brad.

" As an extract," answered Jean; " it is used to give permanency to very fleeting scents, as it undergoes slow decomposition and possesses very little volatility; both musk and ambergris contain a substance which clings pertinaciously to woven fabrics, and not being soluble in weak alkaline lyes, is still found upon the material after passing through the lavatory ordeal.

" When ambergris is powdered, it is used in the manufacture of cassolettes, little ivory boxes, perforated, which are made to con-

19

tain a paste of odoriferous substances, to carry in the pocket or reticule, also in the making of peau d'Espagne, or Spanish skin, used for perfuming writing paper and envelopes."

"Queen Elizabeth," I said, "had a cloak of this Spanish leather, the value of which may be estimated by stating that pieces of "Peau d'Espagne" are sold by Boston Perfumers at seventy-five cents the square inch; even her shoes were perfumed."

"I can't say that I admire its odor," said Brad, smelling of a piece of the ambergris.

"Its odor now is of course too powerful," said Jean, "as are most all crude substances, but when prepared correctly it gives entire satisfaction. Its odor then is agreeable, peculiar, diffusive, and ethereal. Its chief constituent is *ambreine*, which crystallizes on cooling from a saturated solution of ambergris in boiling alcohol."

"But how came you to think of diving to the bottom of the ocean to find it?" asked Brad.

"Well, Captain, I will tell you," said Jean. "Reading and thinking over the many observations on ambergris, I came to the conclusion that it is nothing more nor less than the fæces of the spermaceti whale under certain conditions and food, probably stoppage; in this conclusion I am upheld by many others, as Captain Buckland, Homberg, and G. W. Septimus Piesse.

"It is known that the ambergris whale feeds on cuttle-fish. This creature is armed with a sharp, pointed, curved, black horn, exceedingly hard, tough, and indestructible. On breaking up good specimens of ambergris, I always find perfect specimens of this beak, and I remember one large ball of ambergris that Mr. Montague bought of a sea captain, who had taken it out of a whale, which was completely studded on the outside with cuttle-fish beaks.

"You will notice them in that piece, Captain, if you look closely," and Jean handed Brad a small piece from the bag. "These beaks appear to escape, or to be incapable of digestion, and are thus excreted with the biliary matter. On these facts and suppositions I determined at the first opportunity to visit one of the places noted for its finds of ambergris, and explore.

"I knew it was found floating on the sea near the coasts of Japan, China, India, and the western coast of Ireland, near the counties of Sligo and Kerry, besides at this place. The other places I did not think so favorable as this.

"The largest piece I ever heard of, was one weighing one hundred and eighty-two pounds which the East India Company bought of the King of Thydore, and there is also an account of a piece found on the beach near here in the year 1691, which weighed fifty-two ounces, and was bought on the spot for one hundred dollars, but which afterwards was sold in London for more than five hundred dollars.

"My experiment has proved my conclusion, as well as others, to be true, for that small lot in the bag bears the same relation to the size of the whole deposit as a cask of guano bears to the deposits on the Islands of Chili, and like them has been ac-cumulating for centuries.

"The pieces found floating on the water, or cast up on the beach, are merely lighter portions detached from the masses in different parts of the sea, by some disturbance, either natural or artificial. At the spot I visited there is a perfect mine of it, and will furnish the perfumers of the world, and those who admire its odor, with this costly perfume substance for ages to come."

By this time we had reached the ship, and we climbed on board. Jean had obtained enough ambergris to last some time, and taking bearings of the exact spot, he told Brad he had finished his explorations.

After we got aboard, Brad gave orders to bout ship, and heave ahead; we started for Bantry Bay to stop at Bantry for Patsey, whom we had let off to visit his parents.

We were not long in the offing before we saw a boat coming towards us, and Patsey in the stern standing up and waving his hat.

We welcomed him back, for he was not certain that he should return, but would remain in Ireland with his friends.

"Did you find your folks, Patsey?" I asked, after he had finished receiving the congratulations, for he was a great favorite.

"Faith an' I did sir, all but the dead ones; me poor ould muther died a year ago, and me faythur was that glad to see me he couldn't stand at all. Two brothers of mine started for Ameriky some six months ago, and a sisther who was but a wee bit of a colleen whin I left home, takes care of me ould daddy."

"Have you enjoyed yourself, while away, Patsey?" inquired Susie.

"Oh! bless yer eyes ma'am, I did iver so much," he replied. I wint to a fair — a regular tearing Irish fair — at Donnybrook, an' carried off siveral prizes, an' thereby won the admiring glances of all the bright oiyed lasses, an' the hate of all the fellers; an' I wint around visiting me frinds, an' attinded two wakes; such fun; och! my! how drunk they all were!"

"But I hope you did not drink, Patsey?" my wife asked anxiously. "I never saw you the worse for liqu)r, or use tobacco, and I truly hope you did not."

"Do yees think me lower than the bastes, ma'am?" he replied.

"Oh, no!" she answered. "I supposed you had more sense than they, for it is well known that all animals possess enough not to touch either."

"Faith, ma'am, an' do ye think I could have a stidy oiye, an' a clear head, if I used them nasty things?" he replied.

For once we saw Patsey serious.

"Whin I mate anyone who uses naythur, I know I have a compititor of whom to be afeered; but when I know he has ayther of those bad habits, I troubles meself but little; he may go on safely and surely fur a long while but at the rale time for action his brains and iverything fails him. Let them idjuts who wish to endulge do so, sure an' then for those who do not there is a better chance,—th' drunkards are soon left bahind.

"While I live I manes to live, and give all me faculties ivery odvantage. To be sure, I hev not hed the binefits of edycation, but I hev hed the upportunity of cultiveting me body, an' I hev brought that almost to parfection; ivery muscle obeys me will, an' is thrue to me, an' ivery narve is steady an' niver fails me; me health is parfect in any clime, be it hot or could.

"Do yees think I'm crazy anough to un'ermine all thase, and live a loife of narvousness, sickness, and misery, to gratife a vile appetate for rum an' baccy? No!"

How much better, I thought, would be the condition and happiness of many others, far better educated, and priding themselves upon having more brains, if they but followed the teachings of this uneducated, but smart and sensible Irish boy.

Leaving Bantry Bay, we steamed on, night and day, nothing out of the common course of events happening. At every night's close we were glad we were one day's journey less from the old Hub, and home.

At last we made Cape Cod Light, from which we first took our bearings; we felt now as if we were really within the influences of home; familiar landmarks continued to appear until we were surrounded with them, then that feeling of safety and surety of rest and peace came over us, and we felt more than content. It seemed perfectly natural to break forth in song, and the words of that well beloved one, "Home, Sweet Home," were truly sweet to hear, as carolled by such voices as Susie, Millie, and Jean possessed, and under such circumstances; as by one accord, sailors and all joined in the chorus as if in praise and gladness. As the ship rubbed against the wharf, was secured, and the gang plank laid, we could hardly realize we had but to make a step, and we should be in our native city.

The word "Home" had a new meaning to us, and we felt truly thankful that we had been protected in our wanderings, and had been so successful in our undertakings.

Since our arrival, the friend of my boyhood, our Captain, and his bride, together with old Captain Cole and John Gagler, have sailed for old England; and we are soon expecting another couple will be joined together, — our faithful Jean and Millie, — for which occasion grand preparations are being made.

Jean's father is with us, and likes America exceedingly, especially as Jean is now as wealthy, and perhaps more so, than any of us, from his Ambergris mine.

By the pecuniary aid of Brad, Jean, and myself, Patsey is the owner and manager of one of the largest circuses and menageries in the United States, and is in his element and contented as can be imagined.

As for my wife and self, we are as settled and sedate as become a couple of our age, and happy as we can wish to be, and
hope that all the readers of the past pages, may never have cause
to feel less joyful than do those who sailed upon the *Cynthia*, in
search of CAPTAIN JACOB COLE.

INDEX.

www.ingramcontent.com/pod-product-compliance
Lightning Source LLC
Chambersburg PA
CBHW032302280326
41932CB00009B/668